D1096066

Making Great
BOXES

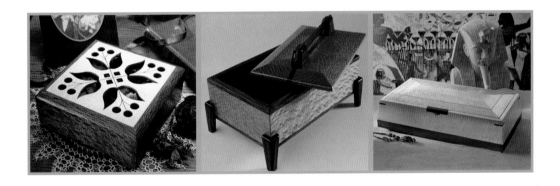

Sterling Publishing Co., Inc.
New York

Editor: Peter J. Stephano

Library of Congress Cataloging-in-Publication Data Available

10 9 8 7 6 5 4 3 2 1

Published by Sterling Publishing Co., Inc.
387 Park Avenue South, New York, NY 10016
© 2006 by WOOD® magazine editors
Distributed in Canada by Sterling Publishing
C/o Canadian Manda Group, 165 Dufferin Street
Toronto, Ontario, Canada M6K 3H6
Distributed in the United Kingdom by GMC Distribution Services
Castle Place, 166 High Street, Lewes, East Sussex, England BN7 1XU
Distributed in Australia by Capricorn Link (Australia) Pty. Ltd.
P.O. Box 704, Windsor, NSW 2756, Australia

Printed in China

Sterling ISBN-13: 978-1-4027-0763-6
        ISBN-10: 1-4027-0763-0

For information about custom editions, special sales, premium and
corporate purchases, please contact Sterling Special Sales
Department at 800-805-5489 or specialsales@sterlingpub.com.

Contents

Acknowledgments iv

Introduction 1

Chapter 1: Boxes with Different Faces. 3
❏ The Great Cover-up: Veneering 101 4
❖ Special Feature:
  Buying Veneers and Inlays 12
❏ Create a Marquetry Mirage 14
❏ Quilt-Top Wood Box. 20
❏ A Keepsake Box 26

Chapter 2: Bandsaw Boxes 31
❏ Four Basic Boxes. 33
❏ Making More Bandsaw Boxes 35

Chapter 3: A Bevy of Bandsaw Boxes. 41
❏ A Whale of a Container 42
❏ A Box with a Beak 44
❏ Sweetheart Jewelry Box. 47
❏ One Cool Catch-all 51
❏ Trinket Treasure Chest 55
❏ Shoot the Moon 58
❏ A Cottontail that Flips Out. 63

Chapter 4: An Assortment of Handsome Boxes 67
❏ Potpourri Box 68
❏ A Contemporary Keepsake 71

❏ Patina-topped Jewelry Box 77
❖ Special Feature:
  Patina Technique Through Basic Chemistry . . 79
❏ Stack 'em Up! 86
❏ Dovetailed Jewelry Box 90
❏ A Standout Box With Fine Splines. 97

Chapter 5: Beautiful Boxes You Can Put to Use. 101
❏ A Tool Chest That's Top Drawer 102
❏ Colonial Pipe Box 111
❏ A "Nutty" Idea for a Box 115
❏ Magazine Keepers. 123
❏ A Perfect Box for Your Photos 126
❏ First-Class Letter Box. 130
❏ Batter Up! for a Baseball-card Box 134
❏ Classic Candle Box 140
❏ Flip-up Pen Box 144

Chapter 6: Boxes with Flair to Spare 147
❏ A Beveled Beauty. 148
❏ Crown Molding Boxes 155
❏ A Roomy Jewelry Box. 162
❏ Aspen-leaf Treasure Chest 169

Patterns Appendix 175

Index. 189

Metric Equivalents Chart 191

Acknowledgments

My greatest appreciation goes to the past and present design and editorial staff of the Meredith Corporation's *Better Homes & Gardens® WOOD®* magazine for the technical advice, projects, tips, and techniques that you'll find in this book. A special thanks also to woodworking craftsman Jerry Patrasso for his bandsaw skills; designer and boxmaker John Russell for his knowledge; and Sal Marino for his technical assistance with veneering. Individual project designers are also noted as appropriate. Finally, my gratitude to Administrative Assistant Sheryl Munyon at *WOOD* magazine, Jackie Keuck, Meredith's Art Library Manager, and Bob Furstenau, head of Meredith's Information Systems and Technology Department, for their efforts in helping assemble the material for this book.

Peter J. Stephano

Introduction

Boxes: more than just storage

*I*f *you've ever watched a toddler entertain himself for hours playing with the cardboard box the new TV just came in, you have to agree that there's something innately fascinating about boxes. Whether it's the anticipation of what's inside or the possibility of secret contents, who knows? But in addition to being practical, decorative boxes of all shapes and sizes—from toy boxes to jewelry boxes to storage boxes—surround us in our daily lives.*

This book will teach the woodworker how easy it can be to create a wide variety of boxes that will both come in handy and make great gifts!

In some form or another, boxes have always been a significant aspect of daily life in cultures all over the world. Sure, they began as strictly utilitarian storage containers with simple sides, bottoms, and lids, but over time, they have involved into highly decorative items as well. The nomadic Sami people of Arctic Scandinavia, for example, require sturdy, functional boxes in which to store and protect their daily necessities—sugar, tea, flour, and so on. But no matter what the box's purpose or raw material—be it birch-bark, reindeer-skin, or wood—each and every container is adorned with

carving, leather lacing, or jewel-like pieces of antler, and becomes a much-treasured possession handed down through generations.

In less harsh environs, boxes also play important roles. As a child, you learned early on to organize and collect your toys, crayons, and such in boxes. As an adult, you expanded and elaborated on this practice with jewelry boxes, sewing boxes, bread boxes, recipe boxes, and numerous others. It seems that the need for boxes never ends. That's why the editors of *WOOD Magazine* have compiled this book, dedicated to boxes and the tech-

niques for building them.

Although all boxes share the basic elements of bottom, sides, and (most of the time) a lid, you'll discover that there is a myriad of ways to arrive at that configuration. Chapter 1 shows you how to use veneers to turn simple boxes into eye-catching ones. In Chapter 2, you'll learn to create imaginative boxes at the bandsaw from a single piece of wood. In the remaining chapters, you'll jump right into making boxes of your own from more than three dozen outstanding designs that range from the utilitarian to the utterly fanciful. Have fun!

1

Boxes with Different Faces

*W*hen you're making decorative boxes, there's one technique that will come in handy time after time—veneering. This chapter will give you the basics of this woodworking "trick" and introduce you to two box projects in which the technique works well.

THE GREAT COVER-UP: VENEERING 101

Woodworkers have been applying veneers and adding banding inlays to furniture for centuries, but today there are some practical reasons to learn how it's done. Veneer will allow you to turn a box made from inexpensive or featureless wood into a real gem! You can even utilize particleboard, medium-density fiberboard (MDF), or plywood for your basic box, and after veneering, you'll be the only one who knows.

Next, place the workpiece to be covered on the veneer, allowing for at least 1" of waste all around, as shown in **Photo A.** Boxes require the grain to match on neighboring sides, so label consecutive pieces of veneer on the inside face with large letters. Label the mating box sides, too. Try to envision an application order that will provide the best appearance. With a box, glue on the back veneer first, the sides second, and then the front. Add the top last.

Cutting veneer and inlay bandings

You can crosscut and ripcut standard or figured veneer with either a sharp veneer saw or a crafts knife and a metal straightedge. The veneer saw works best on denser woods.

Pictured above are the basic tools used in veneering: veneer and masking tapes, a sponge, a small roller, a veneer saw, a crafts knife with a No. 1 blade, metal straightedge, metal push pins, a combination square, a sanding block, and a pencil. You should be able to find all of these at most art supply and hardware stores.

Laying out the veneer

First, select the veneer types that best suit your project. Look over your veneer carefully to take advantage of its grain patterns or figure and to avoid any flaws. If your veneer has uneven edges, trim them to create true ones.

A

Make your cuts on a flat, firm surface such as particleboard. Start by ripcutting one true or straight edge on your veneer piece. When ripcutting, score and cut from one veneer end to the other, following your straightedge. Make two to four scoring passes as needed to establish a straight line before cutting. If you use the saw, score with just the front corner of the blade. Make final cutting passes by pulling the saw in from one end, with the teeth parallel to the work surface. If you're using a crafts knife, just apply more pressure on each succeeding cut, following the straightedge and score. Be careful that wayward wood grain doesn't pull you off course. If using a crafts knife, change your blades often. (Remember, dull blades can lead to mistakes.)

Now you are ready to crosscut square corners, which is particularly important when cutting pieces for an assembled face (more on this later). Align your true veneer edge with the true edge of the cutting surface. With a metal square or combination square held firmly against the true veneer edge, begin a square crosscut by scoring the wood with two to four passes, cutting in from each edge toward the center of the work to avoid breakout, as shown in **Photo B**. Similarly, make final saw and knife cuts by applying greater pressure on the tool.

For miter cuts, use a combination square, scoring toward the center, then cutting with added pressure, as shown in **Photo C**.

To miter-cut inlay, first miter-cut a length of ¾ × ¾" pine and nail or glue it to a piece of particleboard. Place a strip of inlay as shown in **Photo D**. Then, take a sharp block plane blade, holding the flat side against the mitered pine and over the inlay. Strike the blade with a mallet for a crisp, clean cut.

Jointing edges for perfect seams

Many veneering projects will call for joining pieces edge to edge. To do this, sandwich mating veneers tightly between two edge-jointed boards, allowing less than 1/32" of the veneers to stand proud of the board edges (see **Photo E**). Clamp where needed to prevent movement along the exposed veneer edges. Now, sand or block-plane the edges carefully without bending them over. Make several passes, removing the exposed veneer until it is flush with the board edges.

Joining like veneers to make bigger pieces

To join veneers edge to edge, lay the pieces good-side up on a flat surface. Check that they mate well with no gaps between. Then, pin one piece down, pressing pushpins in through the veneer and into the work surface, angling them away from the joint. Locate the pins ½" from the mating edge, spaced 4–9" apart, depending on the length of the pieces. Be careful not to split the wood. Place the joining piece snugly against the pinned piece, and pin it down as shown in **Photo F**.

After taping these pieces together (see the next section), flip them over and apply a thin bead of yellow woodworker's glue on the underside seam for added strength.

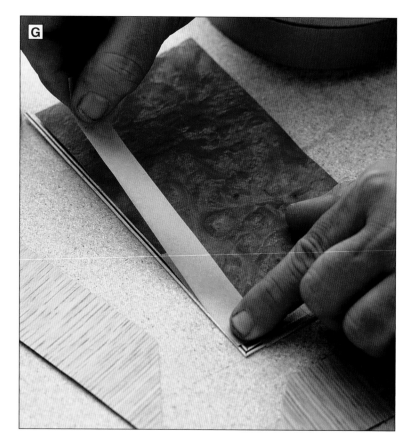

Keep in mind that you should not use flexible veneer (which has a wood veneer thickness of 1/64") for any inlay work or assembled faces. Otherwise you risk sanding through when sanding inlays flush to the surrounding surface. Apply tape to the good side, and remove once the piece is glued in place.

Taping veneers together

Once you have dry-fitted your pieces, you're ready to tape them together into a bigger sheet or an assembled decorative face. To do this, start with two joining pieces of veneer

or inlays—any kind will do. Spot-tape them together, checking for alignment and snugness. Use water-activated veneer tape here, wetting it with a dampened sponge. Then apply a full-length piece, as shown in **Photo G**.

When making an assembled face consisting of several pieces, start from the middle of the assembly and work outward, taping up one piece completely before moving to the next. Roll out the tape for a good bond.

Gluing veneer to a substrate

Select a glue from the "Veneering Glues at a Glance"

chart on *page 9*. (We used a solvent-based contact cement here.) If you use a contact cement, first thin it by 20 percent with contact-cement thinner, then apply two evenly spread coats to each of the mating surfaces with a disposable brush.

With yellow, white, or urea-formaldehyde glues, you may get by with one thin, even coat on one surface. Or, on more porous surfaces, you could roll out a thin coat on each mating surface.

Then, either center the veneer over the substrate material, or vice versa—whichever is easier—and carefully press the veneer in place.

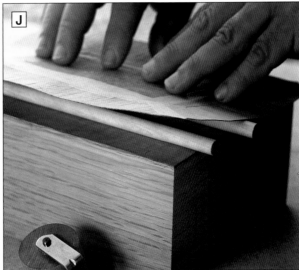

With an assembled face where precision centering is a must, first mark positioning lines on the mating side of the veneer as shown in **Photo I**. Work from one end, allowing for even waste all around. If using contact cement, use dowels or a slip sheet (kraft paper, for instance) while applying the veneer or assembled face. (See **Photo J**.) Remove these as you carefully press the veneer down.

Once the veneer is in place, roll it out, starting from the center as shown in **Photo H**. If you're using something other than contact cement, apply uniform clamping pressure across the entire veneer surface. To do this, apply 2-mil plastic, then a flat piece of particleboard over the glued veneer using as many clamps and weights as needed. The plastic will prevent any glue squeezeout from bonding to the particleboard.

VENEERING GLUES AT A GLANCE

GLUE TYPE	APPLICATIONS	PROS/CONS
WHITE (POLYVINYL RESIN)	Close-grained woods (maple, cherry, etc.); ideally suited to large projects requiring more open time.	Long open time; slightly gummy, doesn't sand as well as yellow glue; weighting or clamping overnight necessary. Bubbles resulting from poor contact can be heated and pressed into place.
YELLOW WOODWORKER'S GLUE (ALIPHATIC RESIN)	Close-grained woods; works best for medium and small projects; could penetrate pinholes and pores of figured veneers.	Short open time (5–10 minutes) and early tack; less time than white glue to move veneers into place; uniform clamping required for at least 2 hours.
CONTACT CEMENT (SOLVENT-BASED ONLY)	Best used for paperback (flexible) veneers or small projects; avoid on large projects with highly figured woods due to control problems and potential for uneven bonding.	Sets on contact; eliminates presses and clamps; slight chance of delamination on highly figured woods; slip sheet required during application while positioning veneer.
UREA-FORMALDEHYDE RESIN	Best all-around glue for applying veneer (standard and paperback) on any surface (particleboard, stable solid wood, etc.).	Doesn't bleed through or allow veneers to creep; must mix by weight; weighting and clamping required.

SHOP**TIP** *Flattening and repairing figured veneer*

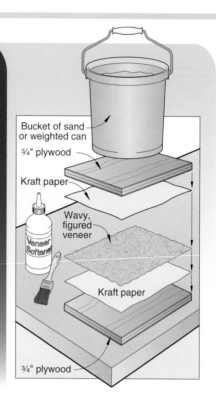

Burl, crotch, and other figured veneers frequently get wavy due to wood stress. They also have cracks, checks, and pinholes that need correcting. Most of these problems need to be dealt with before application.

You can flatten wavy veneer before application by wetting it with a softening solution (available wherever you buy veneer). Brush it onto both sides and let it stand a few minutes. Next, press out the veneer in a sandwich of flat boards and kraft paper, placing a weight on the stack as shown in the drawing here. Let the veneer sit overnight. Repeat if necessary Remember, the results are temporary—you'll only have a 48-hour working window before waviness returns.

You'll have to correct cracks before application, too. You can do this by first applying a piece of masking tape to the veneer's good side to hold the crack together. Then, mix a small batch of epoxy and color-matched sawdust, and gently work it into the crack from the back side, Do not leave any excess on the surface. Later, after the patch has cured and you've glued the veneer in place, remove the tape.

To fill pinholes, first apply the veneer. If you want a glasslike finish, use a color-matching paste filler over the defective area. Wipe off the excess, and then sand away the residue (don't sand through the veneer!). If you're adding a Danish or other penetrating-oil finish, don't bother with pinholes. The finish will fill them.

Bucket of sand or weighted can
¾" plywood
Kraft paper
Wavy, figured veneer
Kraft paper
¾" plywood

Trimming and cleaning up

Holding a metal straightedge along your workpiece and using a crafts knife, trim the excess prior to adding a neighboring piece. (See **Photo K**.) Score and cut as described earlier. Block-sand the remaining fine edge flush.

To remove veneer tape on assemblies, allow the glue to set overnight. Then, moisten 1–2" of the tape at a time to reactivate the adhesive. Next, carefully lift up the moistened tape with a thin, rounded crafts knife or putty knife blade. (See **Photo L**.) Try to avoid making scratches.

Finally, with the tape removed and the edges block-sanded flush and slightly eased, finish-sand the veneered surfaces using a sanding block or finish sander, as shown in **Photo M**. Be careful not to sand through. Move from 180- through 220-grit.

On assembled faces, start sanding the outside edges, moving steadily toward the center. Be aware that inlay typically stands proud of adjoining veneer surfaces, so you'll need to sand it flush. Remove any sanding dust with a clean cloth or vacuum, and you're ready for finishing.

How to finish

Because glues take time to fully cure, wait at least 72 hours before finishing

veneered projects. Oil-based clear finishes, such as polyurethane, work best on veneered projects. However, avoid using lacquer on veneer bonded with contact cement—it reacts with this glue, causing it to loosen.

SPECIAL FEATURE: BUYING VENEERS AND INLAYS

One of the most enjoyable parts of working with veneer or prefabricated inlays is buying it! The range of choices is incredible, and the combinations are practically limitless. If you can't visit a woodworking specialty store, you can always shop by catalog.

Veneer is traditionally sold by the square foot or by a sheet of a particular size. Inlays are usually sold by linear foot or by the piece. Following are descriptions of the different types of veneer.

Standard (or raw) veneer

Made when a cutter knife slices across the face of a water-soaked half log, this so-called flat-cut veneer offers patterns that range from tapering grain to a distinctive cathederal look. (See *below*.) The raw veneers are then dried and stacked in flitches in numbered order, making them ideal for bookmatching. (This is where sequentially sawn pieces of near-identical grain patterns are placed side by side in a veneering project, such as in a cabinet door or drawer front.)

Thicknesses of standard veneer range from $1/28$" to $1/42$". Sheets come in random widths from 3" to 12", and between 3' and 10' long. Costs range from $.50 to $2.75 per square foot.

Figured veneer

Like standard veneer, figured veneer is flat-cut and stacked in flitches, but figured veneers are the showiest in the veneer line-up—they consist of only the most fanciful grain patterns. Woodworkers tend to favor these most because of the wide variety of possibilities for decorative projects, from box tops to drawer fronts.

These veneer slices come from tree parts where extreme grain patterns are manifested— growths, roots, and places where trunks split into large branches. From these we get burls, curly, quilted, and crotch woods. But one thing to remember is that figured veneers tend to be unstable. Often, sheets of figured veneer are wavy, containing cracks and pinholes. These imperfections will necessitate flattening and some minor repair work before you apply it. (See the Shop Tip on *page 10*.)

Though the thickness of figured veneer is the same as that of other flat-cut veneer, pieces tend to be smaller, starting around 10 × 10". Prices are higher than for standard veneer, with premium walnut and elm burls costing more than $4 per

Quartersawn oak

Walnut burl

Mahogany crotch

Flat-cut rosewood

Birdseye maple

Dyed veneers

Flexible veneer

Decorative inlay bandings

square foot. To get the best look and to avoid problems in the veneer, allow for 50 percent waste when ordering.

Quartersawn veneer

This veneer type comes from logs quartered lengthwise, through which cuts are made at a right angle to the annular growth rings. The process yields veneers with straight, parallel grain lines and high wood stability. Quartersawn veneers, such as oak, create a pleasant, consistent design and can often be seen in mission furniture pieces. Sheet sizes are the same as those of standard veneer, but expect higher prices.

Dyed veneer

Made from fine-grain, flat-cut hardwoods, dyed veneer features solid, rich colors penetrating through $\frac{1}{28}$"-thick sheets. Colors include black, red, orange, green, blue, and yellow. Dimensions range between 6" and 10", with lengths up to 3'. Priced around $2.75 per square foot, woodworkers often rely on dyed black veneers to serve as an ebony look-alike, and other dyed veneers to help create striking accents and surfaces.

Other veneers

Because of interest among builders, architects, and cabinetmakers, manufacturers developed other veneer types with special advantages. These,

in general, reduce application time and labor costs while covering larger areas and solving such tricky tasks as veneering curved surfaces.

One such type is *paperback* or *flexible veneer*. The easiest special type to work with, this veneer costs about two to three times more than standard veneer. Sold in 18"- to 48"-wide rolls 8' long, paperback veneer consists of a $\frac{1}{64}$" layer of smooth, factory-sanded veneer (such as walnut) applied to a 5- or 10-mil paper backing. It can be cut with scissors, though sanding through the thin veneer can present a problem. For this reason, paperback serves better as attractive covering for jobs such as large tables and cabinet sides.

Another variety of flexible veneer, *peel-and-stick* or *pressure-sensitive veneer*, has an adhesive backing that sticks to a substrate's surface when pressed or ironed in place. This veneer requires a very clean surface during application; otherwise, failure may result.

Rotary-cut veneer takes shape when logs spin on a large lathe while a sharp horizontal knife peels off long, thin layers of wood. The layers are cut and dried, and later go into the making of plywoods. The final look features repetitive cathedral patterns.

Decorative inlays

Inlays come in two types, inlay bandings and inlay faces. The former begins as solid wood

Decorative
inlay faces

laminations made up of two or more contrasting woods. Strips are cut from the laminations and then sanded to $\frac{1}{28}$" thick. The resulting multicolored strips, measuring between $\frac{1}{16}$" and $1\frac{1}{2}$" wide, let you spice up projects with attractive accents and borders. Strips are sold in 3' lengths and are priced by the running foot. The wider and more complex they are, the higher the price usually is.

Inlay faces, by contrast, consist of marquetry pieces, pictures, or designs made from various veneers. With these, you may find images of shells, flowers, sunbursts, and so on. Applied as an inlay or overlay (glued onto a wood surface), inlay faces are available for prices ranging from $3 to $50 each. More elaborate faces look great on box tops.

CREATE A MARQUETRY MIRAGE

Mirages are optical illusions arising from the refraction if light passing through different air layers. Sure, you'll see them in hot oppresive desert heat and on cold winter seas…but on a box?

Yes, says New Yorker John Russell. He's been creating them with wood veneer for decades. So, follow along as he walks you through the building of one such box. Be sure to heed his tips along the way.

Note: the full-size patterns for the project shown here can be found on pages 175-177.

Materials List

Part	FINISHED SIZE				
	T	W	L	Matl.	Qty.
A sides	¼"	4⅞"	4⅞"	M	4
B ends	¼"	5"	5"	M	2
C liners	⅛"	3¼"	4½"	M	4

Material Key: M–mahogany

Supplies: glue, silica sand, finish

Start by building a hollow cube

1 From a ¾ × 5½ × 36" piece of stock, resaw and plane a blank to ¼" thick for the sides (**A**) and ends (**B**). Plane a 22"-long piece of the remaining stock to ⅛" thick for the liners (**C**), and set it aside.

2 Cut the sides (**A**) to the dimensions listed in the Materials List. With a single blade from your dado set in your tablesaw, cut grooves with the grain in the edges of the sides (**A**), as shown in the Corner Detail of the Box Assembly drawing (*right*).

3 Attach an auxiliary fence to your tablesaw rip fence, position it so the blade just grazes it, and form the tongues by cutting rabbets on the edges opposite the grooves as shown. Be sure to make test cuts in scrap to ensure a snug fit of the tongues in the grooves.

4 Dry-assemble the four sides. Check the dimensions for the ends (**B**) and cut them to size. Install a ¼" dado blade in your table-saw, and cut the dadoes in the ends as shown. A snug fit of the ends in the assembled sides will keep the box square.

5 Glue and clamp the sides and ends together. When the glue is dry, sand the outside of the box to 120-grit. To keep the sides flat and the edges crisp, adhere a sheet of sandpaper to a flat surface, and

move the box in a circular motion on the sandpaper. Set the box aside.

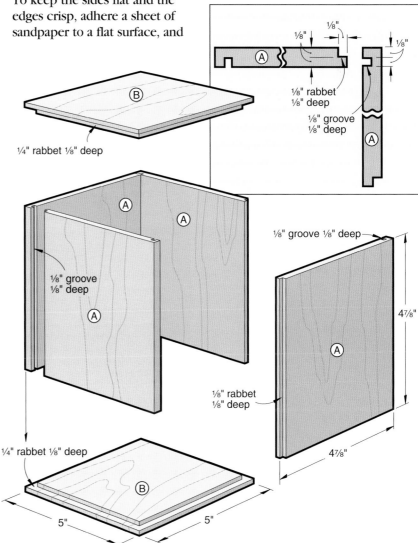

¼" rabbet ⅛" deep

⅛" groove ⅛" deep

¼" rabbet ⅛" deep

⅛" rabbet ⅛" deep

⅛" groove ⅛" deep

4⅞"

4⅞"

⅛" rabbet ⅛" deep

5"   5"

⅛"   ⅛"   ⅛"

⅛" rabbet ⅛" deep

⅛" groove ⅛" deep

Create a veneer illusion

1 For your box, you'll need one 3½" × 36" strip each of tulipwood, wenge, and maple veneers. Rough-cut the veneer to the following: four pieces of tulipwood 5½" long and one 7" long; four pieces of wenge 6½" long and one 7" long; and two pieces of maple 6½" long and one 5" long. Straighten one edge of each piece on your jointer (see Shop Tip *above right*).

2 To create an invisible joint where the jointed edge of the veneer abuts another piece, bevel the back edge. To do this, hold the veneer at an angle and sand a slight bevel as shown in the drawing *below*. Use a sheet of 120-grit sandpaper adhered to a flat surface. To avoid confusion as you assemble the veneers, mark the jointed and beveled edges on the back of each piece. The back is the side with the heel of the bevel.

SHOP TIP

To get a perfectly straight edge on several pieces of veneer at once, sandwich the veneer between two clamped blocks of wood and joint the edge of this sandwich, as shown here. Orient the veneer grain as you would when jointing a board. Set the jointer for a light cut—about ⅟32" or so.

3 The three-dimensional illusion on this box depends heavily on a shadow effect created on one corner of each of the maple triangles. This shading is the result of singeing the veneer in hot sand (see the Shop Tip *below*). Put 1" of sand in a steel cake pan and place it on a burner over medium heat for about 10 minutes. Slice the 7"-long pieces of maple cut in Step 1 into 3 ⅟3" squares.

SHOP TIP
The Secret's in the Sand

For shading the veneer, purchase silica sand, intended for sandblasting, from your local home center.

Hot sand will cause the veneer to shrink and distort slightly, so cut your project pieces to a larger size and trim them after shading. You can trim each piece so as to precisely position the shading on it.

Use extra veneer to experiment. The shading effect can vary considerably depending on heat intensity and the thickness and species of your veneer. Be careful not to burn the veneer by leaving it in the sand too long or letting it touch the bottom of the pan.

The hot sand singes the veneer, creating a shaded effect.

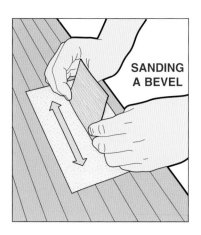

SANDING A BEVEL

Immerse one corner of each square in the hot sand as shown, until you achieve the desired amount of shading.

4 Using the full-size patterns on *pages 175–177*, and using a crafts/utility knife, metal ruler, and combination square, cut the veneers to final size. (Read "How to be a Cutup Artist," *right.*) Cut the squares of tulipwood and wenge from the 7" pieces that you cut in Step 1. Mark the backs of the pieces as you cut them. The backs are the sides with the knife plow.

How To Be a Cutup Artist

When cutting veneer, always use a fresh blade. A dull blade will tear the wood fibers and make rough, inaccurate edges. Guide your cut with a steel ruler, and to avoid tearing the veneer, cut in from both edges toward the middle. Complete the cut in several passes. Most hardwood veneers require two or three passes; exotic woods such as wenge can take up to five or six swipes with a knife.

To get super-tight joints, always position the veneer face-down when cutting. This way, the knife edge creates a "plow" on the back side of the veneer, as shown in the Knife Plow drawing. The plowing action will create beveled edges that make for nearly invisible joint lines when you tightly butt together two edges as shown in the Veneer Joint drawing.

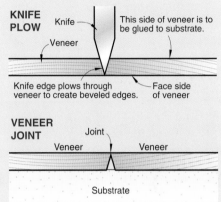

KNIFE PLOW — Knife — This side of veneer is to be glued to substrate. — Veneer — Knife edge plows through veneer to create beveled edges. — Face side of veneer

VENEER JOINT — Joint — Veneer — Veneer — Substrate

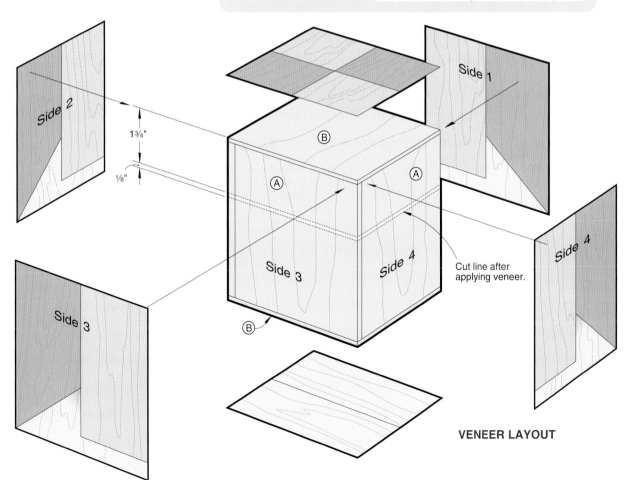

Side 2

Side 1

1¾"

⅛"

Ⓑ

Ⓐ   Ⓐ

Side 3   Side 4   Side 4

Cut line after applying veneer.

Ⓑ

Side 3

VENEER LAYOUT

5 Assemble the veneers for each side of the box, placing them with their marked sides down, on a flat surface. Tape them together as shown on the Veneer Layout drawing on *page 17*. Make sure all the mating edges are straight and the veneer joints are tight.

Give your illusion substance

1 Draw center lines both ways on the top and bottom of the box. Cut a ¾ × 6½ × 6½" piece of particleboard for a clamping platen, cover it with a piece of waxed paper, and place the first side veneer assembly face-down on it. Spread a thin coat of glue on one side of the box, and position it on the veneer as shown in the drawing *below*. Because veneer has a tendency to shift when pressure is applied, use a little yellow glue for a fast grab. Clamp the box to the platen.

2 After the glue dries, place the box, veneer-side-down, on a piece of cardboard and trim the excess veneer as shown in **Photo A**. Be sure to cut from both edges to the center. Sand the edge flush with a firm sanding block.

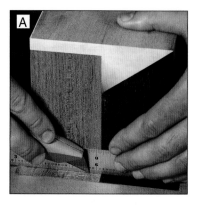

3 Repeat the veneering sequence in Steps 1 and 2 for the other three sides, then for the top and bottom, as shown on the Veneer Layout drawing. Sand the box lightly, and soften the corners with 320-grit sandpaper, taking care not to sand through the veneer.

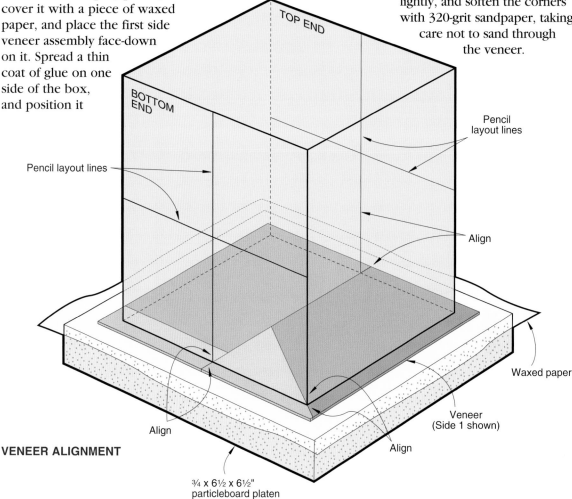

Pencil layout lines

Pencil layout lines

Align

Align

Waxed paper

Veneer (Side 1 shown)

Align

TOP END

BOTTOM END

VENEER ALIGNMENT

¾ x 6½ x 6½" particleboard platen

Turn your veneered cube into a box

1 Raise your tablesaw blade to cut 7/32" deep, and position the rip fence 1¾" from the blade. With the box top against the fence, cut all the way around. Apply masking tape to the box in the path of the blade and back your cuts with a follower block to avoid chipping the veneer as the blade exits the back of the cut.

2 Separate the lid from the box as shown in **Photo B**. Remove the remaining waste from the saw kerf with your sanding block.

3 Rip your ⅛" stock to 3¼" wide. Miter-cut four pieces to fit tightly inside the box for the liner

(**C**), as shown in the drawing *below*. Sand round-overs on the top edges, and slide the liners into place. The liner protrudes ¼" to provide a lip for the lid.

4 Because the tulipwood and wenge veneers are porous, apply a paste wood filler following container directions. (A transparent, water-based filler was used here.) Top off with two coats of gloss spray finish, sanding lightly with 320-grit sandpaper between coats. Only the outside of the box will require finishing.

SHOP TIP

Excess glue isn't such a big deal when it squeezes out of typical woodworking joints, but too much glue can totally ruin a veneering project. That's because the excess adhesive will squeeze right through the pores of veneer. Even if you succeed in sanding the extra glue off the surface without sanding through the veneer, the glue will still be visible in the pores.

To avoid this calamity, apply just a thin layer of glue to one surface—the substrate. Move the glue around with a plastic spreader or an ink roller to get a thin, uniform coating.

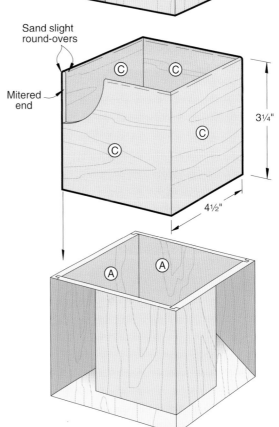

Sand slight round-overs

Mitered end

3¼"

4½"

Carefully slice through the last 1/32" by cutting down the center of the saw kerf with a utility knife.

QUILT-TOP WOOD BOX

Sure, the "quilt-top" design seems perfect for storing yarn or sewing supplies, but don't limit yourself. It would also be great for holding your playing cards and poker chips.

Although the box shown actually employs ⅛"-thick, diamond-shaped wood pieces for the star-patterned lid, veneer can be substituted. However, you'll have to adjust the groove dimensions in the lid to allow for the thinner material. Either way, you'll enjoy making this box that's sure to please whoever uses it.

Note: *for a full-size pattern you can use in creating the top of this box, refer to page 25.*

Begin with the base and lid pieces

1 Rip and crosscut a piece of ½" walnut to 1" wide by 26" long for the lid pieces (**A**) and a second ½" piece to 2¼" wide by 26" long for the base pieces (**B**). Notice on the Cutting Diagram how we cut these two pieces side-by-side from the same stock so

the grain would match between the lid and base.

2 Using the Forming the Lid Profile drawing *(page 22)* for reference, machine the 1"-wide lid strip. Repeat the process using Forming the Base Profile drawing *(page 22)* to shape the base strip.

3 Miter-cut eight pieces at 22½° to 2⅞" long to form the lid pieces (**A**). Number the pieces in the order in which they were cut so you can align the grain when gluing them together later.

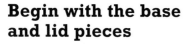

FULL-SIZE DIAMOND PATTERN

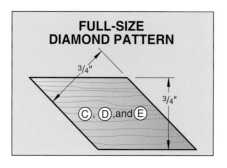

¾"

¾"

Ⓒ, Ⓓ, and Ⓔ

Materials List

Part	Finished Size			Matl.	Qty.
	T	W	L		
A lid sides	½"	1"	2⅞"	W	8
B base sides	½"	2¼"	2⅞"	W	8
C walnut diamonds	⅛"	¾"	¾"	W	8
D maple diamonds	⅛"	¾"	¾"	M	16
E oak diamonds	⅛"	¾"	¾"	O	40
F panels	¼"	6½"	6½"	P	2

Pieces are cut oversized to start. See the how-to instructions for cutting the pieces to the finished sizes shown above.

Materials Key: W–walnut, M–maple, O–oak, P–walnut or oak plywood.

Supplies: clear finish.

4
Repeat step 3 to cut and number the eight base sides (**B**).

Miter-cut the diamonds

1
Build the jig shown in the Miter Jig drawing at *right*. Angle your miter gauge 45° from center. Position the jig against the miter gauge so the adjustable stop is ¾" away from the blade as shown in the drawing. Drill pilot holes and screw the jig to the miter gauge.

2
Cut a piece of walnut to ⁵⁄₃₂ × ¾ × 18", two pieces of maple to ⁵⁄₃₂ × ¾ × 18", and four pieces of oak

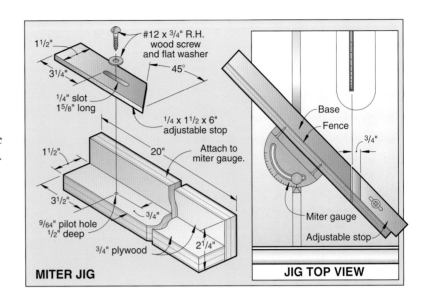

MITER JIG

#12 x ¾" R.H. wood screw and flat washer

1½"

3¼"

45°

¼" slot 1⅝" long

¼ x 1½ x 6" adjustable stop

1½"

20"

Attach to miter gauge.

3½"

¾"

⁹⁄₆₄" pilot hole ½" deep

¾" plywood

2¼"

JIG TOP VIEW

Base

Fence

¾"

Miter gauge

Adjustable stop

to ⁵⁄₃₂ × ¾ × 20". Make a 45° miter-cut at one end of each

strip. These strips will be used for the diamonds (**C**, **D**, **E**).

3
Raise the blade on your tablesaw ¼" above the surface of the jig base.

4
As shown in **Photo A**, place the mitered end of one of the strips against the stop, and miter-cut a test diamond. Position the wood diamond on the Full-Size Diamond Pattern *(page 25)*.

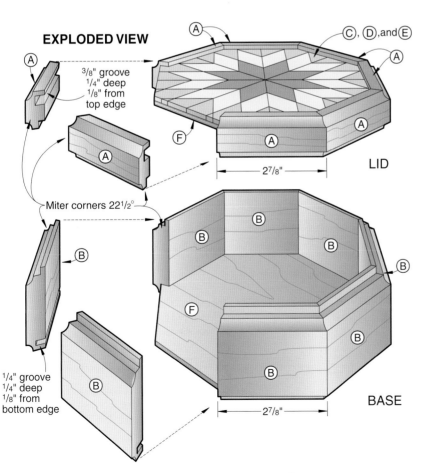

EXPLODED VIEW

ⓐ

⅜" groove ¼" deep ⅛" from top edge

ⓐ

ⓐ

Ⓒ, Ⓓ, and Ⓔ

ⓐ

ⓐ

Ⓕ

ⓐ

LID

2⅞"

Miter corners 22½°

Ⓑ

Ⓑ

Ⓑ

Ⓑ

Ⓕ

Ⓑ

¼" groove ¼" deep ⅛" from bottom edge

Ⓑ

Ⓑ

Ⓑ

BASE

2⅞"

A

Using the miter jig, miter-cut the diamond pieces to size from the hardwood strips.

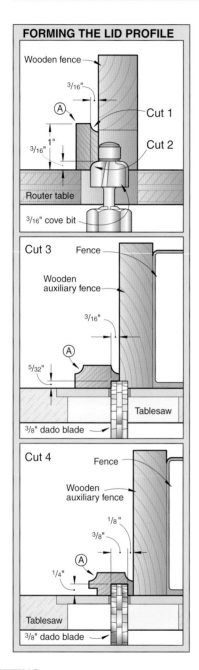

FORMING THE LID PROFILE

Wooden fence

3/16"

(A)

Cut 1

Cut 2

1"

3/16"

Router table

3/16" cove bit

Cut 3   Fence

Wooden auxiliary fence

3/16"

(A)

5/32"

Tablesaw

3/8" dado blade

Cut 4   Fence

Wooden auxiliary fence

1/8"

3/8"

(A)

1/4"

Tablesaw

3/8" dado blade

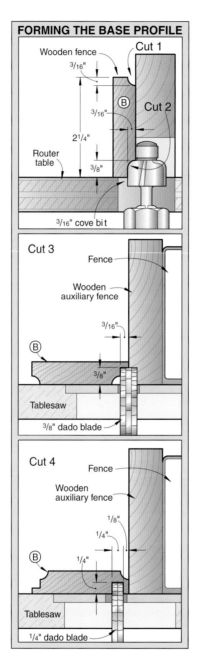

FORMING THE BASE PROFILE

Wooden fence   Cut 1

3/16"

(B)   Cut 2

3/16"

2 1/4"

Router table

3/8"

3/16" cove bit

Cut 3

Fence

Wooden auxiliary fence

3/16"

(B)

3/8"

Tablesaw

3/8" dado blade

Cut 4   Fence

Wooden auxiliary fence

1/8"

1/4"

(B)

1/4"

1/4"

Tablesaw

1/4" dado blade

If necessary, adjust the stop and jig angle so the piece just cut is the same length and shape as the full-size pattern.

5 Miter-cut the diamonds from each strip. (We used the eraser end of a pencil to hold the diamond being cut in place.) After pushing the strip through the blade to make the cut, remove the diamond from the jig before moving the jig back across the blade for the next cut.

Glue the diamonds to the top panel

1 Cut two 6-1/2" square pieces of 1/4" walnut or oak plywood for the top and bottom panels (**F**). Mark centerlines on the top panel as shown in the Lid Panel drawing on *page 22*.

2 Cut two 3¼" squares from ⅛" hardboard. Stick the two 3¼" squares caddy-corner from each other on the unveneered face of the ¼" plywood top panel (**F**) with double-faced tape. Use a square to make sure the 3¼" hardboard squares are positioned at a right angle to each other.

CUTTING DIAGRAM

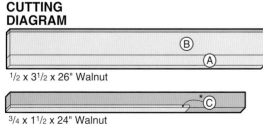

(B)

(A)

1/2 x 3 1/2 x 26" Walnut

(C)

3/4 x 1 1/2 x 24" Walnut

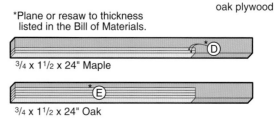

*Plane or resaw to thickness listed in the Bill of Materials.

(D)

3/4 x 1 1/2 x 24" Maple

(E)

3/4 x 1 1/2 x 24" Oak

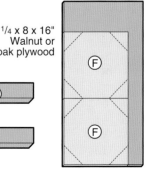

1/4 x 8 x 16" Walnut or oak plywood

(F)

(F)

3 Spread glue on one of the exposed square areas of the top panel. Position the diamonds (**C**, **D**, **E**) tightly into the corners and against each other on glue-covered areas as shown in **Photo B**. (You might use white glue for its extended working time.) Position wax paper and a clamp block on top of each glued-up pattern, observing the pieces closely so they don't spread apart.

4 Remove the two taped-on 3¼" hardboard squares from the top panel, and repeat the process to cover those areas with the hardwood diamonds. Now, before the glue is fully dried, clamp the top panel to a flat surface to keep it from cupping. (Left unclamped, the top panel might cup as the glue dries.)

5 Fit your bandsaw with a fine-toothed blade and trim the overhanging portions of the diamonds flush with the edges of the top panel (**F**). Sand the cut edges flat.

6 Position the top panel upside down on your workbench. Mark cut-lines on the plywood to form a perfect octagon. See the Lid Pattern drawing, *above right,* for reference. Bandsaw along these lines to cut the top panel to final shape. Repeat for the bottom panel.

7 Sand the top surface of the top panel smooth and until it fits into the ⅜" groove in the lid pieces (**A**).

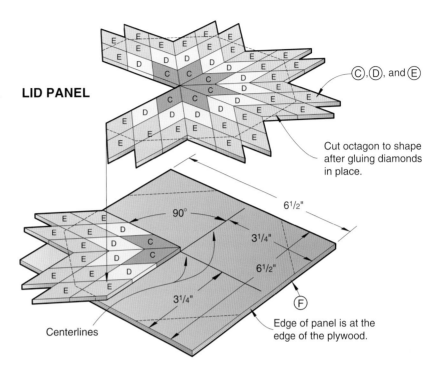

LID PANEL

Ⓒ,Ⓓ, and Ⓔ

Cut octagon to shape after gluing diamonds in place.

90°

6½"

3¼"

6½"

3¼"

Ⓕ

Centerlines

Edge of panel is at the edge of the plywood.

B

Use two square positioning blocks to align the diamonds when gluing them to the top panel.

Assembling the pieces

1 Line up the base sides in the order in which they were cut and numbered, inside face down. This will allow the grain to wrap around the base. Use masking tape to tape the pieces together at the miter joints, using a straight-edge to keep the edges flush. See **Photo C** for reference.

2 Wrap the taped-together pieces around the bottom panel to check the fit; adjust if necessary.

3 Use a small brush to spread an even coat of glue on the miter joints.

4 Roll the taped-together base side pieces around the bottom panel (**F**) as shown in **Photo D**. Use a band clamp or rubber bands to clamp the box sides to close the joints tight. Wipe off any excess glue with a damp cloth. Then, place the clamped-together assembly on a flat surface with a weight on top of it to hold it flat while it dries. Let the assembly dry overnight.

5 Repeat the process with the lid sides and lid panel. Wipe off any glue squeeze-out with a damp cloth, and place the lid on the base to test the fit of the two assemblies. Let the glued-together lid dry while fitted to the base.

6 Finish-sand the box and lid (you might consider wrapping sandpaper around a ⅜" dowel to sand the coves.) Apply a clear finish (satin polyurethane works nicely) to the base and lid.

Use a straightedge to align one edge of the base pieces when taping them together at the miter joints.

Wrap the taped-together side pieces around the base panel. Use a band clamp to pull the joints tight.

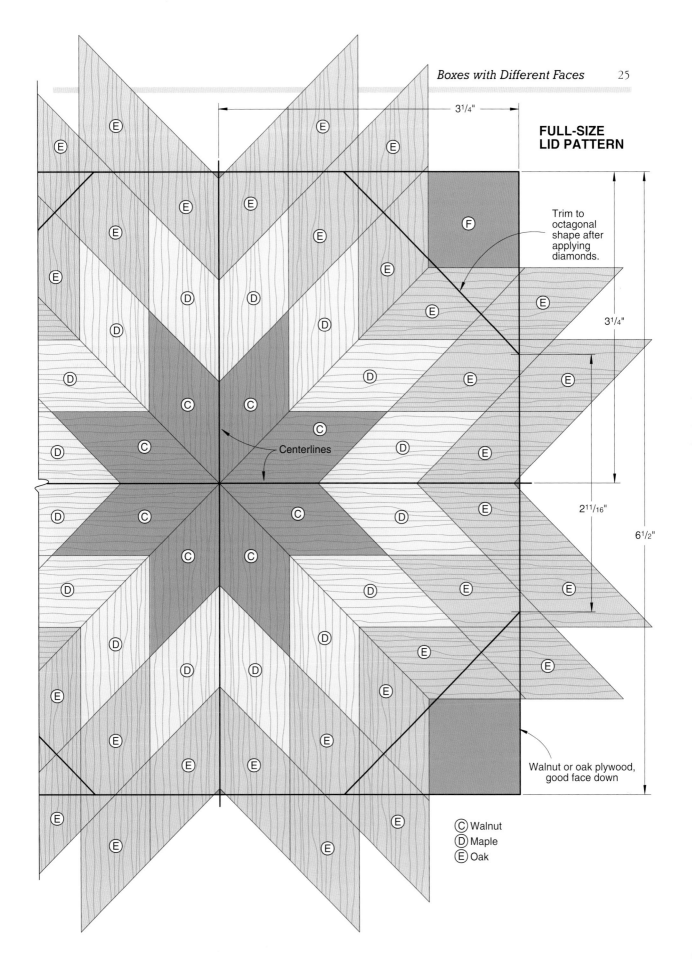

3 1/4"

FULL-SIZE LID PATTERN

Ⓕ

Trim to octagonal shape after applying diamonds.

3 1/4"

Centerlines

2 11/16"

6 1/2"

Walnut or oak plywood, good face down

Ⓒ Walnut
Ⓓ Maple
Ⓔ Oak

A KEEPSAKE BOX

If you need a great example of a handsome box that you can create with veneer, you've found it! Use quartersawn oak veneer for the sides and top banding that surrounds a veneer of madrone burl banded by inlay. Or, choose other species for a different special effect.

Start with the basic box

1 Cut the box front and back (**A**), sides (**B**), and top and bottom (**C**) to the dimensions in the Materials List. (Maple was used in this project.)

2 Rout ⅜" rabbets ⅛" deep in the front and back as shown in the Box Assembly drawing.

3 Glue and clamp the front, back, and sides together, checking for square.

4 Glue and clamp on the box top and bottom (**C**). Remove any squeeze-out.

5 Finish-sand the box with 150-grit sandpaper in preparation for the veneers and inlay. Maintain sharp corners all around.

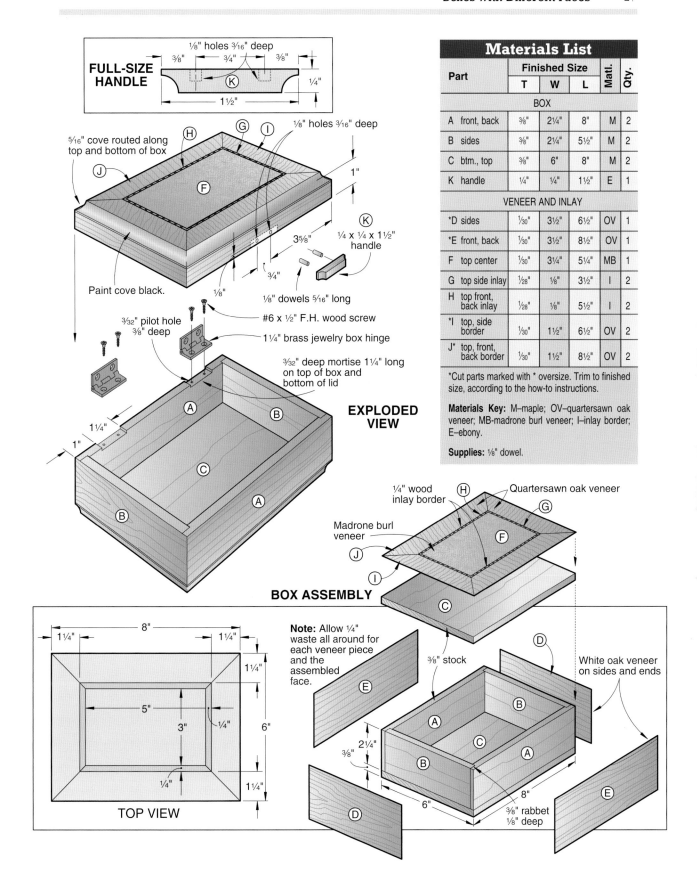

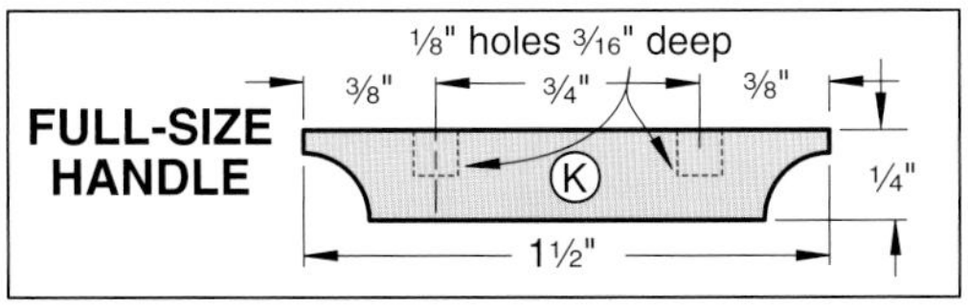
FULL-SIZE HANDLE
1/8" holes 3/16" deep
3/8"
3/4"
3/8"
K
1/4"
1 1/2"

Materials List

Part	Finished Size T	W	L	Matl.	Qty.
BOX					
A front, back	3/8"	2 1/4"	8"	M	2
B sides	3/8"	2 1/4"	5 1/2"	M	2
C btm., top	3/8"	6"	8"	M	2
K handle	1/4"	1/4"	1 1/2"	E	1
VENEER AND INLAY					
*D sides	1/30"	3 1/2"	6 1/2"	OV	1
*E front, back	1/30"	3 1/2"	8 1/2"	OV	1
F top center	1/30"	3 1/4"	5 1/4"	MB	1
G top side inlay	1/28"	1/8"	3 1/2"	I	2
H top front, back inlay	1/28"	1/8"	5 1/2"	I	2
*I top, side border	1/30"	1 1/2"	6 1/2"	OV	2
J* top, front, back border	1/30"	1 1/2"	8 1/2"	OV	2

*Cut parts marked with * oversize. Trim to finished size, according to the how-to instructions.

Materials Key: M–maple; OV–quartersawn oak veneer; MB-madrone burl veneer; I–inlay border; E–ebony.

Supplies: 1/8" dowel.

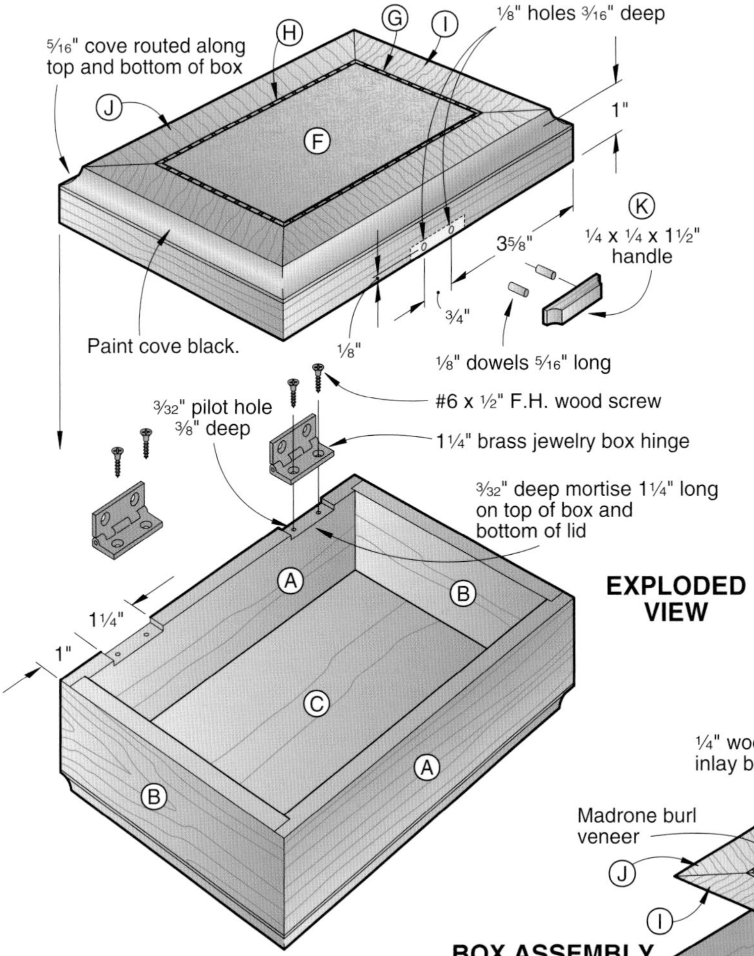
5/16" cove routed along top and bottom of box
H
G
I
1/8" holes 3/16" deep
J
F
1"
K
1/4 x 1/4 x 1 1/2" handle
3 5/8"
3/4"
Paint cove black.
1/8"
1/8" dowels 5/16" long
#6 x 1/2" F.H. wood screw
3/32" pilot hole 3/8" deep
1 1/4" brass jewelry box hinge
3/32" deep mortise 1 1/4" long on top of box and bottom of lid
A
B
1 1/4"
1"
C
A
B
EXPLODED VIEW

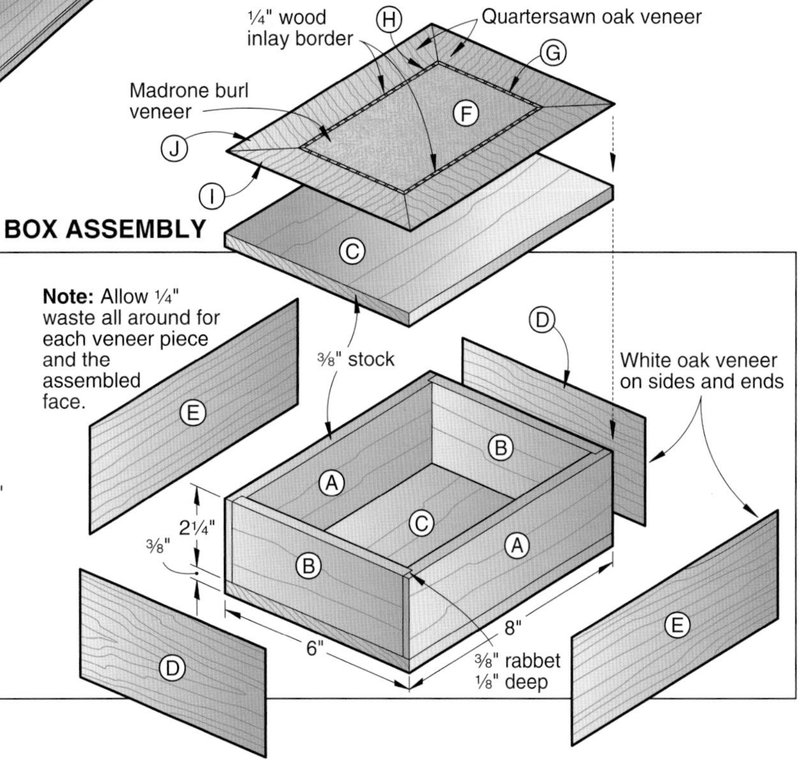
1/4" wood inlay border
H
Quartersawn oak veneer
G
Madrone burl veneer
F
J
I
BOX ASSEMBLY
C
Note: Allow 1/4" waste all around for each veneer piece and the assembled face.
3/8" stock
D
White oak veneer on sides and ends
E
B
A
C
A
B
2 1/4"
3/8"
8"
6"
3/8" rabbet 1/8" deep
D
E

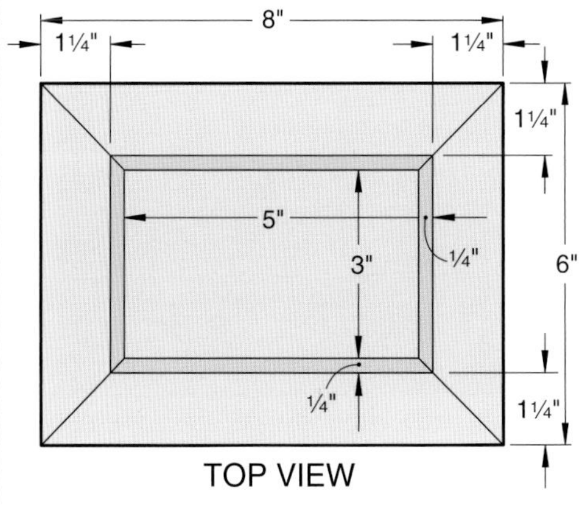
8"
1 1/4"
1 1/4"
1 1/4"
5"
1/4"
3"
6"
1/4"
1 1/4"
TOP VIEW

Jazz up your box with veneers and inlays

1 Feel free to select any combination of veneers and inlay that you like, or go with our choices, spelled out in the Materials List.

2 Cut the veneer sides (**D**), and front and back (**E**), leaving ¼" extra all around (refer to the cutting instructions starting on *page 5* for these and all subsequent cuts.)

3 Glue on the side pieces, then the front and back, using solvent-based contact cement or another adhesive. (Referring to the techniques on *page 10*, trim the excess veneer from the box.)

4 Cut out the figured center piece (**F**), ensuring that the corners are square. Then, miter-cut an inlay border (**G** or **H**), taping it to the figured center, as shown in "Taping veneers together" on *page 8*. Cut and tape the remaining inlay borders, and then add the oak surround pieces (**I, J**) to complete the assembled face.

Once the tape dries, lay the assembled face on its taped side and dry-fit the box on top of it. (We aligned the mitered corners of the oak surround with the box corners, penciling the box outline on the face to mark exact placement of the box.)

5 Apply the assembled face to the box top. (Because we used contact cement, we had to use dowels to separate the face and box top while aligning the box with the placement lines on the face. We then flipped the box and carefully removed the dowels, pressing the face out with a roller for a full bonding.) Once the glue cures, trim the excess and sand flush.

6 Remove the tape and finish-sand the veneered box. Be careful not to sand through the veneer.

Cove the edges and create the lid

1 Chuck a ⁵⁄₁₆" cove bit in a table-mounted router. (if possible, use a new, sharp bit to reduce the chance of splintering.) Making ¹⁄₃₂" incremental passes, rout around the top and bottom edges. Holding the box firmly and snugly to the fence, begin by climb-cutting the coves while pulling the box toward you as shown in **Photo A**. Before reaching the end of the cut, pull the box away from the fence and bit. Finish the pass by placing the box on the

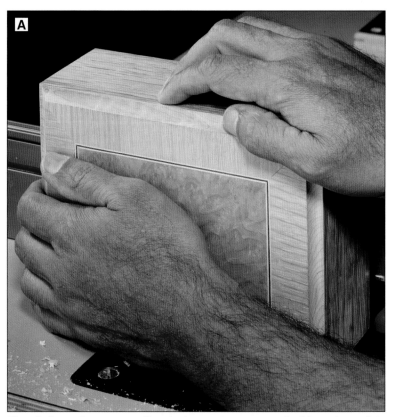

First climb-cut the coves, pulling the box partway across the bit, and complete the cut, moving in the reverse direction.

opposite side of the bit and routing the remaining portion of the edge. Again, this approach will help reduce splintering. Continue routing until you reach the cove depth shown in the drawings.

2 Note on the Exploded View drawing where the box base and lid divide. Now, apply masking tape around the box at this location to reduce splintering when sawing the box in two. Also, cut four 1 × 1" shims to the thickness of your tablesaw blade.

   Raise the saw blade to ½", adjust the fence, and begin sawing off the box lid. Cut the sides first and then insert and tape shims in the kerfs. Saw the box front, add two more shims, and then saw the box back as shown in **Photo B**. Block-sand the sawn edges to remove marks.

3 Chuck a ½" straight bit in your table-mounted router, raising it ³⁄₃₂" above the table. Adjust the fence 1" from the bit and rout the hinge mortises as shown in **Photo C**. Adjust the fence as needed to complete the mortises. Test-fit the hinges and drill the pilot holes for the screws.

4 Carefully finish-sand the box and wipe it clean with a cloth. Wait at least 72 hours after gluing before applying a finish. (We brushed on three coats of polyurethane, sanding between coats with gray ultra-fine pads. Then we masked around the coves and painted these areas with black enamel. Finally, with extra-fine pads, we smoothed the surfaces with paste wax.) Once the finish dries, screw the hinges into place.

5 Scroll saw and sand the lid handle to shape using the pattern in the Exploded View drawing. Drill ⅛" dowel holes in the handle and box lid as shown. Cut two ⅛" dowels ⁵⁄₁₆" long, glue them into the handle, then glue the handle to the lid.

Separate the box lid by raising your saw blade 1⁄2" and cutting evenly around the box perimeter as shown.

Rout the mortises for the 11⁄4" jewelry-box hinges. Test-fit the hinges in the openings to check the depth and width.

2

Bandsaw Boxes

*B*andsawn boxes may seem complex, but they're actually quite simple—
all you need to get started are a sturdy bandsaw and a few good ideas.
But before you get ahead of yourself, start with the four simple box projects
presented on the following pages.

If you've never tried making bandsawn boxes before, it's a good idea to make the practice boxes from scraps of glued-up 2 × 4s. You can move on to fancier (and costlier) woods later.

After a few practice cuts, you'll know if your bandsaw is up to the task of cutting thick wood. You'll always get the best results if you use a sharp, ¼"-wide, 6-teeth per inch, hook-tooth blade. Be sure to adjust the saw for a cut that's at exactly a 90-degree angle to the table. (For tight cuts, you'll also need a similar ⅛" blade.) Start by cutting both some softwoods and hardwoods up to 5" thick. If your saw can't muster the power to

cut these (or a least a couple of inches of thickness), you might want to invest in a saw with at least a ¾-horsepower motor. A good set of blade guides will keep the blade from bowing sideways.

When you're ready, follow the instructions on the following pages to create the four basic bandsawn boxes. Each successive one increases a bit in complexity and introduces you to a different technique. After the first four basic lessons, you'll move on to learn some tips and techniques from a professional boxbuilder.

1. Small box
2. Side stock
3. Large blank
4. Medium blank
5. Small blank
6. Large box
7. Raw material (redwood burl)
8. Medium box

FOUR BASIC BOXES

Following the step-by-step illustrations here, you'll be able to make all of these boxes. You won't find any dimensions, though, because you can make them as large or small as you like, depending on your needs and the stock available. Burled wood looks great for these, or you can give them a more modern look by laminating a block from a combination of different species—say, a walnut stripe glued between blocks of maple.

When using plain-grained wood, be sure to make your entry cuts *with the grain*. These cuts are easier to conceal when you glue and clamp them later on.

Remember, use sharp bandsaw blades, and round off their backs by touching a file or whetstone against the back corners as the saw runs. This helps keep the blade negotiable through tight turns. Hold the file or stone firmly on the table, and lightly touch it to the blade. *Always* remove dust from your bandsaw to prevent sparks from igniting a fire. If you plan to also use a ⅛" blade, round its back, too.

Note: *a full-sized pattern for the heart-shaped box can be found on page 40.*

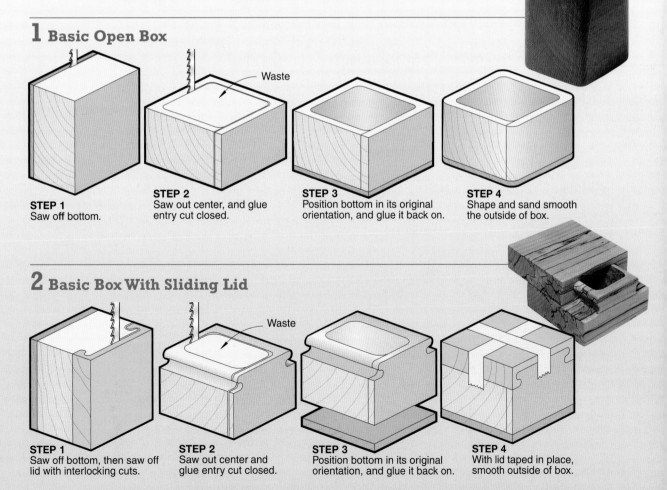

1 Basic Open Box

STEP 1
Saw off bottom.

STEP 2
Saw out center, and glue entry cut closed.

STEP 3
Position bottom in its original orientation, and glue it back on.

STEP 4
Shape and sand smooth the outside of box.

2 Basic Box With Sliding Lid

STEP 1
Saw off bottom, then saw off lid with interlocking cuts.

STEP 2
Saw out center and glue entry cut closed.

STEP 3
Position bottom in its original orientation, and glue it back on.

STEP 4
With lid taped in place, smooth outside of box.

3 Basic Box With Lift-Out Tray

Waste

STEP 1
Saw off bottom of box. Saw out center, and glue entry cut closed. Glue bottom of box back on.

STEP 2
Saw out center of "waste" to be used as tray bottom.

¹/₈" blades

STEP 3
Saw out two sections to create tray. Glue entry cuts closed.

STEP 4
Saw out center section to create tray support. Glue entry cut closed.

Tray

Bottom

Tray support

STEP 5
Glue center section formed in Step 2 to bottom of tray.

STEP 6
Glue section formed in step 4 to bottom of box to form a support for the tray to sit on.

4 Basic Box With Locking Lid Pin

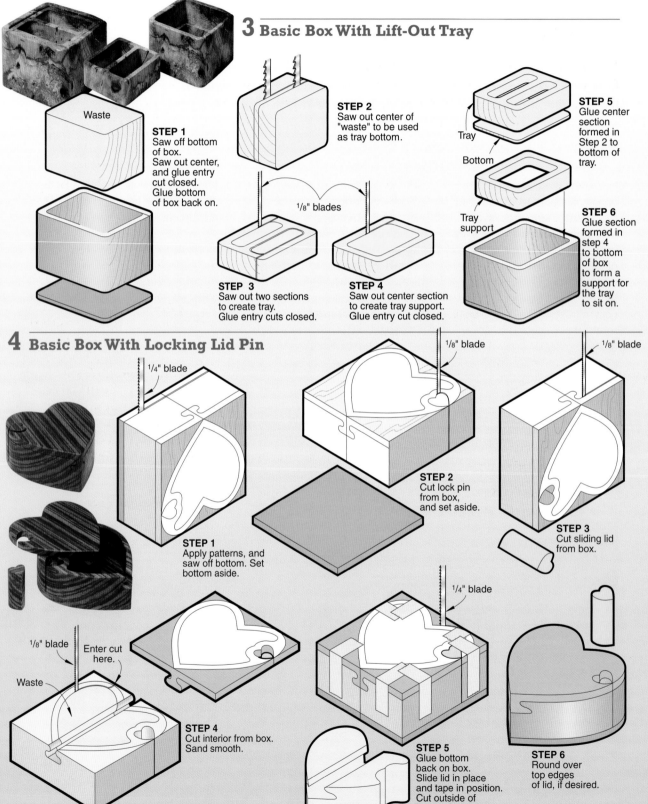

¹/₄" blade

STEP 1
Apply patterns, and saw off bottom. Set bottom aside.

¹/₈" blade

STEP 2
Cut lock pin from box, and set aside.

¹/₈" blade

STEP 3
Cut sliding lid from box.

¹/₈" blade   Enter cut here.

Waste

STEP 4
Cut interior from box. Sand smooth.

¹/₄" blade

STEP 5
Glue bottom back on box. Slide lid in place and tape in position. Cut outside of box to shape.

Waste

STEP 6
Round over top edges of lid, if desired.

MAKING MORE BANDSAW BOXES

You've got to hand it to Colorado boxmaker Jerry Patrasso—with his bandsaw, he can create three boxes from a single block of burl in no time flat. This section will explain his tips and techniques so that you can do it, too— but remember, practice makes perfect!

Jerry Patrasso with a boxelder burl that he discovered in a public park and saved from a certain fate as firewood.

Jerry seems to have the art of bandsawing great boxes down to an exact science. After all, he estimates that over the years he's made about 10,000 of them! And as you'll see, making three boxes with hinged lids isn't as hard as you might imagine, especially when you do it his way. (Each of the boxes fits together as shown in the Exploded View drawing on *page 36.*)

1 Jerry starts with a block of wood that's about 3¾ × 5¼ × 6". The block should be square and flat in all three dimensions. First, he bandsaws two ¼"-thick pieces off one of the 5¼ × 6" sides of

the block for "side stock" to be used later. Smooth the just-sawn face of the block. (A stationary disc sander with 80-grit paper will work well.) Recheck that the block is square.

2 On a 3 × 5¼" piece of stiff paper (like card stock), mark three concentric templates as shown in the Box Blank Template drawing on *page 38.* You will use the templates later to mark the bandsaw cuts onto one end of the block.

3 Note that Jerry allows about ³⁄₃₂" of space between each template for a bandsaw kerf and sand-

ing. Cut the three templates to shape with a pair of scissors, but *do not* cut along the lid lip cuts or the cuts below the hinge pins. Mark the locations for the lid lips, lid clearance, and hinge pins on the card-stock templates.

Using the templates, you can determine how much

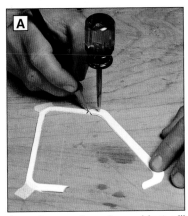

An awl or another sharp object will serve as a pivot point for marking the lid clearance on the template.

Mark the template outline on the end of the block. Also, mark the lid lip and hinge clearance.

Hold the block firmly on the table with one hand and use a pushstick to guide the portion of the block near the blade.

stock you'll need to remove to allow the hinged lid to swing freely. If you intend to make a set of larger boxes, you can determine this clearance by using a pencil and awl as shown in **Photo A**. Just cut the template lid off, then pin the lid down with the awl at the hinge pin location. Pivot the lid, and follow it with a pencil to mark the necessary clearance.

Place the largest template on the block and trace its outline as shown in **Photo B**. Transfer the lid lip, lid clearance, and hinge pin locations onto the block of wood. Place

the template on the opposite end of the block to mark the other hinge pin location.

4 To make the large blank, enter the cut through the lid lip, saw out the inner blank, and back out of the cut through the lid lip (see **Photo C**). Hold the block down firmly as you saw it to ensure 90° cuts.

Set the inner block aside so you can use it later for creating the medium and small boxes. In the following steps, we'll continue building the large box. Simply repeat all steps beginning with #3 to

complete the medium and small boxes using the inner block. Remember to square the inner block on your disc sander before marking it for the medium blank. (If your bandsaw cuts are square, you'll just have some light sanding to do.) Do the same before cutting out the small blank.

A sanding spindle with an aggressive abrasive, such as 50-grit, will quickly smooth out any bandsaw blade marks.

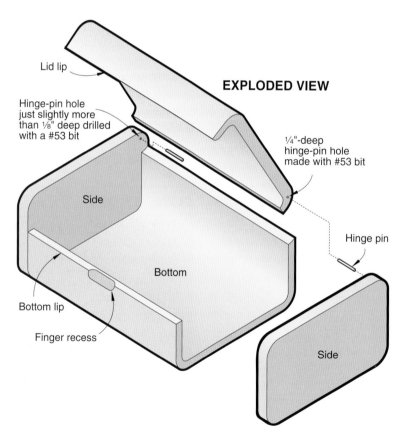

EXPLODED VIEW

Lid lip

Hinge-pin hole just slightly more than ⅛" deep drilled with a #53 bit

¼"-deep hinge-pin hole made with #53 bit

Side

Hinge pin

Bottom

Bottom lip

Finger recess

Side

Use a #53 bit to drill the hinge-pivot holes into both ends of the box blank. Stabilize the bit with stop collars.

Lightly touch one end of the lid to a disc sander to reduce its width by about ¹⁄₆₄" uniformly along the end.

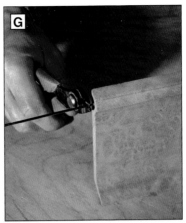

Brass or bronze brazing rod makes for sturdy hinge pins. Nip the pins so that they stick out ⅛" from the lid.

Use the hinge pin already placed in the lid to mark its matching location on the side pieces.

5 Smooth the inside of the box with a ¾" sanding spindle outfitted with 50-grit abrasive as shown in **Photo D**. Jerry uses his drill press, but an oscillating spindle sander works well, too.

6 With a #53 bit, drill a ¼"-deep hole at both hinge pin locations in the lid, as shown in **Photo E**. Jerry uses four stop collars (only two are visible in the photo) to stabilize the bit and prevent it from bending or breaking. The collars also come in handy if your drill-press chuck won't go down to the small diameter of a #53 bit. Just be sure to mount the collars to the bit so the bit stays centered in the chuck.

7 Jerry uses a #53 bit because it's just slightly smaller than a ¹⁄₁₆" bit. That way, the ¹⁄₁₆" hinge pin has enough friction to hold the lip up and prevent it from slam-

ming down due to looseness.

Separate the lid from the blank by cutting away the lid-clearance material. ***Tip: You might consider removing*** slightly *too much material to avoid a lid that won't swing freely later.*

8 Straighten the bottom lip as marked on the Box Blank Templates drawing. Jerry does this on his stationary disc sander.

9 Smooth the inside surfaces of the lid and bottom with 120- and 220-grit abrasives. Then, narrow the width of the lid by about ¹⁄₆₄". Again, Jerry turns to his trusty disc sander for this task, as shown in **Photo F**.

10 Determine which sides of your side stock surfaces will face the inside of the boxes. Then, sand out the bandsaw marks on those sides with an

80-grit belt in your stationary sander. Smooth these surfaces further with a hardwood sanding block and 120- and 220-grit abrasives. Be careful to keep the sanded surfaces flat.

11 Insert a length of ¹⁄₁₆" bronze or brass brazing rod into a hinge pin hole and nip it off so ⅛" of the rod protrudes, as shown in **Photo G**. Repeat for the other hinge pin.

12 Cut two pieces of side stock to 3⅛ × 5⅛". Place one piece flat on a bench, inside surface up, and position the lid as shown in **Photo H**. Mark the position of the hinge pin on the side stock by pressing the pin into the side. Be sure to position the lid so there is excess side stock along its edges. (You'll sand this away later.) Repeat Steps 11 and 12 for the other piece of side stock.

With the #53 bit, drill holes just a hair more than ⅛" deep at the marked indents on the sides.

13 Align the pin holes on the sides with the pins in the lid, and dry-clamp the side pieces to the box lid and bottom. Position the pieces with excess side stock all around the edges of the lid and bottom. Check to make sure the lid will open. If it doesn't, remove more stock from the hinge clearance area.

Once you're satisfied with the fit of these parts, disassemble them and apply yellow glue to the ends of the box bottom, as shown in **Photo I**. Repeat this process on the other side and reclamp the assembly. Check the gaps at the hinge and lid lip—you can usually equalize small gaps by shifting the clamps slightly.

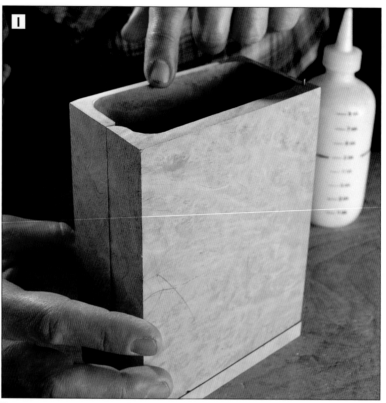

Prevent squeeze-out on the inside of the box by wiping the glue bead away from the inside edges of the lid and bottom.

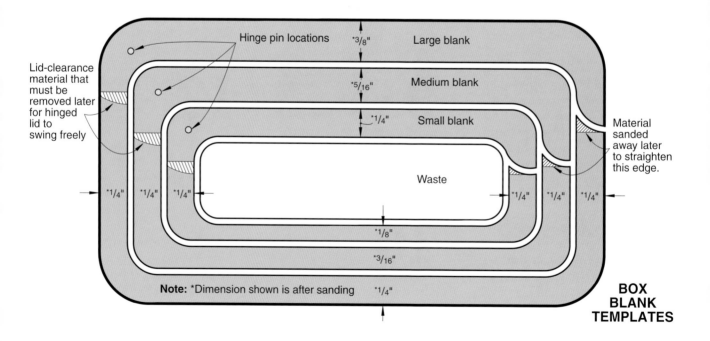

Hinge pin locations   *³/₈"   Large blank

Lid-clearance material that must be removed later for hinged lid to swing freely

*⁵/₁₆"   Medium blank

*¹/₄"   Small blank

Material sanded away later to straighten this edge.

Waste

*¹/₄"   *¹/₄"   *¹/₄"   *¹/₄"   *¹/₄"   *¹/₄"

*¹/₈"

*³/₁₆"

Note: *Dimension shown is after sanding   *¹/₄"

BOX BLANK TEMPLATES

Use a gentle touch with a disc sander to equalize the gaps between the box lid and sides.

Use a spindle sander to make a 1"-long finger recess along the bottom front edge of the box.

14 Allow the glue to dry, and remove the squeeze-out with a sharp chisel. With a disc sander and 80-grit abrasive, sand the bottom, back, and front surfaces of the box, in that order, to bring the sides flush with those surfaces. Use a light touch and don't overheat the wood—that might cause it to warp. Next, equalize the gaps on both ends of the lid with a light sanding as shown in **Photo J**. Then, sand the top of the box. Go back to the disc sander and round-over the four long edges of the box.

15 Remove all sanding marks on the outside of the box with a 150-grit belt in a stationary sander. Then, hand-sand the outside with 220-grit abrasive and sand the entire box with 400-grit paper.

Make a centered mark on the bottom lip. Mark ½" on both sides of the center, and use a drum sander to cut a shallow finger recess, as shown in **Photo K.**

Blow, vacuum, or brush all dust from the box and apply the finish of your choice. Jerry wipes on his own polyurethane/tung oil mix, but you can achieve similar results by applying an oil/varnish blend. After the finish dries, Jerry uses a bench grinder and buffing wheels to buff the outside with tripoli compound, and polishes the surfaces with carnuba wax.

Now, go ahead and put your new expertise to work. Chapter 3 contains an exciting variety of bandsaw box projects for you to master!

FRONT VIEW

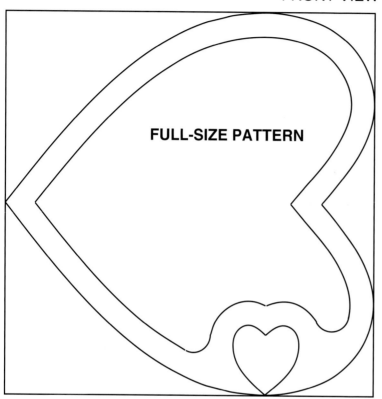

FULL-SIZE PATTERN

SIDE VIEW

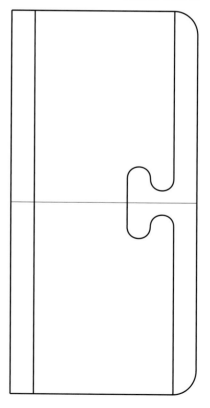

A Bevy of Bandsaw Boxes

So you think you're ready to test your bandsaw skills? The seven project designs on the following pages were developed to give you and your bandsaw a workout. They are sure to bring you hours of enjoyment—plus, you'll be creating some pretty neat and unusual gifts.

A WHALE OF A CONTAINER

The box shown here is so simple to make that with the right bandsaw, Shamu himself could build it. It was made from 1¾"-thick walnut stock using a ⅛" bandsaw blade. (You can also use a scrollsaw—just note the blade-start hole location on the pattern.) Feel free to use any type of wood you like, but be sure to make the cuts in the order described here.

Referring to the full-sized Side View pattern shown *opposite*, draw the red outside cutting line, designated no. 1, on one face of a 1¾ × 1¾ × 6" piece of stock. Saw around the line. Sand the edges as necessary.

Stand the workpiece on its bottom—the flattest edge—and mark a cutting line along the curved upper surface ¼" from the back, shown by the green line (no. 2) in the Top View drawing. Saw along the line to cut off the thin back piece. Set the back aside for later use.

Now, draw the removable keys—the yellow lines shown as no. 3 on the Side View pattern. Saw the keys (the mouth and the tail). Set the keys aside and turn the workpiece onto the flat bottom again.

Draw the purple cutting line for the lid (no. 4) onto the curved surface, facing up. Saw along that line, then slide the lid piece off and set it aside.

With the lid off, draw the blue interior cutting line (no. 5) as shown. Next, carefully saw through the back at an angle to access and cut out the center section of the body. After removing the center section, glue and clamp together the access kerf in the back.

On the cutout part, draw a line about ³⁄₁₆" below the keyed edge and parallel to it, shown by line no. 6 on the Inner Lid and Supports drawing. Cut off the inner lid, then saw the ends from the remaining piece where shown by the line(s) labeled no. 7.

To assemble the box, first glue the thin back piece to the body with woodworker's glue. Align the front end and edges, and clamp. Remove any squeeze-out in the key slots or the interior.

Glue the inner lid supports into position at the front and back of the interior cavity. You can use woodworker's glue or cyanoacrylate adhesive for these parts.

After the glue dries, sand as necessary. Set the inner lid into place, slide the lid onto the body, and drop the keys into position. Sand the outside of the box. Remove the keys and lids, and then apply a clear oil finish to all parts, taking care not to let it build up so thick that the parts won't fit together. When dry, reassemble the box.

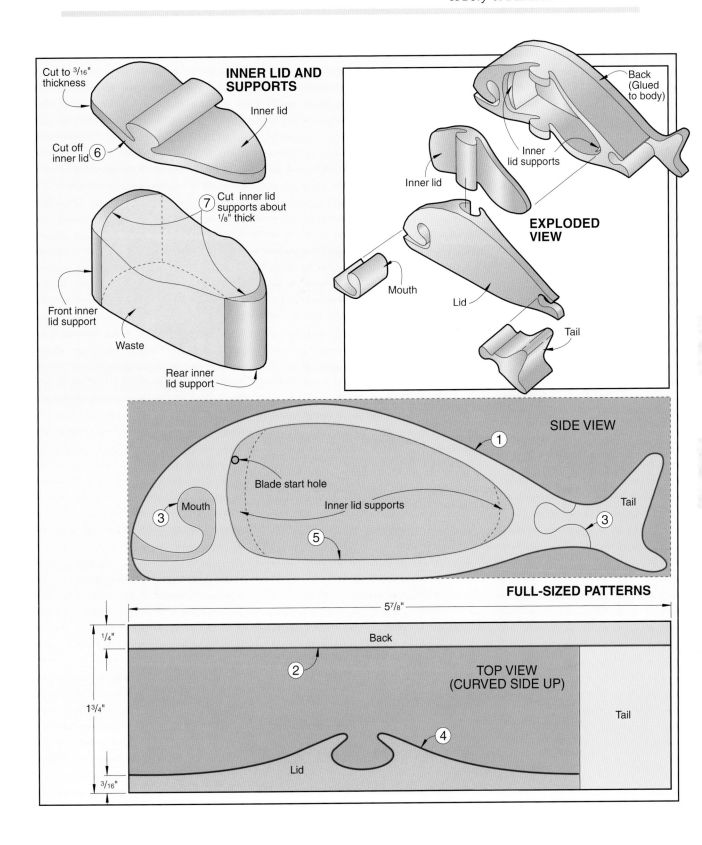

INNER LID AND SUPPORTS

Cut to 3/16" thickness

Inner lid

Cut off inner lid ⑥

⑦ Cut inner lid supports about 1/8" thick

Front inner lid support

Waste

Rear inner lid support

Back (Glued to body)

Inner lid supports

Inner lid

EXPLODED VIEW

Mouth

Lid

Tail

SIDE VIEW

Blade start hole

①

Mouth

③

Inner lid supports

Tail

③

⑤

FULL-SIZED PATTERNS

5 7/8"

1/4"

Back

②

TOP VIEW (CURVED SIDE UP)

1 3/4"

Tail

④

Lid

3/16"

A BOX WITH A BEAK

It's a bird! It's a bandsawn box! It's a woodworker's whimsy! Whatever you want to call Russell Greenslade's fanciful creation, you'll surely find it a lot of fun to build...and to have around the house.

1 Photocopy the top and side views of the full-size pattern of the body found on *pages 178–180*. Using rubber cement or a spray adhesive, adhere the top-view pattern to the top edge of a 1¾ × 4¼ × 12¾" blank. (This bird's body was cut from cocobolo.)

2 Bandsaw the outline of the pattern. Reattach the cut-off sides to the blank with double-faced tape, as shown in **Photo A**. Slide the cut-off pieces back to make a flat surface as shown.

3 Fasten the side-view pattern to the blank. Align the end of the tail on the side pattern with the tail end of the blank. The pattern should hang over the sides of the blank at the tip of the beak, as shown in **Photo B**.

4 Transfer the centers for the leg holes from the top-view pattern to the bottom of the blank. Drill the eye, hinge, and leg holes in the body.

Tape the sawn-off sides back onto the blank to provide flat surfaces for pattern attachment and sawing.

The side-view pattern will extend past the taped-on side. Cut smooth curves out to the tip of the beak.

To saw a sharp corner, cut into it from both directions. Carefully stop each cut at the pattern line.

5 Bandsaw the outside pattern outline as shown in **Photo C**. A ⅛" bandsaw blade was used for both the inside and outside cuts in the project shown. Saw slightly outside the pattern line, then sand to the line. (We sanded to the pattern line with a 1" bench-top strip sander.)

6 Following the arrows on the pattern, bandsaw the inside of the box as shown in **Photo D**. Free the lid with a final cut in from the back of the body, as shown in **Photo E**.

7 Sand the inside of the box and the lid. A spindle sander will do most of the job, but you'll need to hand-sand the corners with a sandpaper-wrapped dowel. Peel off all of the patterns.

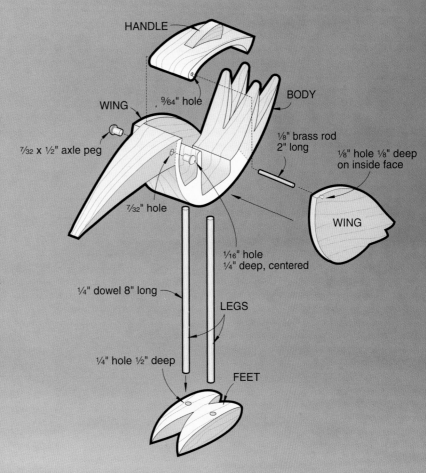

HANDLE

9/64" hole

WING

7/32 x 1/2" axle peg

BODY

1/8" brass rod 2" long

1/8" hole 1/8" deep on inside face

WING

7/32" hole

1/16" hole 1/4" deep, centered

1/4" dowel 8" long

LEGS

1/4" hole 1/2" deep

FEET

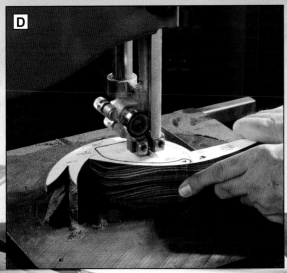

A ⅛" bandsaw blade will help you saw the sharp inside corners in the box.

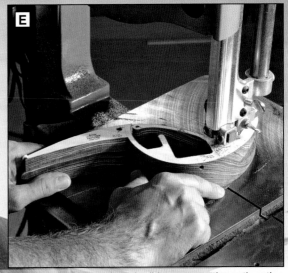

Make the final cut to free the lid as a smooth continuation of the curve that comes down the top of the tail.

The wings are the box sides

1 Laminate two ¼ × 3⅛ × 6½" wing blanks together with double-faced tape. (We cut the wings from bocote.) Put the best faces to the inside.

2 Adhere a photocopy of the Wing Full-Size pattern (found on *page 180*) to one face of the stacked blanks. Transfer the hole center to the other face of the stack. Drill the ⅛" hole ⅛" deep in each blank.

3 Bandsaw (or scrollsaw) the wings to shape. Sand the edges as necessary and remove the pattern.

4 Saw the handle from ⅜" stock. Lay a piece of 100-grit sandpaper, abrasive side up, on the lid. Then, position the handle on the lid as shown and slide the handle from side to side, sanding its bottom contour to match the lid's curvature. Glue the handle to the lid.

5 Glue and clamp a wing to one side of the body, locating it where indicated on the body pattern. The hole in the wing should face toward the inside of the box.

6 Cut a 2" length of ⅛"-diameter brass rod for the hinge. Slide the rod through the hole in the lid, and insert one end into the hole in the installed wing. Without gluing, clamp the other wing in place, trapping the brass rod's other end in its hole. Open and close the lid. If it binds against the wings, sand its edges to allow free movement.

7 With the lid in place, glue and clamp the other wing to the body.

Add the feet and finish the box

1 Cut two 8" lengths of ¼" dowel for the legs (or you can stand your bird on shorter legs if you like). Since we built our box from exotic woods, we decided to make our own bocote dowels for the legs. If you want to make your own leg dowels, here's how.

Start with a ¼ × ¼ × 12" blank for each dowel. Chuck a ⅛" round-over bit in your table-mounted router, and set a fence. Clamp stopblocks to the fence 4½" from each side of the bit. (This stops the cuts short of each end, leaving the ends of the workpiece square for easier control on the router table.)

Using a pushstick and holding the stock against the fence and router table with featherboards for safety, round over the four corners of the blank. Hand-sand as necessary. Cut off the ends and trim the dowels to length.

2 Photocopy the top and side views of the Feet Full-Size patterns (*page 180*). Adhere the top-view pattern to a ⅞ × 2⅜ × 4¼" blank. (We cut the blank out of scrapwood left over from the body.)

3 Drill two ¼" holes ½" deep for the legs as shown.

4 Bandsaw the pattern outline. Tape the cut-off pieces to the sides of the blank as you did for the body.

5 Apply the side-view pattern. Cut the feet to shape. Remove the patterns and sand away all of the saw marks.

6 Glue the legs into the body holes and the feet onto the legs.

7 Drill a centered ¹⁄₁₆" hole ¼" deep into the large end on each of two ⁷⁄₃₂" toy axle pegs. Glue the pegs into the eye holes as shown on the Exploded View drawing.

8 Finish-sand the completed box with 120-, 180- and 220-grit sandpaper. Apply a clear finish overall. (This box was finished with two coats of antique oil finish.)

SWEETHEART JEWELRY BOX

You're sure to win your loved one's affection with this unique gift. The lid and trays rotate open to display fine earrings, rings, and necklaces, and they swivel closed, making an eye-pleasing dresser-top showpiece.

Get started

1 From 1¹⁄₁₆"-thick cherry, cut a 7"-square piece for the base (A), two pieces to 5½" square for the trays (B), and one piece of ¾"-thick bird's-eye maple to 5½" square for the lid (C).

2 Mark centerlines on the bottom surface of the four blanks as shown in the Parts View drawing. Then, using a combination square, mark 45° reference lines on the bottom surface of the two trays and lid blanks.

3 Using a compass, mark a 3¼"-radius and 2"-radius circle on the base blank. See the Parts View for reference. Mark 2"-radius and 2½"-radius circles on the tray blanks (B). Mark a 2½"-radius circle on the maple lid blank (C).

4 Mark the center-points, and drill the pivot holes as shown in the Parts View drawing. For the base pivot hole, first drill a ⅝" hole ¼" deep on the bottom side. Then, drill a ¼" hole centered inside the ⅝" hole.

Cut and sand the pieces to shape

1 Fit your bandsaw with a ¼" blade. Then, following the centerline marked parallel with the grain, bandsaw the base and trays in half.

Materials List

Part	Finished Size			Matl.	Qty.
	T	W	L		
A* base	1¹⁄₁₆"	6½" diam.		C	1
B* trays	1¹⁄₁₆"	6½" diam.		C	2
C* lid	¾"	5" diam.		BM	1
D interiors	¼"	4" diam.		P	3

*Initially cut parts oversized. Then, trim each to finish size according to the how-to instuctions.

Materials Key: C-Cherry, BM-bird's eye maple, P-Plywood

Supplies: ¼" pivot cap or ¼"nut, ¼" dowel stock, red enamel paint, clear finish, cork.

2 Bandsaw the inner marked circle on the tray and base pieces to cut the interiors to shape.

3 Spread glue on the kerfed areas, and glue the tray and base halves back together, making sure the top and bottom edges are flush.

4 Cutting just outside the outermost marked circle, bandsaw the base, two trays, and lid to shape. Later, sand the outside edge of the base to the marked circumference lines to finish the shaping.

5 Using your largest diameter drum sander, sand the inside of the base and trays, sanding to the inner marked circle.

6 To make the bottom (D) for the base (A), position the base on a piece of ¼"-thick stock (we used plywood). Marking along the inside of the base wall, transfer the shape to the ¼" stock. Cut and sand the base bottom (D) until it fits snugly inside the base and the bottom edges are flush. Glue the bottom in place. Repeat the process for the two trays.

7 Mark the stop-dowel centerpoints on the bottom side of the trays and lid. Drill the holes.

More machining, more details

1 Cut the pivot dowel to 3¹⁵⁄₁₆" long. Dry-fit (no glue) one end of the dowel into the hole on the bottom side of the lid. Sand the rest of the dowel until the trays rotate easily on it.

2 To sand the edges of the trays and lid flush, use double-faced (carpet) tape to adhere the trays and lid—one on top of the other—with the outside edges flush and the pivot pin inserted through the pivot pin holes in the trays and into the ¼"-deep hole in the lid.

3 With the assembly upside down and resting on the lid, disc sand the outside edges of the pieces flush. Switch to a palm sander, and remove sanding marks left by the disc sander.

4 Use a splash of lacquer thinner or acetone to weaken the double-faced tape joints. Now, separate the parts, and remove the tape and sticky residue.

5 Cut a V-block router-table fence like that shown in **Photo A.** The fence will provide support when you're routing the base and lid coves and help keep your fingers safely away from the spinning router bit. Rout a ⅜" cove along the top outside edge of the lid (C). Then, switch bits and rout a ½" cove along the top outside edge of the base (A). To minimize

To rout the base and lid coves, fit your router with a V-block fence to help keep your fingers safely away from the rotating router bit.

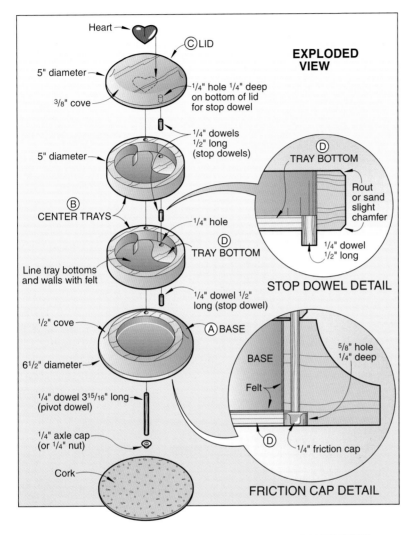

Heart

©LID

5" diameter

³⁄₈" cove

¼" hole ¼" deep
on bottom of lid
for stop dowel

5" diameter

¼" dowels
½" long
(stop dowels)

Ⓑ
CENTER TRAYS

¼" hole

Ⓓ
TRAY BOTTOM

Line tray bottoms
and walls with felt

¼" dowel ½"
long (stop dowel)

½" cove

ⒶBASE

6½" diameter

¼" dowel 3¹⁵⁄₁₆" long
(pivot dowel)

¼" axle cap
(or ¼" nut)

Cork

**EXPLODED
VIEW**

Ⓓ
TRAY BOTTOM

Rout
or sand
slight
chamfer

¼" dowel
½" long

STOP DOWEL DETAIL

BASE

⅝" hole
¼" deep

Felt

Ⓓ

¼" friction cap

FRICTION CAP DETAIL

chip-out when routing the coves, do it in three passes, increasing the depth of cut for each pass.

6 Sand a ¹⁄₃₂" chamfer along the top and bottom edges of each tray, and along the bottom edge of the lid. See the Stop Dowel detail *left* for reference.

7 From ¼" dowel stock, cut the three stop dowels to ½" long. Again, see the Stop Dowel detail for reference. Glue the stop dowels in place.

Make the heart

1 Transfer the full-sized heart pattern, *page 50*, to a piece of ⅜" thick maple. Bandsaw the heart to shape, and then sand the cut edges smooth.

2 For stability, adhere the heart to one corner of your benchtop or to a large piece of scrap material.

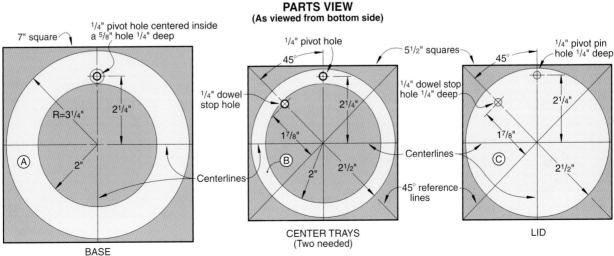

PARTS VIEW
(As viewed from bottom side)

7" square

¼" pivot hole centered inside
a ⅝" hole ¼" deep

R=3¼"

2¼"

Ⓐ

2"

Centerlines

BASE

¼" pivot hole

45°

5½" squares

¼" dowel
stop hole

2¼"

1⅞"

Ⓑ

2"

2½"

Centerlines

45° reference
lines

CENTER TRAYS
(Two needed)

45°

¼" pivot pin
hole ¼" deep

¼" dowel stop
hole ¼" deep

2¼"

1⅞"

Ⓒ

2½"

LID

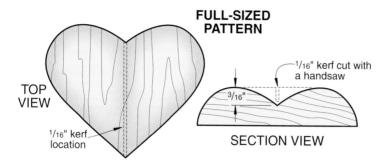

FULL-SIZED PATTERN

TOP VIEW

¹/₁₆" kerf location

¹/₁₆" kerf cut with a handsaw

³/₁₆"

SECTION VIEW

Using a handsaw, cut a ³/₁₆"-deep kerf down the middle of the heart as shown *above*.

3 Sand or chisel the contours of the heart to the shape shown in the drawing and photo *below*. Finish-sand the heart to its final rounded shape.

4 Seal the heart's top surface with a spay lacquer. When dry, paint the sprayed surface with a bright red enamel.

Add the finish and lining

1 Finish-sand the base, trays, and lid. Apply a clear finish to the individual pieces.

2 Once the finish dries, lightly sand the tray and base interiors. (A roughed-up finish makes for better adhesion when applying the felt jewelry box linings.) Next, cut pieces of felt to fit as shown in the Exploded View drawing. Glue the bottom pieces and then the wall pieces in place.

3 Glue the pivot dowel into the hole in the lid bottom. Slide the dowel through the pivot holes in the trays and base. To align the outside edges of the trays and lid when closed, you may have to sand the side of the stop dowels slightly. Check the alignment and sand further as necessary.

4 Tap a ¼" friction cap onto the bottom end of the pivot dowel. The cap will allow the dowel to swivel when you open the trays. You can also thread a ¼" nut onto the bottom of the dowel and secure it with a drop of instant glue.

5 Lightly sand the bottom surface of the base and adhere ¹/₁₆"-thick cork (cork gasket material will also work). Using an X-acto knife, carefully trim the edges of the cork flush with the outside edges of the jewelry box case.

6 Rough-up a small area on the top of the lid, opposite the pivot pin, and glue the heart into place.

Chiseled and sanded smooth, the painted wood heart adds an element of romance to this trayed jewelry box.

ONE COOL CATCH-ALL

This clever little box is perfect for containing all the random knick-knacks that clutter up your desk. But be warned—building this bandsawn beauty is so simple, you might be asked to make several for family and friends.

1 Cut two pieces of stock 1¹⁄₁₆ × 4 × 5¾" for the lid (A) and bottom (B). (We used walnut here.) Stack them and then look at the edges. The grain should be running in the same direction, giving the appearance of one thick piece of stock. If it isn't, turn one piece around or flip it over to achieve the most seamless look. Mark the mating faces for orientation.

2 Chuck a ⅜" round-over bit in your table-mounted router. Rout the upper edges of the lid and the lower edges of the bottom as shown in the Lid and Bottom Side View drawing.

3 Transfer the inside cutting lines from that drawing to the lid (A) and bottom (B). You can photocopy the drawing, cut it into the two parts, and adhere them to the stock. Or, you can lay out the cutting lines directly on the stock, measuring from the drawing.

4 Adjust your bandsaw for a 6" cutting depth. Then, standing the lid (A) on its unpatterned end, saw along the inside line.

Next, saw the bottom, as shown in **Photo A** on *page 52* .

5 Sand the lid and bottom (inside and out) with 100-, 150-, and 220-grit sandpaper. Wrap your sandpaper around a length of dowel rod to sand the inside corners, as shown in **Photo B**. With a disc sander, sand about ¹⁄₁₆" off of one end of the lid, making it slightly shorter than the body. This will allow the lid to open freely after assembly.

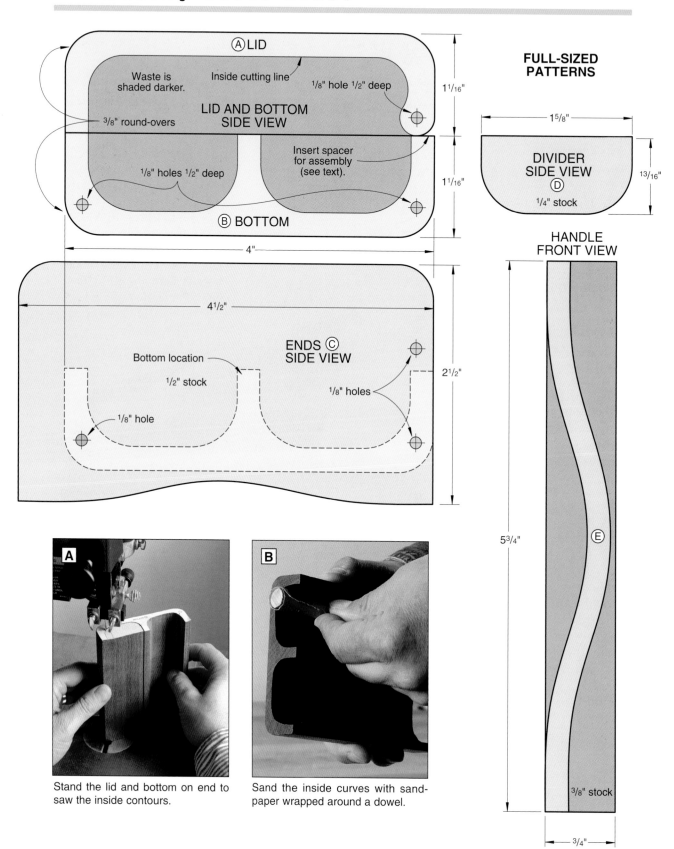

FULL-SIZED PATTERNS

Ⓐ LID

Waste is shaded darker.

Inside cutting line

1/8" hole 1/2" deep

3/8" round-overs

LID AND BOTTOM SIDE VIEW

1 1/16"

1/8" holes 1/2" deep

Insert spacer for assembly (see text).

1 1/16"

Ⓑ BOTTOM

4"

DIVIDER SIDE VIEW Ⓓ

1 5/8"

13/16"

1/4" stock

HANDLE FRONT VIEW

4 1/2"

ENDS Ⓒ SIDE VIEW

1/2" stock

Bottom location

1/8" hole

1/8" holes

2 1/2"

Ⓔ

5 3/4"

3/8" stock

3/4"

Stand the lid and bottom on end to saw the inside contours.

Sand the inside curves with sandpaper wrapped around a dowel.

Make the ends

1 With double-faced tape, laminate two ½ × 3 × 5" pieces of stock, good faces together, for the ends. Choose a wood that contrasts with the body. (We used maple.)

2 Photocopy the Ends pattern. Attach the copy to the laminated stock with rubber cement or spray adhesive.

3 Drill three ⅛" holes through both ends as shown. If possible, use a drill press for accuracy. Back the workpiece with scrapwood to prevent tearout.

4 Bandsaw around the outer pattern line. For a smooth edge, saw slightly outside the pattern line, then sand down to it. Remove the paper pattern and separate the two pieces. Remove any traces of adhesive with lacquer thinner.

5 Rout a ⅜" round-over along the front, back, and top edges of the outer face on each endpiece. Rout the parts facedown on a router table, making multiple shallow cuts.

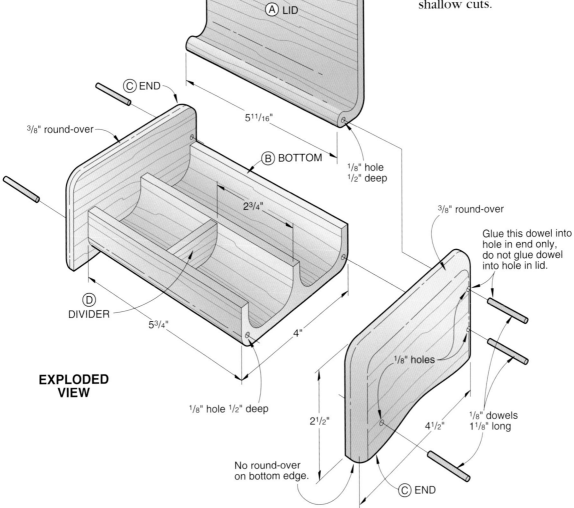

⅛" round-overs

Ⓔ HANDLE

Ⓐ LID

Ⓒ END

⅜" round-over

5¹¹/₁₆"

Ⓑ BOTTOM

⅛" hole ½" deep

2¾"

⅜" round-over

Glue this dowel into hole in end only, do not glue dowel into hole in lid.

Ⓓ DIVIDER

5¾"

4"

⅛" holes

⅛" dowels 1⅛" long

2½"

4½"

EXPLODED VIEW

⅛" hole ½" deep

No round-over on bottom edge.

Ⓒ END

Glue on the ends

1 Sandwich a spacer about 1/16" thick between the top and bottom (We used the cardboard back from a memo pad.) Bind the pieces together with masking tape as shown in **Photo C**, keeping the ends and edges flush.

2 Clamp the ends to the bottom/lid assembly. Position the ends flush with the top of the lid and the back (hinge side).

3 With a drill press, drill two 1/8" holes in each end of the body and one in each end of the lid, using the holes in the ends as guides. Drill 1/2" deep. (The total depth of the holes from the face of the end should be 1".)

4 Remove the ends. Sand both sides of the two ends with 100-, 150-, and 220-grit sandpaper.

5 Cut six 1 1/8" lengths of 1/8" dowel rod. Apply glue to one end of the bottom (B), and attach the appropriate end (C) to the bottom. Push a dowel pin into the two lower holes on the end. Repeat for the other end. Clamp until dry.

6 Attach a photocopy of the divider pattern (D) to a 1/4 × 1 × 2" piece of stock. (We used maple to match the ends.) Cut out the divider, place it in position, and sand it to fit. Then, finish-sand the divider and glue it into the middle of the front tray.

Dress up the lid

1 Photocopy the handle pattern (E). Attach the copy to the best face of a piece of stock 3/8 × 3/4 × 5 3/4". (We cut the handle from maple to match the box ends.)

2 Bandsaw or scrollsaw the handle. Remove the paper pattern, and sand 1/8" round-overs along both edges of that face. Finish-sand the handle.

3 Glue the handle to the front of the lid (A), the side without holes drilled into it. Center the handle and position it so the lower surface fits flush with the lower edge of the lid at the ends. Clamp with rubber bands. When dry, sand the ends flush with the lid.

4 Slightly sand 1/2" at one end of each remaining dowel pin for a snug, rotating fit in the lid holes. The lid will hinge on these pins. Then, place the lid in position. Push a dowel pin, sanded end first, through the end holes into the lid. Glue the pins to the ends.

5 After the glue dries, sand the dowels flush with the ends. Finish as desired. We sprayed on a clear, semigloss finish inside and out.

Insert a 1/16" spacer between the lid and bottom before fitting the ends.

TRINKET TREASURE CHEST

Whatever kind of trinkets you're looking to stash, they will find a good home inside this handsome hardwood box. It's fairly compact, but its two trays and a drawer provide plenty of room to organize your watches, jewelry, or other small valuables.

For this project, a stable hardwood such as walnut, cherry, or mahogany will work well, but tropical woods are another way to go. You should glue up the block for this box from milled stock; you'll need a board at least 1½ × 6 × 26". You'll also need to resaw and plane a board of the same species into ¼"-thick and ⅜"-thick for the drawer end caps and box side panels *(see Exploded View drawing on page 56)*.

1 Glue up four pieces of 1½"-thick stock for the center block. The finished block should measure 5¾" high by 5⅛" wide by 5⅛" long. With a bandsaw and a stationary disc sander, trim an oversized block to the required dimensions and true up all the faces. Or, you can mill each of the four layers exactly to size, and use clamping cauls to keep all the edges and faces properly aligned while the glue dries.

2 After you clean off any glue squeeze-out and sand the block smooth, use spray adhesive to affix a copy of the Core Side View pattern onto one end of the block.

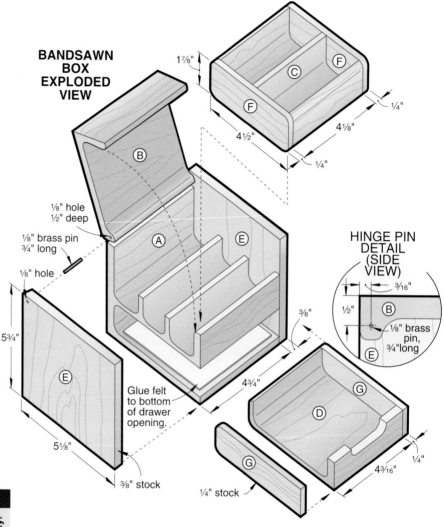

BANDSAWN BOX EXPLODED VIEW

1⅞"

4½"

4⅛"

¼"

¼"

⅛" hole
½" deep

⅛" brass pin
¾" long

⅛" hole

HINGE PIN DETAIL (SIDE VIEW)

³⁄₁₆"

½"

⅛" brass pin, ¾"long

⅜"

5¾"

5⅛"

⅜" stock

Glue felt to bottom of drawer opening.

4¾"

4³⁄₁₆"

¼"

¼" stock

Materials List

Part	Finished Size			Matl.	Qty.
	T	W	L		
A box core*	5⅛"	5⅛"	4¾"	**	1
B lid*	1⅞"	5⅛"	4¾"	**	1
C tray body*	1⅞"	4⅜"	4⅛"	**	1
D drawer body*	1⁹⁄₁₆"	4⅞"	4³⁄₁₆"	**	1
E side panels	⅜"	5⅛"	5¾"	**	2
F tray end caps	¼"	1⅞"	4½"	**	2
G drawer end caps	¼"	1⁹⁄₁₆"	4⅞"	**	2

* Note: These parts feature irregular shapes due to the nature of the project design and technique. The dimensions shown reflect the overall space they occupy, but not the specific contours. See the patterns for details.

Cut the basic box parts

Note: *For best results, install a new ⅛" blade on your bandsaw and tune the table so it's dead square to the blade. Any error will produce a box that doesn't fit together cleanly.*

1 Following the pattern's outlines and easing through the corners, bandsaw the lid (B), the tray body (C), and the drawer body (D) from the box core (A). Then cut the three "pockets" in the box core's fixed tray.

2 Sand all of the cuts smooth with 100-grit and then 150-grit sandpaper. (For the inside curves, it helps to wrap the sandpaper around a dowel.)

Next, set your tablesaw's rip fence to 4⅛" and cut the drawer and tray bodies to that length. You'll need this clearance to add the end caps.

3 Using your bandsaw and a ¼" or wider blade, resaw ⅜" stock for the side panels (E) and ¼" stock for the drawer and tray end caps (F, G). Plane or sand the stock smooth and cut it to the sizes shown in the Materials List.

4 Test-fit the parts by clamping the side panels to the box core (without glue); then insert the drawer and lift-out tray parts (including end caps) to see if they fit with the correct clearance. Recut the center portion of either assembly if it proves too long.

5 Once everything fits properly, you're ready to glue up the box. Use Epoxy so that when the finish is applied, the exposed adhesive will be nearly invisible.

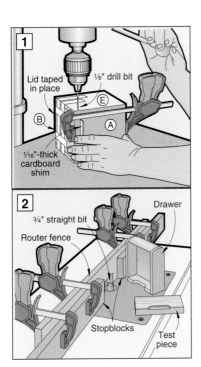

Place one side panel (E) on waxed paper (outside face down). Use a cotton swab to spread a uniform layer of epoxy on one end of the box core (A), then carefully place it on the side panel. No clamps are required, but allow the epoxy patterns handling the assembly or gluing on the other side panel. Repeat this procedure for the tray and the drawer.

After the epoxy in all the joints has cured (times will vary according to the resin type and the ambient temperature), sand off any residue from the outside surfaces.

Fit the lid and the hinge pins

1 Cut or sand about ¹⁄₃₂" from the length of the lid to provide clearance for it to open and close without binding. When you've got a good fit, use a cardboard spacer as a shim between the back edge of the lid and the upper edge of the box core. Then, tape the lid in place.

2 Lay out marks at the rear corners of the box, where the hinge pins will go (see Hinge Pin Detail). With the lid taped in place, drill a ⅛" hole ¾" deep through each side panel into the ends of the lid, as shown in **Drawing 1**.

3 Cut two 1½"-long pins from a length of ⅛"-diameter round brass rod; lightly chamfer the leading end

on each. Now tap them into the holes you drilled. Make sure the lid opens and closes properly. If you need to adjust it or trim more length, pull the hinge pins and remove the lid. After you get a good fit, reinstall the pins, trim them off, and sand them flush.

One last detail, then finish

1 To keep the outside lines of the box clean, we opted for a drawer pull cutout rather than a knob. To do this, first install a ¾" straight bit in your router table, and then clamp stopblocks to the fence as shown in **Drawing 2**. This will control the drawer's travel from side to side. Make a test cut on a scrap block the same size as the drawer front, and limit the cut depth to about ⅛". When the setup is right, make a first pass in the drawer. Raise the bit again in ⅛" increments for another two passes or until the cutout is routed clear through the drawer front.

2 Apply several coats of a penetrating oil finish. When dry, line the drawer opening with felt or cork.

Closed up, this box makes for compact storage of keepsakes.

SHOOT THE MOON

You've always wanted to give your loved ones the moon and the stars—well, here's your chance! This lunar-inspired box that holds a mysterious surprise is just the right place for stashing some out-of-this-world jewelry.

1 Start with a 2 × 6 × 9" hardwood blank (the box shown is of tiger maple). Make three copies of the full-size pattern found on *page 62.*

[Note: Resawing a 6"-wide blank requires a 14" bandsaw. If yours is smaller, start with a smaller blank and reduce the pattern to a manageable size when you photocopy it.] With spray adhesive or rubber cement, adhere one copy of the pattern to the blank face, orienting it with respect to the grain (as shown on the pattern).

2 Fit your bandsaw with a sharp ⅛" blade, then saw the moon to shape, keeping your blade outside the line and cutting wide around the tip of the star. Next, make the carrier jig shown on *page 61* and attach the blank to it with double-faced tape. Then, using your bandsaw's rip fence, saw a ³⁄₁₆"-slice off the bottom of the blank.

Note: If you've opted for a smaller blank (less than 2" thick), use a separate piece of stock for the bottom. Plane or resaw it to ³⁄₁₆", then adhere a copy of the pattern. Bandsaw it to shape, keeping your blade about ¼" outside the cut line.

3 Cut out the star, centering your blade on the line. Then, sand the edges and points of the star. (We used our 1" belt sander.) Next, fit your table-mounted router with a ¼" round-over

bit, and rout the top edges of the blank (with the star removed). To avoid tearing out the stock at the points of the moon, it's a good idea to make two separate passes to rout the inside and outside curves of the box.

Rough out the lid and interior

1 Using the Lid Profile detail shown *below* as a guide, draw the profile on the edge (outside curve) of the blank as shown in the "Drawing the Lid Profile" **Drawing A** on the top of *page 60*. Reattach the blank to your carrier jig (with the points down) using fresh tape.

Supplies
Quick-set epoxy, double-faced carpet tape, spray adhesive, duct tape, oil enamel (for flocking), finish, and paste wax.

SHOPTIP

For securing your stock during bandsawing, we recommend using cloth-backed double-faced carpet tape. It has more holding power than the less expensive vinyl-backed tapes. To remove stubborn tape, splash a little acetone or lacquer thinner on the edge, and let it penetrate the adhesive.

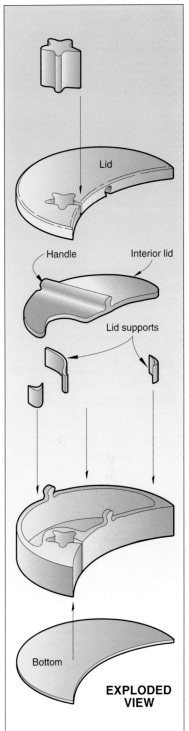

Lid

Handle

Interior lid

Lid supports

Bottom

EXPLODED VIEW

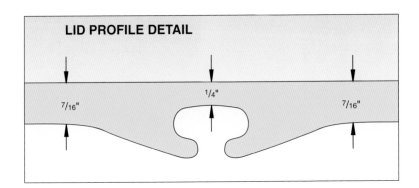

LID PROFILE DETAIL

7/16"   1/4"   7/16"

DRAWING THE LID PROFILE

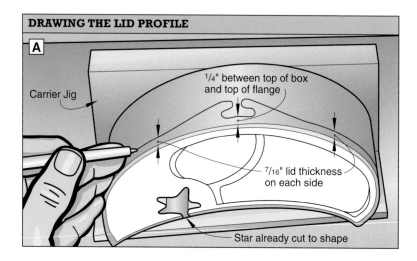

A

Carrier Jig

¹⁄₄" between top of box
and top of flange

⁷⁄₁₆" lid thickness
on each side

Star already cut to shape

Now, bandsaw the lid from the blank as shown in the "Bandsawing the Lid" **Drawing B**, keeping your blade on the line as much as possible.

2 Cut your second copy of the full-sized pattern *widthwise* into two

roughly equal parts. Position and adhere the two pieces to ensure a uniform wall thickness on all sides of the cavity. Since the two pattern pieces will ride up over the handle in the middle, you'll need to extend the lines across this area with a pencil.

3 Before you start your bandsaw, back the blade into the star cavity. Then, saw an entry/exit kerf as shown on the pattern, and begin sawing out the interior cavity, following the arrows. *Note: If at any point you feel you're getting into trouble, switch off your machine, reposition, and then resume sawing.* When you've cut out the entire cavity, turn off your saw, back the blade out through the same kerf, and remove the core.

4 Now, close up the entry/exit kerf. To do this, place the box on waxed paper. Mix up a small quantity of quick-set epoxy and apply it to the mating edges. Then, clamp the joint by stretching a length of duct tape across the box. Remove any epoxy squeeze-out from the star cavity.

5 Using 150-grit sandpaper, round the edges throughout the interior,

BANDSAWING THE LID

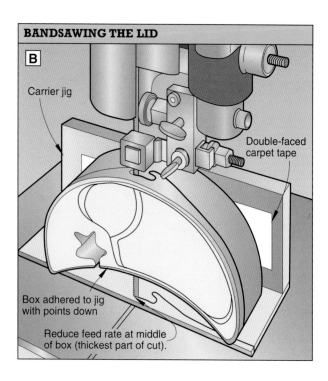

B

Carrier jig

Double-faced
carpet tape

Box adhered to jig
with points down

Reduce feed rate at middle
of box (thickest part of cut).

SHOP TIP

When you bandsaw the lid, remember that you are resawing a considerable—and also varying—thickness. Sawing will go more quickly at the start than in the center, speeding up again towards the end. Adjust your feed rate to avoid excessive stress on the blade, and take your time to prevent the blade from flexing in the wood.

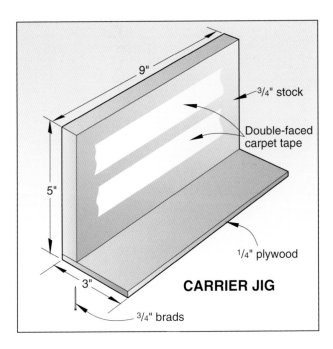

9"

3/4" stock

Double-faced
carpet tape

5"

1/4" plywood

3"

CARRIER JIG

3/4" brads

including the star and its cavity. Next, epoxy and clamp the bottom panel to the box. When the epoxy has cured, sand the box sides and bottom smooth. Then, fit your table-mounted router with a ¼" round-over bit, and rout the bottom edge of the box.

Cut the cavity lid and add lid supports

1 Using fresh carpet tape, attach the flat bottom face of the interior core to the carrier jig. Then, lay out and saw a ¼"-thick slice off the top to make the cavity lid.

Note: Be careful to maintain a uniform thickness by following the contours of the top face.

2 Cut out the cavity section from your third copy of the pattern. Sand the contoured top face of your remaining core until just smooth, and adhere the pattern to it. Now, saw out the three lid supports as shown. Remove the pattern pieces from the supports, then epoxy and clamp them into the box cavity. Wipe away any squeeze-out and allow the epoxy to cure.

Clean up, finish, and flock

1 To sand the box exterior, attach the outer lid to the box using small strips of carpet tape. Then, sand all surfaces and edges smooth using a palm sander. To smooth the round-overs, use a flap sander chucked into your drill press.

2 Sand the cavity lid and the top edges of the lid supports sufficiently so that the lid will rest as flat as possible in its recess. Now, sand the cavity floor and walls smooth.

3 Finish-sand any areas that still need it. Then, apply your choice of finish (an aerosol lacquer will work fine). Add as many coats as needed, rubbing between coats with extra fine steel wool. A final coat of paste wax will add more luster.

4 Flocking the interior cavity adds a royal touch (flocking supplies can be found at most craft supply stores). To flock the interior surface, including the lid supports, first apply an oil enamel that matches the flocking. Then blow the flocking into the paint, trying to achieve uniform coverage.

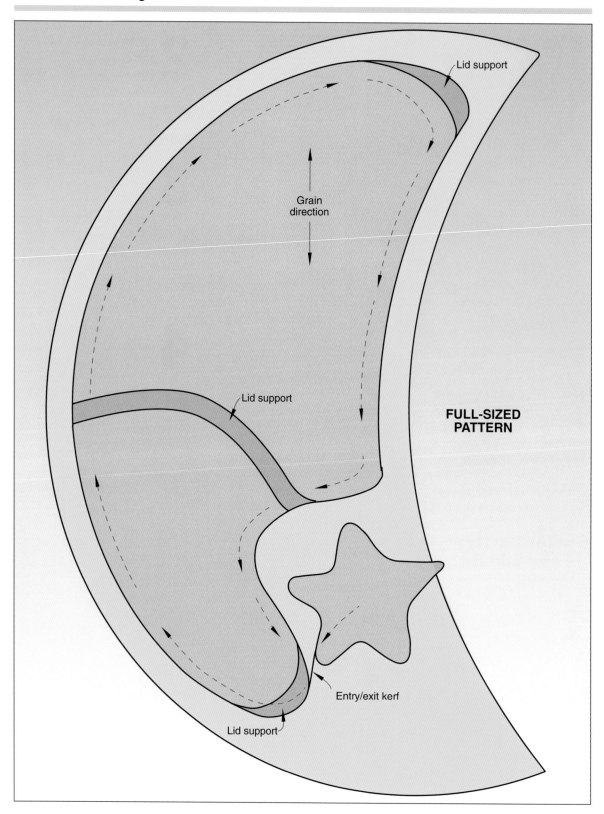

Lid support

Grain
direction

Lid support

**FULL-SIZED
PATTERN**

Entry/exit kerf

Lid support

A COTTONTAIL THAT FLIPS OUT

No, we're not talking about Bugs Bunny having a nervous breakdown here, we're referring to a bunny box that actually "flips" out!

Bandsaw your bunny

1 To make a blank, rip and crosscut a 4 × 6" piece of 1¾"-thick hardwood stock (cherry is shown). Or, you can laminate thinner stock to arrive at this thickness. Next, make two copies of the full-size pattern on *page 66* and adhere one of these to one face of the blank with spray adhesive or rubber cement. Using your bandsaw and a sharp ⅛" blade, follow along the outside pattern line to cut the rabbit to shape, keeping your blade just outside the line.

Materials List

Part	Finished Size			Matl.	Qty.
	T	W	L		
A sides	¼"	3⅜"	5¾"	C	2
B lid	1⅛"	2¼"	5³⁄₁₆"	C	1
C base	1⅛"	1⅜"	5¼"	C	1

Materials Key: C—cherry.

Supplies: 3⁄16" birch dowel; felt; oil finish.

2 Drill a 3⁄16" hinge-pin (eye) hole as shown on the pattern. To do this, use a brad-point bit in your drill press, and place a backup board under your stock to prevent tear-out.

Note: For your backup board, be sure to select scrap stock of a hardness similar to that of your workpiece. Also, see Shop Tip at top right.

3 Rip a ¼"-thick side (A) from each face of the rabbit cutout using your bandsaw and rip fence. Then, adhere the second copy of the pattern to one face of the center block. Starting at one of the entry-exit kerf lines, bandsaw through the middle of the center cavity where marked on the pattern, and exit at the other kerf line. *Note: It's critical that you make the entry-exit kerfs where shown on the pattern so that the box will open properly.* Now, bandsaw along the inside pattern line on both pieces as in **Drawing A** *(opposite)* to form the lid (B) and base (C).

Machine the parts, then assemble your rabbit

1 Sand the inside faces of all four parts smooth. (For the contoured surfaces, we used a ¾"-diameter drum sander in our drill press.) Next, sand the entry-exit kerfs smooth with a 1" belt sander, if possible. Remove the patterns from parts B and C (but not from A), then sand the edges of the lid (B) slightly so that it will open freely. We laid a sheet of sandpaper on our bench and hand-sanded, checking frequently for fit.

2 To make a hinge pin, cut a 2½" length of 3⁄16" hardwood dowel (we

used birch for contrast). Place the lid between the two sides (A) with the eye holes aligned, and insert the pin through all three pieces to hold them together. (The pin should be a bit too long.) Now, stand this assembly upside down on your bench, making sure that the lid edges are aligned with the top edges of the sides (with the lid in its closed position).

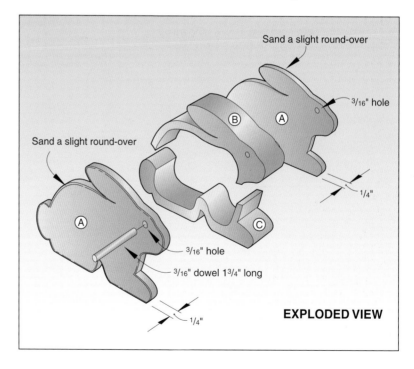

Sand a slight round-over

3/16" hole

Sand a slight round-over

1/4"

3/16" hole

3/16" dowel 1¾" long

1/4"

EXPLODED VIEW

BANDSAWING THE LID AND BASE TO SHAPE

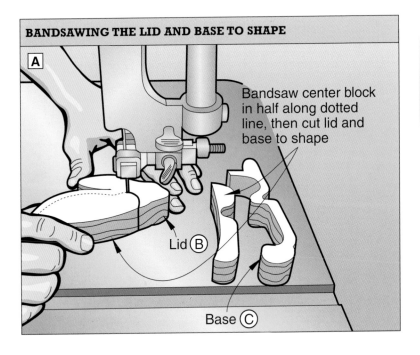

A

Bandsaw center block in half along dotted line, then cut lid and base to shape

Lid (B)

Base (C)

1 Apply glue to the edges of the base (B) and mating surfaces of the sides. Next, position the base between the sides, and slide it up snug against the edges of the lid. Clamp the assembly, then open the lid a little so that glue squeeze-out won't lock it in. Wipe away all squeeze-out, then allow the glue to dry. ***Note:*** *This will put the base out of alignment with the bottom edges of the sides. See Shop Tip below left.*

Fine-tune the bunny and finish

1 To glue in the hinge pin, first back it out on one side until it's recessed about ⅛" on the other side. Using a straightened paper clip, apply a drop or two of glue to the inside of this "eye socket," and push the pin back through until it protrudes just slightly. After the glue has dried, trim the pin ends and sand them flush.

2 With the pattern still in place on one side, sand all edges of the box smooth. (We used our 1" belt sander. For the tight spaces, we wrapped a piece of stiff cardboard with sandpaper.) Next, finish-sand the sides using your palm sander. Now hand-sand a slight round-over on all exterior edges (see Shop Tip *above*).

3 Apply your choice of clear finish to all box surfaces. Two coats of a penetrating oil will work well.

4 Allow the finish to dry overnight. Now, line the base interior with felt. It's a good idea to cut the felt to width before trial fitting it along the base contours. Then, cut the felt to length and adhere it using double-faced carpet tape.

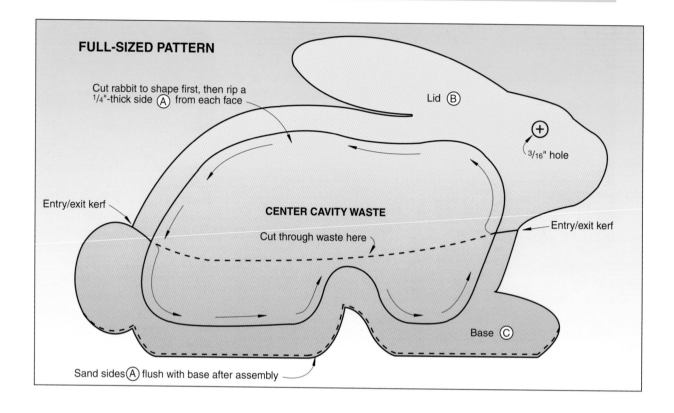

FULL-SIZED PATTERN

Cut rabbit to shape first, then rip a
1/4"-thick side Ⓐ from each face

Lid Ⓑ

⊕
3/16" hole

Entry/exit kerf

CENTER CAVITY WASTE

Cut through waste here

Entry/exit kerf

Base Ⓒ

Sand sides Ⓐ flush with base after assembly

An Assortment of Handsome Boxes

A finely crafted box will always get noticed, but the main reason why is left to the eye of the beholder. A box may owe its good looks to it's joinery, stand out because of the quality of the woods used, or simply have a unique quality about it that defies description.

The six boxes in this chapter were chosen because they displayed one, two, or all three of these reasons. You'll probably agree that each one has it's own distinct appeal—and that's why they've been set apart from the others in this book. We know you'll take pride in building any or all of them, and you'll learn a few techniques along the way, too!

POTPOURRI BOX

So simple you can make it in a single evening, this box has what it takes to maximize the fragrance of whatever you choose to put inside.

1 Cut a piece of ½"-thick hardwood stock (planed-down lacewood was used here) to 2" wide by 24" long.

2 As shown in Steps 1 and 2 of the three-step drawing *(opposite)*, cut a pair of rabbets along the inside surface of the stock.

Now, as shown in Step 3, use a ½" round-over bit to rout a partial round-over along the outside top edge of the board.

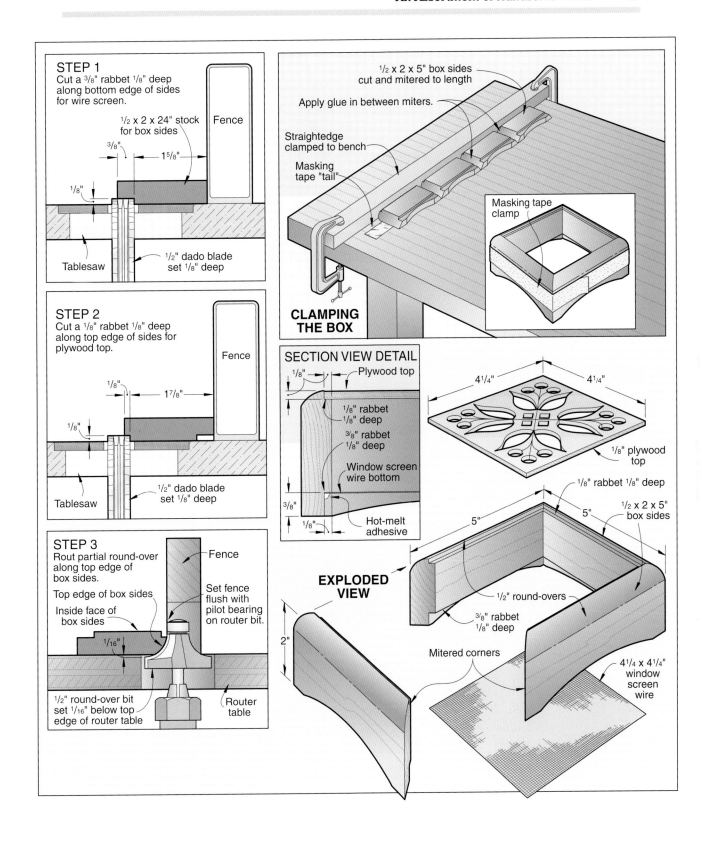

STEP 1

Cut a ³/₈" rabbet ¹/₈" deep along bottom edge of sides for wire screen.

¹/₂ x 2 x 24" stock for box sides

Fence

³/₈"

1⁵/₈"

¹/₈"

Tablesaw

¹/₂" dado blade set ¹/₈" deep

STEP 2

Cut a ¹/₈" rabbet ¹/₈" deep along top edge of sides for plywood top.

Fence

¹/₈"

1⁷/₈"

¹/₈"

Tablesaw

¹/₂" dado blade set ¹/₈" deep

STEP 3

Rout partial round-over along top edge of box sides.

Fence

Top edge of box sides

Set fence flush with pilot bearing on router bit.

Inside face of box sides

¹/₁₆"

¹/₂" round-over bit set ¹/₁₆" below top edge of router table

Router table

¹/₂ x 2 x 5" box sides cut and mitered to length

Apply glue in between miters.

Straightedge clamped to bench

Masking tape "tail"

Masking tape clamp

CLAMPING THE BOX

SECTION VIEW DETAIL

¹/₈"

Plywood top

¹/₈" rabbet ¹/₈" deep

³/₈" rabbet ¹/₈" deep

Window screen wire bottom

³/₈"

¹/₈"

Hot-melt adhesive

4¹/₄"   4¹/₄"

¹/₈" plywood top

¹/₈" rabbet ¹/₈" deep

5"

5"

¹/₂ x 2 x 5" box sides

EXPLODED VIEW

¹/₂" round-overs

³/₈" rabbet ¹/₈" deep

2"

Mitered corners

4¹/₄ x 4¹/₄" window screen wire

3 Miter-cut four equal lengths of stock (ours measured 5" long each) from the 24"-long board.

4 Transfer the full-sized radius pattern to the bottom edge of one of the box sides. Cut and sand the radius to shape. Use this as a template to mark the three remaining box sides. Cut and sand them.

5 Dry-clamp the four pieces to check for tight corner joints. Then, glue and clamp the pieces. For an easy no-clamp method to adhere the mitered corners, start by placing all four pieces inside face down on a flat surface. Use a straightedge to align the bottom edges of all four

box sides. With the mitered joints flush and tight, adhere a strip of masking tape down the center of the four pieces. Flip the assembly over, and apply glue to the mating ends as shown on the Clamping The Box drawing. Fold the pieces together and attach the tape tail to the open end. Later, remove the tape and sand the box.

Make the top and apply the finish

1 From ⅛" Baltic birch plywood, cut a piece 4¼ × 4¼" to fit into the rabbeted top opening in the box.

2 Attach the full-sized pattern (*see page 181*) to the top of the plywood.

To act as a backing board to prevent chip-out, tape a piece of stock to the bottom side of the lid. Using a Forstner bit, drill the ⅜" holes through the lid. Then, scrollsaw the openings in the lid to shape. Drill blade start holes and cut the squares to shape.

3 Remove the pattern and lightly sand with 220-grit sandpaper. Then, apply a clear finish, such as spray lacquer, to the box and lid.

4 Cut a piece of window screen to 4¼ × 4¼" and secure the screen into the bottom rabbet with hot-melt adhesive. Fill the box with potpourri and enjoy.

SIDE
FULL-SIZE
RADIUS
PATTERN

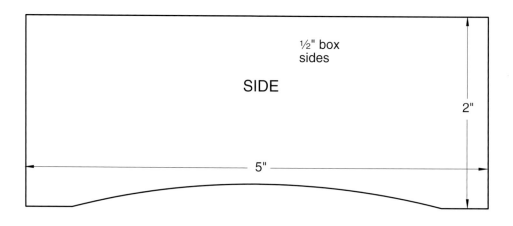

½" box sides

SIDE

2"

5"

A CONTEMPORARY KEEPSAKE

You'll probably have a harder time selecting which woods to use for this box than actually making it! It's shown here in three great combinations, but the possibilites for combinations are endless.

Bird's-eye
maple with
bubinga

Lacewood
with cocobolo

Ash with
cherry

First, make the box

1 From 1/2"-thick stock, cut a 2 × 28" blank for forming the front and back (A) and sides (B) of the box. Also, from 1/2"-thick stock, rip two 1/4 × 28" strips for making the front and back trim (C) and side trim (D).

2 Glue and clamp the trim strips to the edges of the 2 × 28" blank. When dry, remove the clamps and sand or plane the glued-up blank to a thickness of 3/8".

3 From 1/8"-thick stock, cut four 1/8 × 3/8 × 2 1/2" splines for joining the corners of the box. Make the splines from the same type of wood that you use for the trim so the ends of the splines, which will be visible in the assembled box, match the trim.

4 From 1/4" hardwood plywood, cut the bottom (E) to the size listed in the List of Materials. The bottom is slightly undersized to provide a 1/32" clearance on all sides when it's installed in the box.

5 On the inside face of the 2 × 28" blank, cut a 1/4" groove 1/4" deep and 1/4" from the bottom edge to receive the bottom (E), as shown in Drawing 1. Finish-sand the grooved face of the blank to 220 grit.

6 With your tablesaw blade tilted to 45°, miter-cut the glued-up blank to form the front and back pieces (A/C) and side pieces (B/D) to the lengths listed. (It's a good idea to cut test stock first to verify tight miters.) Remember to use a backer board to avoid chip-out.

7 Referring to Drawing 1a and to **Photo A** for setup, cut a 1/8" groove 3/16" deep in the ends of the front and back pieces (A/C) and side pieces (B/D) to receive the splines, as shown in Drawing 1. (We made test cuts in scrap first to verify the groove position and depth.)

Materials List

Part	FINISHED SIZE T	W	L	Matl.	Qty.
A* front and back	3/8"	2"	8"	BM	2
B* sides	3/8"	2"	5"	BM	2
C* front and back trim	3/8"	1/4"	8"	B	4
D* side trim	3/8"	1/4"	5"	B	4
E bottom	1/4"	4 11/16"	7 11/16"	HP	1
F* feet	3/4"	3/4"	2"	B	4
G* lid sides	3/4"	2 1/4"	7 3/4"	BM	2
H* lid center	3/4"	1/4"	7 3/4"	B	1
I* handle braces	3/4"	1"	1 1/4"	B	2
J handle	1/8"	1/2"	6 3/4"	B	1

*Parts initially cut oversize. See the instructions.

Materials Key: BM–bird's-eye maple, B–bubinga, HP–hardwood plywood.

Supplies: Spray adhesive, velvet, cardstock.

Cutting Diagram

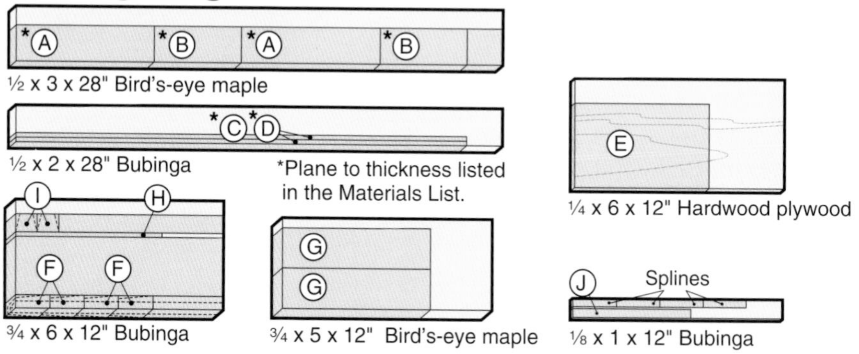

*A
*B
*A
*B
1/2 x 3 x 28" Bird's-eye maple
*C *D
1/2 x 2 x 28" Bubinga
*Plane to thickness listed in the Materials List.
E
1/4 x 6 x 12" Hardwood plywood
I
H
F
F
3/4 x 6 x 12" Bubinga
G
G
3/4 x 5 x 12" Bird's-eye maple
J
Splines
1/8 x 1 x 12" Bubinga

SHOP TIP

Cut the parts in sequence for continuous grain flow

To get continuous grain flow at the corners of a box, miter-cut the pieces in sequence from the blank (e.g., cut the back first, followed by left side, front, and right side). Identify the parts with numbers, where shown, to make it easy to match up the corners during assembly.

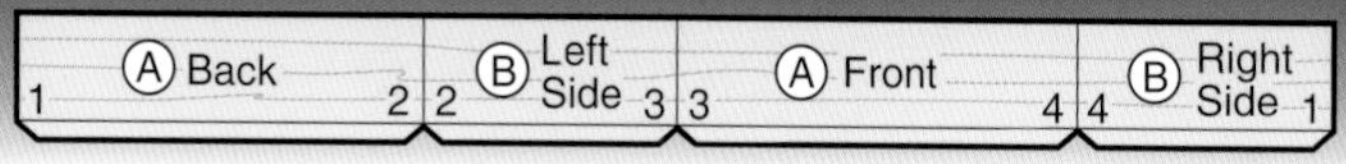

1 A Back 2
2 B Left Side 3
3 A Front 4
4 B Right Side 1

Use a stopblock to ensure consistent positioning of the spline grooves in the mitered ends of the box parts.

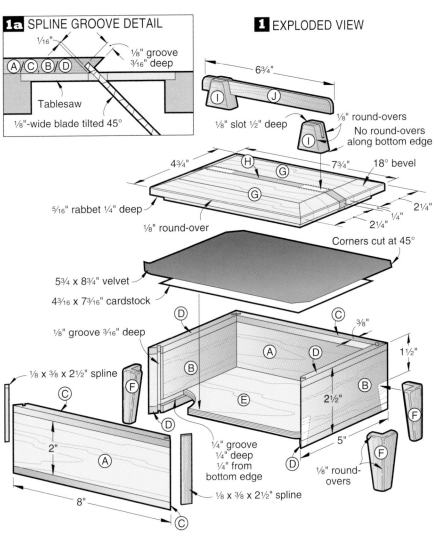

1a SPLINE GROOVE DETAIL

1/16"
1/8" groove 3/16" deep
A C B D
Tablesaw
1/8"-wide blade tilted 45°

1 EXPLODED VIEW

6¾"
I J
1/8" round-overs
No round-overs along bottom edge
I
1/8" slot ½" deep
4¾"
H
G
G
18° bevel
7¾"
5/16" rabbet ¼" deep
1/8" round-over
2¼"
¼"
2¼"
Corners cut at 45°
5¾ x 8¾" velvet
4³/16 x 7³/16" cardstock
1/8" groove 3/16" deep
D
C
3/8"
D
A
D
1½"
B
B
1/8 x ³/8 x 2½" spline
C
F
E
2½"
F
C
2"
A
D
¼" groove ¼" deep ¼" from bottom edge
D
1/8" round-overs
8"
5"
C
1/8 x ³/8 x 2½" spline

8 Cut or sand away a small amount of material at a 45° angle at each corner of the bottom (E) to enable it to clear the splines during box assembly. Then, dry-assemble the front, back, and side pieces, the splines, and the bottom, and check that all joints fit together without gaps. Remove the material from the corners of the bottom little by little until all joints fit correctly.

9 Apply glue to the mitered ends of the front, back, and side pieces, and into the spline grooves and ¼" grooves in these pieces. Now, apply glue to the splines and assemble the pieces with the bottom located in the ¼" groove. Secure the box with a band clamp, and check for square.

Now, do some footwork

1 From ¾"-thick stock, cut a 4 × 12" blank to form the feet (F). Using a wide blank will keep your hands well away from the tablesaw blade when ripping the foot stock from the blank.

2 Cut a ½" rabbet ½" deep along one edge of the blank.

3 Rip a ¾"-wide strip from the rabbeted side of the blank, as shown in **Photo B**.

4 Make four photocopies of the full-size foot pattern, found in Drawing 2. Using spray adhesive, attach the tapered foot part of the pattern to one end of the blank, bending it over the blank at the fold line.

SHOP**TIP**

Forming Tapers on Small Parts Safely

You don't have to risk getting your fingers too close to the moving blade of your tablesaw or bandsaw to form tapers on small parts such as the feet (F). One safe way to do this is to sand the tapers, and to use a 12"-long blank that will keep your fingers out of harm's way. First, mount a belt sander in your vise with the belt up. Then, form the tapers on the end of the blank by sanding to the lines of the attached pattern, as shown here.

With the rabbet facing up, rip a ¾"-wide strip from the blank. This rabbeted blank will form the feet (F).

With the box on a 1" spacer, make sure that all four feet touch the work surface before tightening the band clamp.

2 FOOT FULL-SIZE PATTERN

½" rabbet ½" deep

¾"

¾"

(F)

⅛" round-overs   TOP VIEW

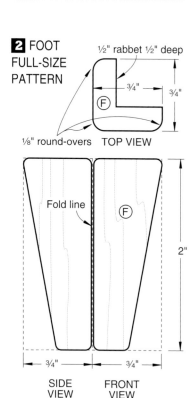

Fold line

(F)

2"

¾"   ¾"

SIDE VIEW   FRONT VIEW

5 Taper the sides of the foot by sanding to the pattern lines. (See the Shop Tip *above*.) Then, crosscut the 2"-long foot from the blank.

6 Using the remaining patterns and following the same process, form the other three feet from the blank.

7 To complete the feet, sand ⅛" round-overs on all outer edges of the feet, as shown in Drawing 1.

8 From a scrap of 1"-thick stock, make a 3¾ × 10" spacer block to support the box at the required height for attaching the feet. Apply glue to the top 1" area on the inside of the feet. With the box placed on the spacer block, as

shown in **Photo C**, position the feet on the box, and secure with a band clamp.

Put a lid on it

1 From ¾"-thick stock, cut two 2¼ × 8½" pieces for the lid sides (G). As shown on the Cutting Diagram, cut these from a

3 SECTION VIEW

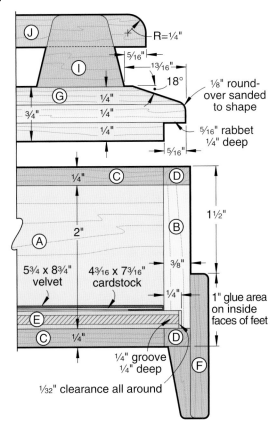

J
R=¼"
⅝₁₆"
13⁄16"
18°
I
G   ¼"
¾"   ¼"
¼"
⅛" round-over sanded to shape
⅝₁₆" rabbet ¼" deep
⁵⁄₁₆"
¼"   C   D
1½"
2"   B
A
5¾ x 8¾"   4³⁄₁₆ x 7³⁄₁₆"
velvet   cardstock
⅜"
¼"
E
1" glue area on inside faces of feet
C   ¼"   D
¼" groove ¼" deep
F
1⁄32" clearance all around

3a BEVEL-CUTTING DETAIL

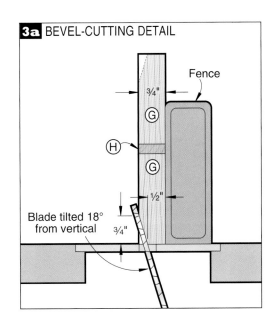

¾"   Fence
G
H
G
½"
Blade tilted 18° from vertical   ¾"

5"-wide piece to maintain grain flow on the lid. Also, from ¾"-thick stock, cut a ¼ × 8½" strip for the lid center (H).

2 Glue and clamp the lid center (H) between the lid sides (G). After the glue is dry, trim the lid (G/H) to its finished length of 7¾".

3 To cut the 18° bevel on the lid as shown in Drawing 3, tilt your saw blade to 18° from vertical. Position your fence ½" away from the base of the blade as shown in Drawing 3a. Cut the bevel on the ends of the lid first; then, cut the sides. Cutting in this sequence will minimize chip-out.

4 Using your tablesaw or a rabbeting bit in your table-mounted router, cut a ⁵⁄₁₆" rabbet ¼" deep around the perimeter of the lid (G/H) on the bottom side, as shown in Drawing 3. To avoid chip-out, make several passes around the lid, raising the blade or bit a little at a time with each pass.

5 Sand the ⅛" round-over on the top outer edges of the lid (G/H) as shown in Drawing 3. Finish-sand the entire lid to 220 grit.

6 To make the handle braces (I), first cut a 1 × 12" blank from ¾"-thick stock.

7 Install a ⅛"-wide blade in your tablesaw and set it to ½" high. Adjust your fence to center the blade on the ¾" thickness of the blank. Now, cut a groove along the length of the blank to accept the handle (J), as shown in the end view of the full-size handle brace pattern (Drawing 4). Then, crosscut the blank to make two 1¼"-long pieces.

4 HANDLE BRACE
FULL-SIZE
PATTERNS

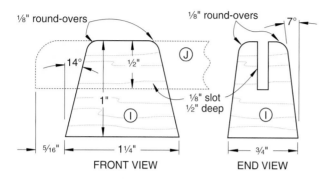

⅛" round-overs

14°   ½"
1"
⑯

⅛" round-overs   7°

⅛" slot
½" deep

⑯   ⑯

5/16"   1¼"   ¾"

FRONT VIEW   END VIEW

8 Make two photocopies of the full-size handle brace pattern (*above*). Using a spray adhesive, attach the front view part of the pattern to the handle brace pieces. Sand to the pattern lines to form the 14° sides and ⅛" round-overs. Remove the patterns. Then, attach the end-view pattern to the braces, and sand to the pattern lines to form the ⅛" round-overs on the outer top edges and the 7° bevel on the handle brace sides.

9 From ⅛"-thick stock, cut the handle (J) to the size listed. Referring to Drawing 3, form the ¼" radius at each end of the handle by sanding.

10 Glue the handle into the slots of the handle braces (I) so that the ends of the handle extend 5/16" from the bottom of the braces, as shown in Drawing 3. Now, glue and clamp the handle assembly (I/J) to the lid as shown in Drawings 1 and 3.

Finish and line the box

1 Finish-sand the box, lid braces, and handle with 220-grit sandpaper. Remove all dust with a tack cloth. Apply three coats of a clear finish of your choice, sanding with 400-grit between coats (aerosol lacquer will work well here.)

2 Finally, cut a piece of cardstock to 4³⁄₁₆ × 7³⁄₁₆", and cut a piece of velvet to 5¾ × 8¾". Referring to Drawing 1, cut the corners of the velvet at 45°. Apply spray adhesive to the bottom of the velvet and to the top of the cardstock. Join the two glued surfaces together, centering the cardstock on the velvet. Fold the outer edges of the velvet onto the bottom of the cardstock. Now, apply spray adhesive to the bottom of the cardstock. Place the cardstock/velvet in the box, and press it into place against the bottom.

PATINA-TOPPED JEWELRY BOX

On the following pages, you'll learn how to make this box's striking copper lid with its Japanese maple leaf pattern. But as you will see, there's more to this container than just an exquisite lid. Although the box shown here was designed with the finest of materials, such as thin cork tray liners to cushion jewelry and brass hardware, you can hold down costs with less expensive hinges, wooden feet, and a flocked interior.

1 Using ½"-thick cherry, rip a 48"-long board to 3⅛" wide for the case front/back (A) and the case sides (B).

2 Set your tablesaw's blade and rip fence to cut the grooves along the top and bottom inner faces of the case pieces (A, B). After you make these cuts, test-fit the thickness of the copper and hardboard for the top panel (C) into its groove. Also test the fit of the cork lining and the hardboard bottom panel (C) into its groove.

3 Cut the case front/back (A) and the case sides (B) to the finished length shown in the Materials List.

4 Referring to Drawing 1 and **Photo A**, set up your router table to cut the spline slots. Use double-faced tape to temporarily join the outside faces of the front/back (A) to one another. Position the stop blocks 2¹⁵⁄₁₆" from the center of the router

bit. Switch on the router and hold the front/back against the right stopblock and the fence. Lower the wood until it comes in contact with the table and support block, and rout the slot by moving the wood to the left until it hits the stopblock. Repeat the process for each of the remaining mitered ends.

5 Referring to Drawing 2, note that the grain of the spline runs along its short dimension. Make the splines by ripping a cherry board 2⅝" wide, and plane or resaw it to ⅛" thick. Then, cut four splines ½" long.

6 Cut two pieces of hardboard for the top/bottom panels (C) to the size listed in the Materials List. Cut the copper panel to the same size, and then apply the decorative finish to the metal using the patina method and the

Japanese maple leaf pattern (see the Special Feature starting *opposite*).

Materials List

Part	T	W	L	Matl.	Qty.
A case front/back	½	3⅛"	14"	C	2
B case sides	½"	3⅛"	7"	C	2
C bottom/top panels	⅛"	6³⁄₁₆"	13³⁄₁₆"	H	2
D handle*	½"	2⅜"	⅞"	S	1
E case divider	⅜"	1"	13"	C	1
F case divider front/back	¼"	1"	13"	C	2
G case sub-dividers	⅛"	1"	2¹³⁄₁₆"	C	10
H tray front/back	¼"	⅞"	6¼"	C	2
I tray ends	¼"	⅞"	5¹⁵⁄₁₆"	C	2
J tray divider	⅜"	⅝"	6"	C	1
K tray sub-dividers	⅛"	⅝"	2¹³⁄₁₆"	C	4
L tray bottom	⅛"	5¹¹⁄₁₆"	6¼"	H	1

*Cut from ½×2½×12" blank and trim to size.

Materials key: C–cherry, H–hardboard, S–scrapwood.

Supplies: Brass feet (4); 1¼×1" brass box hinges with screws (2); #6×¾" brass flathead wood screws (2); .016×6³⁄₁₆×13³⁄₁₆" copper sheet; 6³⁄₁₆×13³⁄₁₆" cork wall covering; 5⅝×6¼" cork wall covering (both paper-thin cork wall covering cork cubed); ⅛×5¹⁵⁄₁₆×12¹⁵⁄₁₆" mirror; label paper printed with leaf pattern for top.

1 SPLINE-SLOT CUTTING

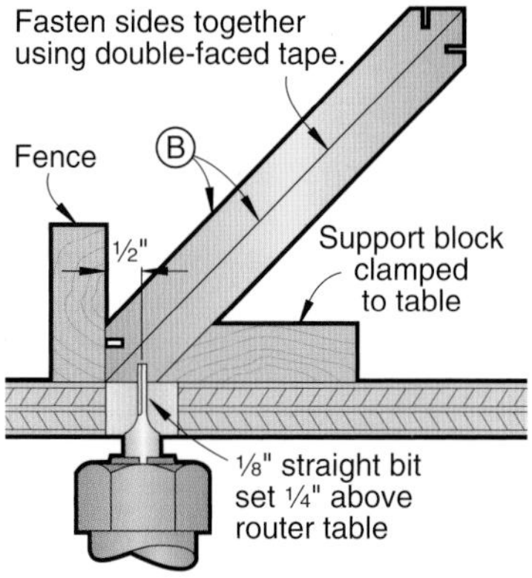

Fasten sides together using double-faced tape.

Fence

Ⓑ

½"

Support block clamped to table

⅛" straight bit set ¼" above router table

A

Position the front/back parts against the fence and right stopblock, and lower them onto the running bit.

SPECIAL FEATURE: PATINA TECHNIQUE THROUGH BASIC CHEMISTRY

Some ammonia fumes are really all you need to give shiny new copper a weathered look, but if you want to include some cool designs, we'll show you how.

Any material that can keep the fumes away from selected areas can act as a "resist" and produce designs on copper. To make the ornamental, Japanese maple leaved panel on the box shown here, we started with some traditional procedures. Eventually, though, we came up with a new twist on the technique that's easier for a beginner, yet still gives reliable, attractive results.

Of course, you don't have to limit your designs to the leaf shapes shown here—feel free to try any natural, geometric,

A sharp-looking design calls for attractive shapes, a good layout, and precise cutting with a sharp knife.

Any coating of salt will bring results, but the density does make a difference. Run a couple of tests before you work on the piece for your project.

or artistic shapes you like. You can find countless samples in clip art books and software. And it isn't just for box lids and house signs, either. It could be just the thing for a serving tray, door panel insert, mailbox, or any number of other applications.

Shopping first

You'll need a sheet of flat, medium-gauge copper, self-adhesive label paper, table salt, non-sudsy household ammonia, and the leaf pattern, plus a plastic container

with a tight-fitting lid. If you prefer to make your own design, read on, because we'll tell you how.

You should be able to find copper at home stores and lumber yards. Or, you can check under "sheet metal work" in the Yellow Pages of your phone book. Those companies often have a supply of copper and will sell you what you need (sometimes at a better price). Look for label paper in your local office supplies store. You can find various sizes of plastic boxes with lids at any department store.

C

Remove the copper when the patina appears complete. Remember to wear a respirator mask whenever you have the lid off your container.

Now for the art part

We used Japanese maple leaves for our design. Put our pattern in a photocopy machine and copy it onto self-adhesive label paper. Or, to make your own design, arrange leaves on the glass surface of the copier, and run a test copy. Rearrange them until you like the design and the leaf edges appear crisp on the photocopy. Then, load self-adhesive label paper into the appropriate tray of the copier, and print the final version.

Of course, there are a number of avenues you can pursue if you're looking for a unique pattern and you're web-savvy and have a fairly decent computer printer. Just make sure the pattern you want to use is clearly printed.

Note: Find the method that works best for you, but paper gave us the most consistent results. Our first efforts involved gluing real leaves to the copper, but that produced varying degrees of crispness along the leaf edges and varying amounts of residue beneath the leaves. Next, we tried plastic leaf shapes, but we got sharp, shiny images that looked too artificial. So we tried self-adhesive paper, and liked what we saw.

Cut the copper to size with shears or a utility knife, and sand it with 180-grit sandpaper until it's uniformly shiny. Clean it with denatured alcohol to make sure nothing remains that will interfere with the next steps. Definitely wear gloves when handling the copper from now until it

goes into the ammonia fumes, so it won't pick up any oil from your fingers.

After the solvent evaporates, peel the backing off the label paper and affix it to the copper. With an X-acto knife, carefully cut around the leaves' outlines as shown in **Photo A**. You also can cut "veins" into the leaves for a more realistic appearance. Remove the white paper surrounding the leaves. Clean off any stubborn adhesive with lacquer thinner, then wait a couple of minutes while the solvent evaporates.

Spray a light mist of water over the copper. Then sprinkle on an even, moderate dusting of ordinary table salt, as shown in **Photo B**. Different amounts will give you different results, so it's best to test the technique on a couple of small pieces of copper first.

And finally, the chemistry

Now you're going to use ammonia to transform that bland copper color into a mottled blue. Ammonia fumes will linger while you carry out this procedure, so set things up outdoors, in the garage, or in some well-ventilated part of the house where the smell won't bother anyone. *Wear a respirator mask*—the strength of those fumes can sneak up on you!

Pour ½" of ammonia into the container. Place blocks of wood or other disposable supports in the box to suspend

Scrub with moderate pressure and check the look of the piece as you go. If you accidentally remove too much patina, carefully add salt where you want it and fume the copper again.

leaves tend to look more natural that way.

Lightly scrub the background, but don't overdo it. You want to eliminate any "muddy" appearance without knocking off all of the blue residue created by the salt and ammonia. As the workpiece dries, you'll see the finished color start to come through.

Let the copper dry, and then apply one or two coats of paste wax. That will protect the patina and give it some luster. Or, you can spray the copper with clear lacquer.

the copper above the ammonia. Lay the copper on the supports and immediately put the lid on the container.

Ammonia fumes by themselves turn copper a dark, olive color. The salt produces a bluish, crusty residue. But each paper leaf acts as a resist, keeping the salt and fumes away from the copper underneath.

Check the progress after about 4 hours to see if the patina is developing evenly. Leave the copper in the fumes

as long as you like, but don't expect much more than very subtle changes after the first 6 hours.

When you remove the copper from the container, as in **Photo C**, you'll see a dark background around the paper leaves. Working on a piece of cardboard or scrap plywood, scrub off the paper with lacquer thinner and a stiff-bristled brush, as shown in **Photo D**. If some dark spots remain on the copper leaf images, that's fine. The

More Patina Possibilities

Want to experiment with variations on this technique? Try these ideas:

■ "Paint" any shape you want with petroleum jelly, which is an excellent resist.

■ For clear, sharp letters, use vinyl lettering from a hobby or department store.

■ After salting the surface, cover it with copper sulfate mixed with sawdust and ammonia instead of fuming. This method creates a warm, brown tone. You can buy copper sulfate at a pharmacy.

■ Use brass or bronze instead of copper to achieve a different look.

Cutting Diagram

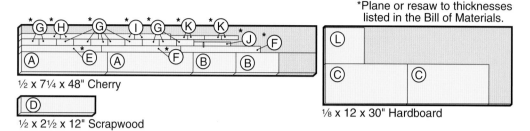

*Plane or resaw to thicknesses
listed in the Bill of Materials.

½ x 7¼ x 48" Cherry

½ x 2½ x 12" Scrapwood

⅛ x 12 x 30" Hardboard

Assemble the box

1 To protect the top-/bottom panels (C) from the protective finish you'll apply later to the wood, cover them with clear plastic food wrap. Wrap about 1" of plastic over each panel edge, and secure it to the back of the panel with masking tape.

2 Dry-assemble (no glue!) the box parts (A, B, C), the copper panel, and the splines to make sure everything fits. If needed, cut a nick out of each panel's corner to get them to fit.

3 To keep glue squeeze-out off the interior corners, place a strip of masking tape along each miter cut, as shown in Drawing 2. Apply glue sparingly to all of the miters and splines, and assemble the box. If the panels bow inward, making it difficult to add the final box side, cut a 2⅝"-long scrapwood spacer strip, and spring it between the panels to separate them. Gently snug up the joints with a band clamp, and make sure the assembly is square and flat while it dries.

Mark for hinges and separate the lid

1 Unclamp the box after the glue dries. Use a pencil and square to

The spacers clamped into the end cuts keep the wood from pinching the blade during the final cut.

Move the lid over a sheet of glued-down sandpaper, and you'll quickly erase saw marks.

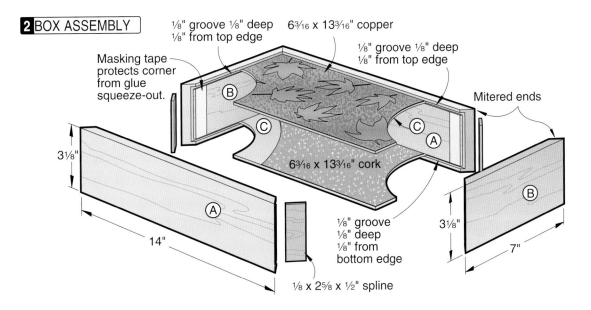

2 BOX ASSEMBLY

⅛" groove ⅛" deep
⅛" from top edge

6³⁄₁₆ x 13³⁄₁₆" copper

⅛" groove ⅛" deep
⅛" from top edge

Masking tape
protects corner
from glue
squeeze-out.

B

Mitered ends

C   C

3⅛"   A

A

6³⁄₁₆ x 13³⁄₁₆" cork

B

3⅛"

14"   ⅛" groove
⅛" deep
⅛" from
bottom edge   7"

⅛ x 2⅝ x ½" spline

mark the hinge locations on the back of the box, as shown in Drawing 2a.

2 Lock your tablesaw's fence ¾" from the inner side of the blade and raise the blade about ⁹⁄₁₆" above the surface of the table. With the top of the box against the fence, make a cut along both ends of the box. Referring to **Photo B**, clamp spacers into the kerfs, and make the cuts along the front and back of the box.

Referring to **Photo C**, remove saw marks by rubbing the cut edges on a full sheet of 100-grit sandpaper spray-glued to a flat surface. Remove the tape from the inside corners of the box and lid.

3 Referring to Drawing 3, use a square to transfer the hinge-location marks from the back of the box bottom and lid to their inner edges.

4 Use a ¼" bit in a small router, as shown in **Photo D**, to remove most of the waste within the hinge's outline. Rout close to the lines, and then finish the mortises with a chisel. Drill pilot holes for the hinge screws, test-fit the hinges, and remove them.

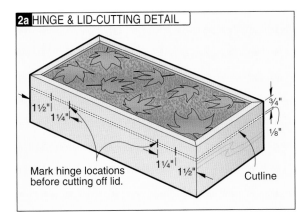

2a HINGE & LID-CUTTING DETAIL

1½"
1¼"

¾"

⅛"

1¼"   1½"

Mark hinge locations
before cutting off lid.   Cutline

D

Clamping a 1½"-wide scrapwood block to the box will provide a no-tip support for the router.

Using a 12"-long blank for the handle will keep your fingers safely away from the router bit.

Make a stylish handle

1 Cut a $\frac{1}{2} \times 2\frac{1}{2} \times 12$" piece of solid scrapwood (any wood that paints well). Referring to Drawing 3a, mark the radius and cutline on the wood. Use a scrollsaw or bandsaw to cut just to the waste side of the radius, then sand to the line.

2 Referring to **Photo E**, put a $\frac{1}{4}$" round-over bit into your table-mounted router, and rout the top and bottom faces of the radius. Use your miter saw to cut the handle to length.

3 Refer to Drawing 3 to drill the handle-mounting holes through the lid. Holding the handle in place, push a finishing nail through these holes to mark the position of the $\frac{3}{32}$" pilot holes in the handle. Screw the handle into place.

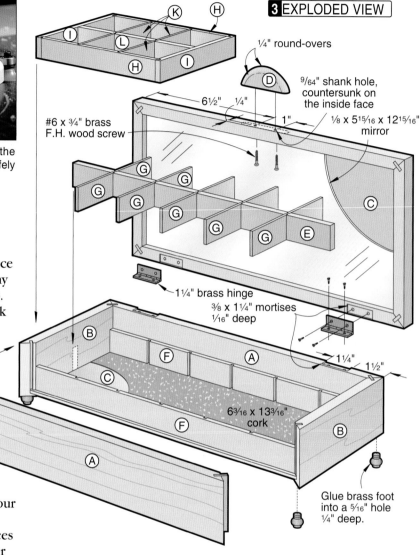

3 EXPLODED VIEW

$\frac{1}{4}$" round-overs

$\frac{9}{64}$" shank hole, countersunk on the inside face

$6\frac{1}{2}$"　$\frac{1}{4}$"

1"

$\frac{1}{8} \times 5\frac{15}{16} \times 12\frac{15}{16}$" mirror

#6 x $\frac{3}{4}$" brass F.H. wood screw

$1\frac{1}{4}$" brass hinge

$\frac{3}{8} \times 1\frac{1}{4}$" mortises $\frac{1}{16}$" deep

$1\frac{1}{4}$"　$1\frac{1}{2}$"

$6\frac{3}{16} \times 13\frac{3}{16}$" cork

Glue brass foot into a $\frac{5}{16}$" hole $\frac{1}{4}$" deep.

Machine and assemble the dividers and tray

1 Referring to the Materials List, prepare blanks for the parts you'll need for the divider and tray assemblies (Parts E, F, G, H, I, J, and K) by planing or resawing cherry to the required thicknesses. Then rip the blanks to width.

2 Crosscut the case divider (E) and the case divider front/back (F) to fit inside the box.

3 Lay out the dadoes on parts E and F as shown in Drawing 4.

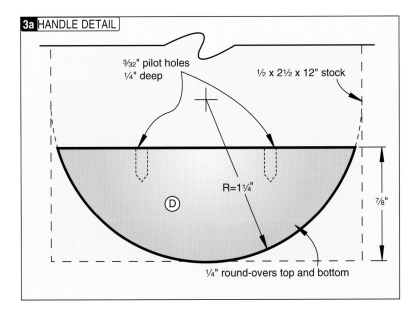

3a HANDLE DETAIL

³⁄₃₂" pilot holes ¹⁄₄" deep

¹⁄₂ x 2¹⁄₂ x 12" stock

R=1¹⁄₄"

Ⓓ

⁷⁄₈"

¹⁄₄" round-overs top and bottom

Finish and final assembly

1 Remove the hinges, the handle, and all the dividers from the tray and box. If necessary, patch the plastic wrap. Do any touch-up sanding that is necessary, but don't sand the divider parts too much—you might change their fit.

2 Apply your choice of finish (three coats of spray lacquer was used here). For the handle, seal first with shellac or diluted clear finish, and then spray on three coats of black enamel.

3 Use a crafts knife to cut away the plastic wrap, and remove the tape. Referring to Drawing 3, drill holes into the bottom of the box for the brass feet. Use a dab of silicone or epoxy to secure the shank of each foot into its hole. Glue and screw the handle into place. Install the dividers, then replace the hinges.

4 Have a ¹⁄₈"-thick mirror cut slightly undersized for the inner lid. We installed ours with four dabs of silicone on the back of the mirror.

4 Center the case divider (E) inside the box, and position the case divider front/back (F), but do not glue any of the pieces. Crosscut and fit the case sub-dividers (G), but don't glue them.

5 Crosscut the tray front/back (H) and the tray ends (I), making sure that the tray ends fit easily between the front and back of the box assembly.

6 Referring to Drawings 5 and 5a, lay out and rout the rabbets, grooves, and dadoes in parts H and I. Note that the horizontal groove in the tray ends (I)

stops at the vertical dado near each corner.

7 Cut the tray bottom (L) from hardboard to the size listed in the Materials List. Glue the cork liner, using the same procedure you used earlier. When the glue dries, cover the piece with plastic wrap and test-fit it. Glue and clamp the tray assembly.

8 Crosscut the tray divider (J) to fit, then rout the dadoes as shown in Drawing 5. Crosscut the tray sub-dividers (K) to fit.

STACK 'EM UP!

Building this stackable jewelry chest requires only the most basic woodworking skills,
but the aniline dyes really set off the figured wood to great effect.

1 Select your stock, paying
particular attention to
grain figure and color
match. Much of the box's
beauty arises from its promi-
nent wood grain display. (We
built our jewelry box from
curly maple.) You will need ¼"
and ⅜" stock for the box—we
resawed ¾" boards.

2 Lay out the parts on
stock of appropriate
thickness. Position
parts A, B, C, D, F, and H for
best appearance—they will be
the most visible parts. (For a

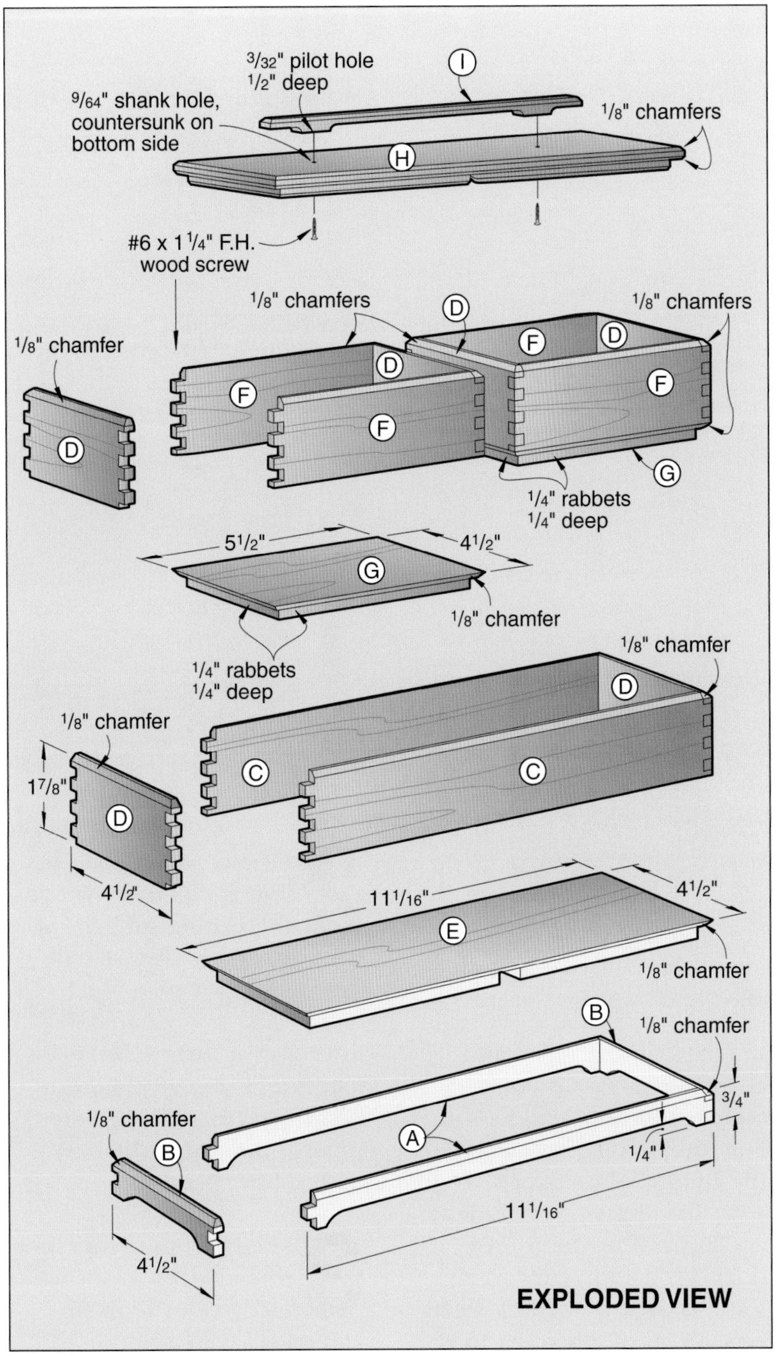

better look at the grain when laying out the parts, wipe the stock with mineral spirits. It will highlight the figure and then evaporate.)

3 Cut out parts A, B, C, D, and F, making them $\frac{1}{16}$" longer than finished size. (Cut parts A and B to the width shown, but do not make the leg cutouts yet.) The extra length will allow you to cut the box-joint fingers $\frac{1}{32}$" longer on each end of each part. After assembly, you can then sand them flush for a perfect fit.

Materials List

Part	Finished Size T	W	L	Matl.	Qty.
A* base side	$\frac{1}{4}$"	$\frac{3}{4}$"	$11\frac{1}{16}$"	M	2
B* base end	$\frac{1}{4}$"	$\frac{3}{4}$"	$4\frac{1}{2}$"	M	2
C* long side	$\frac{1}{4}$"	$1\frac{7}{8}$"	$11\frac{1}{16}$"	M	2
D* end	$\frac{1}{4}$"	$1\frac{7}{8}$"	$4\frac{1}{2}$"	M	6
E long bottom	$\frac{3}{8}$"	$4\frac{1}{2}$"	$11\frac{1}{16}$"	M	1
F* short side	$\frac{1}{4}$"	$1\frac{7}{8}$"	$5\frac{1}{2}$"	M	4
G short bottom	$\frac{3}{8}$"	$4\frac{1}{2}$"	$5\frac{1}{2}$"	M	2
H lid	$\frac{3}{4}$"	$4\frac{1}{2}$"	$11\frac{1}{16}$"	M	1
I** handle	$\frac{3}{8}$"	$\frac{5}{8}$"	$7\frac{1}{4}$"	M	1

*Initially make longer than shown, then trim to finished size in accordance with how-to instructions.

**Initially make both longer and wider than shown, then cut to finished size in accordance with how-to instructions.

Material Key: M–maple

Supplies: Woodworker's yellow glue; aniline dyes—forest green and nigrosine black, jewelry-box liners, #6×$1\frac{1}{4}$" flathead wood screws.

Saw-cut a few box joints

1 Box joints, as used here, normally call for fingers that are typically as wide as the stock is thick, and the width of the box sides must be an increment of the finger width. Otherwise, you'll wind up with less-than-pleasing partial fingers at the box's bottom. For example, with $\frac{1}{4}$"-thick material and $\frac{1}{4}$" fingers, the box sides should be in increments of $\frac{1}{4}$" (5", $5\frac{1}{4}$", $5\frac{1}{2}$", etc.).

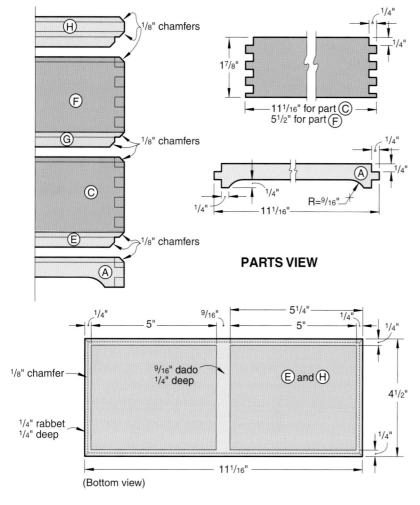

PARTS VIEW

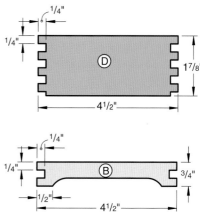

(Bottom view)

But, the 1⅞" width of these boxes' sides and ends (C, D, F) only divides into 7½ increments of ¼". As shown in the Exploded View drawing, the design of the box calls for cutting half-width fingers at the bottom of the sides (C, F). The chamfered edges of the box bottoms (E, G) visually complete the half-fingers to make the joints look even.

2 Lay out the locations and widths of your box-joint fingers and notches on the sides and ends. Then set up your tablesaw with a dado set. For the jewelry box, raise the height of the dado set to 9⁄32"; this allows 1⁄32" extra at each end. Cut the joints, referring to the Exploded View drawing of the jewelry box. (You might want to build the Box-Joint Cutting Jig shown in the Nutcracker Box project in Chapter Five, *page 115*.)

Put the parts together

1 Referring to the Parts View drawings for parts A and B, lay out the leg cutout on the bottom of each piece. Scrollsaw or bandsaw the cutouts, staying slightly outside the line. Sand to the line.

2 Fit one part A and one part B together. Notice the mating surfaces of the joint. Then, disassemble the joint, apply glue to all four joints, and reassemble. After gluing parts A and B together, measure the diagonals to ensure that the base is square, and clamp the base with rubber bands.

3 Similarly, glue together three boxes as shown, using sides C and F and ends D. Square the boxes and clamp.

4 Allow the glue to dry, and then remove the clamps. Sand the sides and ends flush.

Saw the bottoms and the lid

1 Cut the bottoms (Parts E and G) and the lid (H) to size.

2 Glue a bottom to each box, keeping the edges and ends flush with the box sides and ends. Place the half-fingers adjacent to the bottom of each box. Clamp, and clean off the glue squeeze-out.

3 Saw or rout a ¼" rabbet ¼" deep all around the bottom of each box and the bottom side of the lid.

4 Saw a ⁹⁄₁₆"-wide dado ¼" deep across the middle of the long box's bottom (E) and the bottom side of the lid (H), shown in the Parts View drawing. To cut the dado, install a ⅜" dado blade on the tablesaw. Set the fence 5¼" from the blade as a stop. Then, using the miter gauge, saw the dado in two passes, with each end of the lid against the fence.

5 Next, install a chamfer bit in your table-mounted router. Rout ⅛" chamfers around the top and bottom of each box and the lid where indicated.

You can form both chamfers on the bottom with a single setup. Then, lower the bit for the top chamfers. Chamfer the corners inside the ⁹⁄₁₆" dadoes with a hand plane or by sanding.

6 Sand all surfaces and edges until they are smooth and flush.

7 Transfer the full-sized pattern (*below*) for the handle (I) to the stock. Scrollsaw or bandsaw the handle. Sand chamfers on the handle where shown. Sand smooth.

8 Drill ³⁄₃₂" pilot holes through the lid as shown. Then hold the handle in position, and drill through the pilot holes ½" deep into the handle posts. Enlarge the holes through the lid to ⁹⁄₆₄", and countersink them on the bottom.

Color it done

1 Finish-sand all parts to 320-grit.

2 Aniline dye gives figured wood clarity as well as color. We used the water-soluble type because of it's ease in mixing

and color fastness. The colors we choose were a dark forest green and a pure black (names vary by manufacturer). Simply mix according to instructions, then test on scrap wood from the box to check color (the wet, dyed wood represents the final color). Foam brushes work nicely as applicators. To lighten, add more water; to darken, add powder. Remember, adding another coat while the surface is still wet won't deepen the color!

3 Water-soluble aniline dye will raise the wood grain, so you'll have to do some light sanding with 320-grit abrasive after letting it dry for 24 hours.

4 If the dyed wood looks to light in color after sanding, recoat with dye. After it dries, resand lightly.

5 For best results, apply a clear oil finish, following the container instructions. Sand between coats. When the finish has thoroughly dried, add past wax, then buff.

6 Insert velvet or felt liners trimmed to fit (or flock).

Ⓘ FULL-SIZED PATTERN

³⁄₃₂" pilot hole
½" deep

DOVETAILED JEWELRY BOX

Keyed walnut dovetails are really what make this birds-eye maple jewelry box a true standout. But the layers of compartmented trays are pretty cool, too.

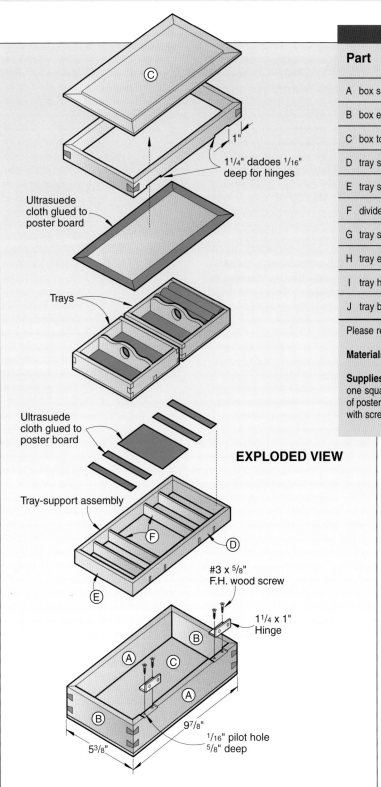

1 1/4" dadoes 1/16" deep for hinges

1"

Ultrasuede cloth glued to poster board

Trays

Ultrasuede cloth glued to poster board

Tray-support assembly

EXPLODED VIEW

#3 x 5/8" F.H. wood screw

1 1/4 x 1" Hinge

9 7/8"

1/16" pilot hole 5/8" deep

5 3/8"

Materials List

Part	Finished Size			Matl.	Qty.
	T	W	L		
A box sides	3/8"	3 3/8"	9 7/8"	M	2
B box ends	3/8"	3 3/8"	5 3/8"	M	2
C box top/bottom	1/4"	5 3/8"	9 7/8"	M	2
D tray support sides	1/4"	1 1/16"	9 1/8"	M	2
E tray support ends	1/4"	1 1/16"	4 5/8"	M	2
F dividers	1/8"	7/8"	4 5/8"	M	4
G tray sides	1/4"	7/8"	4 1/2"	M	4
H tray ends	1/4"	7/8"	4 1/2"	M	4
I tray handles	1/4"	1 1/4"	4 1/2"	M	2
J tray bases	1/8"	4 1/2"	4 1/2"	M	2

Please read all instructions before cutting.

Materials Key: M–birds-eye maple.

Supplies: 3/4×1×20" walnut; 1/3 yard of ultrasuede fabric; one square foot of 1/8"-thick foam rubber; 10×15" piece of posterboard; 1 1/4×1/2" (closed dimensions) stop hinges with screws; finish.

1 For the box sides (A) and ends (B), rip and crosscut to 3 3/8" × 34" a piece of stock that you've planed or resawn to 3/8"-thick (we used bird's-eye maple). Then, adjust the blade on your tablesaw to 45°. Miter-cut the parts to the sizes listed in the Materials List. Use a stopblock to assure that matching parts are identical in length.

2 Mark the bit's center-line on the jig, and screw a stopblock 3/4" from the centerline, where shown in the Dovetail Jig drawing on *page 92*. Now, position the box with the

CUTTING DIAGRAM

*Plane or resaw to thickness listed in Bill Of Materials

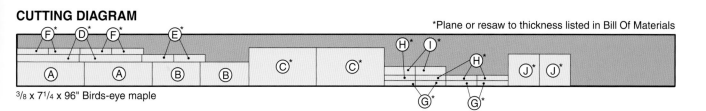

3/8 x 7¹/₄ x 96" Birds-eye maple

bottom against the stop-block as shown in the Using the Dovetail Jig drawing, and rout a dovetail slot through the box's corner. Rotate the box in the jig to rout slots through each of the corners. Then, place the box top against the stopblock, and repeat the procedure to rout four more dovetail slots.

Cut the dovetail slots and keys

1 Make the jig shown *below*. Chuck a ½" × 14 degree dovetail bit into your table-mounted router and set the bit ⁵/₁₆" above the table's surface. Place the jig on the router table, start the router, and slide the jig

across the table to rout a slot through the jig's slanted backboard. Elevate the bit about ³/₁₆", and make another pass. Repeat until you've raised the bit to ¹¹/₁₆" above the table.

2 Mark the bit's centerline on the jig, and screw a stopblock ¾" from the

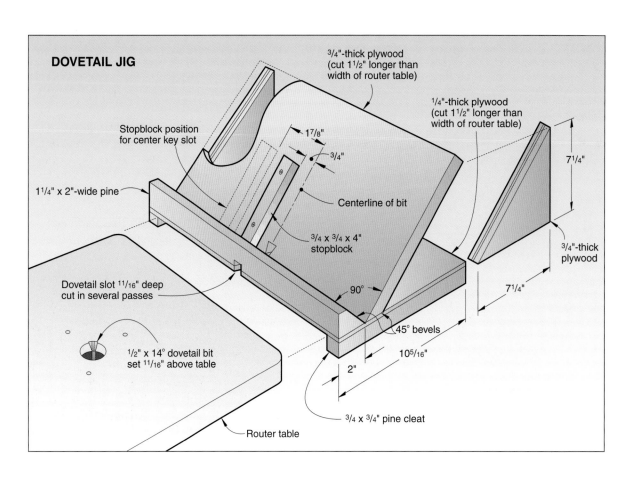

DOVETAIL JIG

¾"-thick plywood (cut 1¹/₂" longer than width of router table)

¹/₄"-thick plywood (cut 1¹/₂" longer than width of router table)

Stopblock position for center key slot

1⁷/₈"

¾"

7¹/₄"

Centerline of bit

1¹/₄" x 2"-wide pine

¾ x ¾ x 4" stopblock

¾"-thick plywood

Dovetail slot ¹¹/₁₆" deep cut in several passes

90°

7¹/₄"

45° bevels

10⁵/₁₆"

¹/₂" x 14° dovetail bit set ¹¹/₁₆" above table

2"

¾ x ¾" pine cleat

Router table

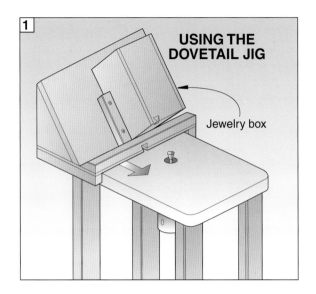

1 USING THE DOVETAIL JIG

Jewelry box

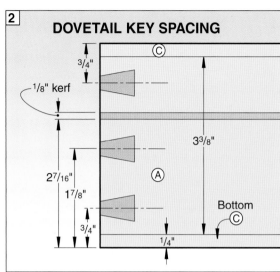

2 DOVETAIL KEY SPACING

3/4"

1/8" kerf

2⁷/₁₆"

1⁷/₈"

3/4"

3³/₈"

Bottom

1/4"

centerline, as shown in the Dovetail Jig drawing. Now, position the box with the bottom against against the stopblock as shown in **Drawing 1**, and rout a dovetail slot through a box corner. Rotate the box in the jig to rout the slots through each of the other corners. Then, place the box top against the stopblock, and repeat

the procedure to rout four more dovetail slots.

3 Referring to **Drawing 2** *above*, move the stopblock to 1⅞" from the bit's centerline. Then, holding the box bottom against the jig's stopblock, rout the center dovetail slot through each corner of the box.

Note: the center dovetail is slightly offset toward the bottom of the box at this time. When the box lid is cut free, the slot will be in the center.

4 Adjust the dovetail bit in your table-mounted router as shown in the "Machining the Dovetail-Key Blank", **Drawing 3**. Align your fence with the bit's centerline, and rout both edges of a 20" length of ¾ × 1" walnut. Refer to the Shop Tip *below* for the method of sizing the dovetail keys perfectly.

3 MACHINING THE DOVETAIL-KEY BLANK

Router table fence

Dovetail-key blank

3/4"

1"

1/2"

1/2" x 14° dovetail bit

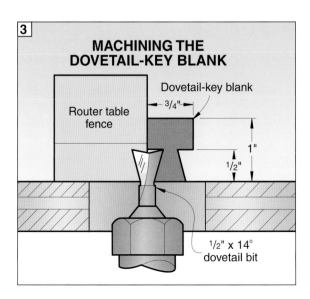

SHOPTIP

When machining the dovetail-key blank, initially set up your router-table fence so that slightly less than half of the bit's width is exposed. Rout both edges of the blank and test the fit. At this point, the key should be too wide. Move the fence slightly to expose more of the bit, and reclamp it. Rout one edge of the blank, and test the key again. Repeat the process until you get a perfect fit.

5 Test the fit of the key stock into the dovetail slots in the box. The fit should not be too tight or you could split the box. Crosscut twelve 1¼"-long dovetail keys. Glue the keys into the dovetail slots, and let the glue dry.

6 Trim the excess length of the keys (we used an offset backsaw, but any fine-toothed handsaw will work well). Carefully sand the keys flush with the surfaces of the box (we used a belt sander with a 150-grit belt).

Create the box lid

1 Adjust your tablesaw blade to 8° from vertical, raise it to ¾", and install an auxiliary wooden fence on your tablesaw's rip fence as shown in **Drawing 4**. Now, cut bevels along the edges and ends of the top and bottom of the box.

2 Adjust your tablesaw blade to vertical, set the blade height to ⁷⁄₁₆", and adjust the rip fence to 2⁷⁄₁₆" from the blade. Make certain that the blade is centered between the top and middle

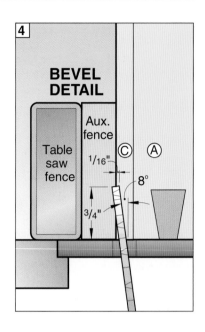

4

BEVEL DETAIL

Table saw fence

Aux. fence

C A

1/16"

8°

3/4"

dovetails. Now, cut the box assembly into top and bottom sections. Start by cutting an end (B), then rotate the box to cut through a side (A). Next, tape ⅛"-thick spacers to support the kerfs, then cut the other end and side. If necessary, sand the cut edges smooth, using a sheet of sandpaper taped to a flat surface.

3 Chuck a ¾" straight bit into your table-mounted router, and set the bit height to ¹⁄₁₆". Adjust your router fence to 1" from the edge of the bit, and rout dadoes for hinges in the base and lid where dimensioned in the Exploded View drawing. Adjust the rip fence to 1½" from the edge of the bit, and widen the dadoes to 1¼".

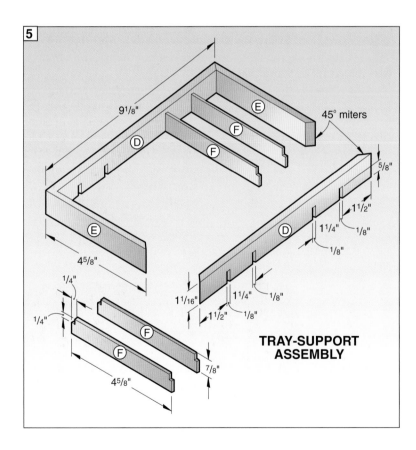

5

9¹⁄₈"

45° miters

E

F

D

F

5/8"

1¹⁄₂"

E

D

1¹⁄₄"   1/8"

4⁵⁄₈"

1/8"

1¹⁄₆"

1¹⁄₄"   1/8"

1¹⁄₂"   1/8"

1/4"

1/4"

F

F

7/8"

4⁵⁄₈"

TRAY-SUPPORT ASSEMBLY

The tray support

1 Rip and crosscut a piece of ¼"-thick maple to 1¹⁄₁₆ × 32" for the tray support sides (D) and tray support ends (E). Next, adjust the blade on your table-saw to 45°. Double-check the inside dimensions of the box assembly. Then, miter-cut the parts to size.

2 Set the height of your tablesaw blade to ⅝", and install an extension on your miter gauge. Next, stack the tray support sides together face-to-face, using double-faced tape. Cut four notches in the tray support sides as shown in **Drawing 5**

(opposite, bottom). Separate the pieces and remove the double-faced tape.

3 Rip and crosscut ⅛"-thick maple into four ⅞ × 4⅝" pieces to form the dividers (F). Stack the four divider pieces together face-to-face with double-faced tape, aligning the edges and ends. Now, adjust the height of your tablesaw's blade, and cut a ¼ × ¼" notch in the upper corners of the dividers. Separate the dividers and remove the tape.

4 Finish-sand all parts of the tray support assembly. Dry-assemble to

check the fit, then glue the pieces into place in the base of the box.

Add the trays

1 Rip and crosscut a piece of ¼"-thick maple into eight ⅞ × 4½" pieces for the tray sides (G) and tray ends (H).

2 Chuck a ⅜" straight bit into your table-mounted router, and adjust the fence to ¼" from the inside edge of the bit, Clamp the four tray sides (G) together, and rout a ⅜" notch ¼" deep centered in both ends of the tray sides where shown in the Tray Assembly drawing on

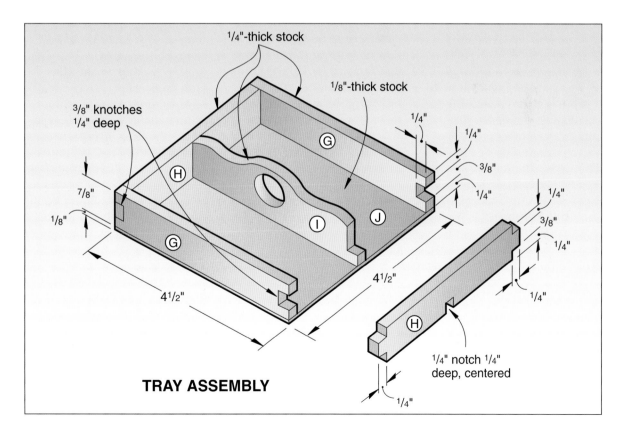

TRAY ASSEMBLY

page 113 (bottom). **Note:**
*Use a backing board in this
step and the next. This will
help prevent tearout where
the router bit exits the stock,
and hold the pieces square
to the fence.*

3 Switch to a ½" straight
bit in the router, and
adjust your fence to
leave ¼" of the bit exposed.
Now, stack the tray ends
together face-to-face, using
double-faced tape, and rout a
notch ¼" deep in each corner
of the tray ends. Switch to a
¼" bit, and adjust the router
fence to 2⅛" from the inside
edge of the bit, and rout a
notch ¼" deep through the
bottom edge of the tray ends.
Separate the tray sides, and
remove the tape. Finally, hand-
sand all tray parts smooth.

4 Rip and crosscut
¼"-thick maple into two
1¼ × 4¼" blanks for the
tray handles (I). Stack the
pieces face-to-face, adhering
them with double-faced tape.
Photocopy the full-size tray
handle pattern shown *below*.
Next, adhere the pattern to
the blank with spray adhesive,
and indent the hole centerpoint where shown. Chuck a
¾" Forstner bit into your drill
press, and drill the finger
holes. Scrollsaw or bandsaw
the contours of the tray
handles to shape. Then, if
necessary, sand the cut edges
of the tray handles.

5 Glue and clamp the tray
sides (G), tray ends (H),
and tray handles (I).
Make sure the assemblies are
square and flat. Next, rip and
crosscut ⅛"-thick maple to
4½ × 4½" for the two tray bases
(J). Glue and clamp until dry.

Finish and fabric complete the job

1 Finish-sand all parts, and
apply several coats of a
penetrating oil finish,
sanding between with extra-
fine abrasive. When the finish
has dried, drill 1/16" pilot holes
for the hinge screws. Adding a
paste wax and then buffing
will add shine and protection.

2 Cut posterboard inserts
1/16" undersized for the
bottom of the lid, the
compartments in the bottom

of the box, and three of the
four tray compartments. Cut
your lining fabric (ultrasuede
will work well) about 1"
larger than each dimension of
the posterboard. Next, apply
spray adhesive to the back
side of the fabric. Center the
posterboard on the fabric, and
fold the excess material over
the edges, mitering the corners neatly. Fasten the covered inserts in place with
double-faced tape.

3 To form the ring rolls,
cut three pieces of
posterboard to ¾ × 4".
Then, wind two thicknesses
of ⅛"-thick foam rubber
around each posterboard
piece. Then, cut three pieces
of fabric (approximately
4 × 5" each) large enough to
completely cover the foam-
wrapped posterboard, leaving
a little overlap on the sides
and ends. Apply spray adhesive to the back side of the
fabric and cover each insert.
Press the three completed
ring rolls, face-to-face, into
place in the unlined tray compartment. Drive the screws in
the hinges to attach the lid to
the box assembly.

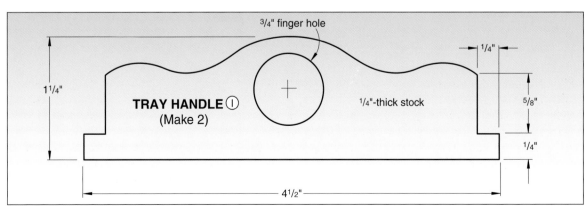

3/4" finger hole

1¼"

TRAY HANDLE ①
(Make 2)

¼"-thick stock

¼"

5/8"

¼"

4½"

A STANDOUT BOX WITH FINE SPLINES

You'll be impressed with the dazzling results of this red oak and walnut box, especially considering how comparatively little work it requires! Plus, it's versatile— you can build it for a man, woman, or child.

1 Begin by planing one edge of a 3½ × 24" piece of ¾" stock on your jointer. Then, rip a 1¾"-wide strip from the jointed edge, and plane or resaw it to ½" thick.

2 To cut a groove for the bottom panel, first check the actual thickness of your ¼"-thick plywood stock. If the stock measures exactly or slightly less than ¼" thick, fit your tablesaw with a ¼" dado set elevated to ³⁄₁₆". If the stock measures closer to ³⁄₁₆", use your regular ⅛"-thick blade, and adjust your fence slightly before making a second pass. Cut a full-length groove ¼" from the edge of one face.

3 Crosscut the box ends (A) and sides (B) to ⅛" longer than the lengths listed in the Materials List. (Cut the parts in A-B-A-B order so the grain will run continuously around the box.) Next, tilt the blade to 45°. Check the angle using your combination square, then miter-cut both ends of each part to finished length. (We attached an extension to our miter gauge and clamped a stopblock to it to ensure accurate cuts.)

4 From ¼"-thick oak plywood, cut the bottom panel (C) to the dimensions listed on the Materials List. Now, dry-assemble the ends, sides, and bottom panel, and sand as necessary until everything fits. Then, glue the two sides to one end. Apply glue to the edges of the bottom panel, and slide it into its groove. Glue the other end in position, then clamp the box. Check for square, and allow the glue to dry.

Machine the lid and face panel

1 To make the lid ends (D) and sides (E), first rip a 1 ⅛ x 24" strip from the same stock you used for A and B. Next, cut a full-length groove on one edge to receive the face panel. Just elevate your tablesaw blade to ¼", set your rip fence ³⁄₁₆" from the blade, and use a pushstick.

2 To bevel-cut the lid stock to thickness, first move your rip fence to the side of the blade opposite the blade's tilt direction, then tilt the blade to 6° from square, as shown in the Step One of the Lid-Cutting Sequence drawing *opposite*. Now, bevel-cut the stock using a push-stick.

3 Next, cut a rabbet on the bottom face of your lid stock where shown in Step 2 of the Lid-Cutting Sequence. To do this, fit your tablesaw with a ⅝" dado set elevated to ⅛". Set your rip fence ½" from the blade, and attach a notched, ¾"-thick wooden auxiliary fence at least 24" long. Set the fence where shown in the drawing, and rabbet the bottom face of your lid stock along the outside edge.

4 Crosscut the lid ends (D) and sides (E) as you did the corresponding box parts, cutting them in D-E-D-E order to finished length plus ⅛". Then, elevate your tablesaw blade to 1¾", and tilt it to 45°, again checking the angle. Using your miter gauge, extension, and stopblock, stand the ends and sides on edge, and miter-cut them to finished length.

Part	Finished Size			Matl.	Qty.
	T	W	L		
A* box ends	½"	1¾"	4½"	O	2
B* box sides	½"	1¾"	7"	O	2
C bottom panel	¼"	3⅞"	6⅜"	OP	1
D* lid ends	⅝"	1⅛"	4½"	O	2
E* lid sides	⅝"	1⅛"	7"	O	2
F face panel	½"	2¾"	5¼"	W	1
G liner panel	⅛"	3⅜"	5⅞"	H	1

BILL OF MATERIALS

*Initially cut part oversized. Please read all instructions before cutting.

Materials Key: O—oak; OP—oak plywood; W—walnut; H—hardboard.

Supplies: Oil finish, velvet, quick-set epoxy.

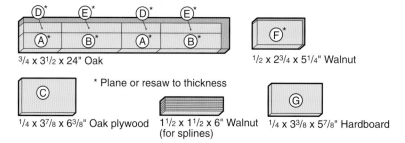

³⁄₄ x 3¹⁄₂ x 24" Oak

½ x 2¾ x 5¼" Walnut

* Plane or resaw to thickness

¼ x 3⅞ x 6³⁄₈" Oak plywood

1¹⁄₂ x 1¹⁄₂ x 6" Walnut (for splines)

¼ x 3³⁄₈ x 5⁷⁄₈" Hardboard

CUTTING DIAGRAM

LID-CUTTING SEQUENCE

STEP ONE

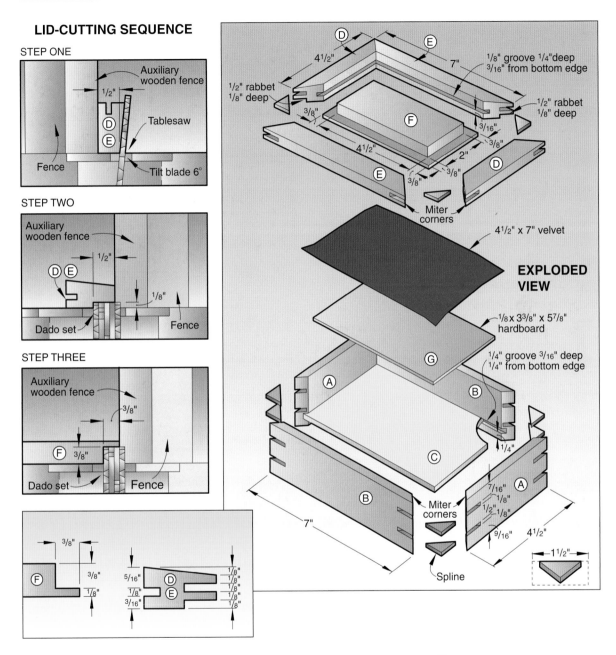

Auxiliary wooden fence

1/2"

D
E

Tablesaw

Fence

Tilt blade 6°

STEP TWO

Auxiliary wooden fence

1/2"

D E

1/8"

Dado set

Fence

STEP THREE

Auxiliary wooden fence

3/8"

F 3/8"

Dado set

Fence

3/8"
3/8"
1/8"

F

5/16"   1/8"   3/16"

D
E

1/8"
1/8"
1/8"
1/8"
1/8"

EXPLODED VIEW

D   E

4 1/2"   7"

1/8" groove 1/4"deep
3/16" from bottom edge

1/2" rabbet
1/8" deep

1/2" rabbet
1/8" deep

3/8"

F

3/16"

3/8"

4 1/2"

2"

3/8"

E

3/8"

D

3/8"

Miter corners

4 1/2" x 7" velvet

1/8 x 3 3/8" x 5 7/8" hardboard

G

1/4" groove 3/16" deep
1/4" from bottom edge

A

B

1/4"

C

B

A

7/16"
1/8"
1/2"
1/8"

9/16"   4 1/2"

7"

Miter corners

Spline

1 1/2"

5 Next, rip and crosscut the face panel (F) to size from ½"-thick stock. (We chose wonderfully figured walnut crotch.) To rabbet the sides, fit your table-saw with a ½" dado set ele-vated to cut ⅜" deep as shown in Step 3 of the Lid-Cutting sequence. Then, adjust the notch depth on your wooden auxiliary fence, and cut the rabbet. Now, sand the face panel smooth.

6 Dry-assemble the lid ends and sides around the face panel, and adjust the fit as necessary. Next, glue and clamp the lid at the corners, allowing the face panel to float without glue.

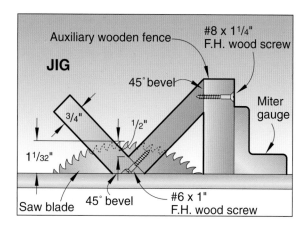

JIG

Auxiliary wooden fence

#8 x 1¼"
F.H. wood screw

45° bevel

Miter gauge

3/4"

1/2"

1¹/₃₂"

Saw blade   45° bevel   #6 x 1"
F.H. wood screw

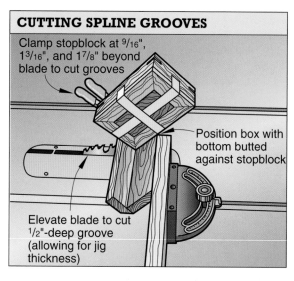

CUTTING SPLINE GROOVES

Clamp stopblock at ⁹/₁₆",
1³/₁₆", and 1⁷/₈" beyond
blade to cut grooves

Position box with
bottom butted
against stopblock

Elevate blade to cut
¹/₂"-deep groove
(allowing for jig
thickness)

Build our simple jig, then add the corner splines

1 To cut the spline grooves, you'll have to first build the jig shown *above*. To do this, cut two 3½ × 12" pieces of ¾"-thick scrap stock. Tilt your tablesaw blade to 45°, and bevel-rip one edge of each piece. Glue and screw the two pieces where shown in the drawing, then remove the screws after the glue has dried. Position and screw the jig to your miter-gauge extension so that it extends 4" beyond the blade path.

2 Sand the top edges of the box until they're smooth and level. Then, place the lid on the box, and sand the lid flush with the box sides. (A stationary belt sander will work for both operations.)

3 Elevate your blade sufficiently to cut ½" above the inside corner of the

jig. (We tested our depth of cut using scrap stock.) Next, measure ⁹/₁₆" beyond the kerf in the jig, and clamp on a stopblock at this point. Secure the lid to the box using masking tape, and place the box in the jig as shown *above right*. Cut a groove in the box corner, then rotate the box to groove all four corners.

4 Reclamp the stopblock 1 ³/₁₆" beyond the kerf, and again groove all four corners. To groove the lid, reset the stopblock at 1¹³/₃₂" beyond the kerf. (This should center the cut on the lid edge).

5 Resaw your walnut spline stock to a rough thickness of ¾". (We used a pushstick.) Then, rip several ⅛"-thick strips from the edge, and crosscut twelve 2"-long splines. Glue the splines into the grooves, and allow the glue to dry. Then, sand the splines flush with the lid and box sides. (Again, you can use a stationary belt sander).

Finish your box and spruce up the interior

1 Finish-sand the box, lid, and interior using 120- and then 220-grit sandpaper. Next, apply your choice of finish. (We applied two coats of a Danish oil, rubbing between coats with 0000 steel wool. After drying we buffed the finish with a soft cotton cloth.)

2 Finally, cut and upholster the liner panel (G). To do this, measure the interior dimensions of the box and cut a piece of ⅛"-thick hardboard that is ¹/₁₆" smaller in both length and width. Cover one face with a 4½ × 7" piece of burgundy velvet, and then epoxy and clamp the edges to the back face (quick-set epoxy will work). When the epoxy has cured, epoxy and clamp the liner into the bottom of the box.

Beautiful Boxes You Can Put to Use

*I*n this chapter, you'll see why it's never correct to say "a box is just a box." That's because each of the nine box designs chosen was designed for a specific purpose. A few of them were based on practical boxes from historical periods. With some small changes, you could adapt some others to alternate uses. But we'll leave those choices up to you. So read on, and get ready for more "boxing."

A TOOL CHEST THAT'S TOP-DRAWER

Whether you have some wonderful old tools or some great ones you purchased just yesterday, precision tools and sharp edges last longer and work better when they are properly protected. This Arts and Crafts design has felt-lined trays that do just that, and you can take your tools traveling in the removable tote.

Begin with the sides

Note: *Throughout this project, sand all the parts to 220 grit before assembly.*

1 Begin by edge-joining a ¾ × 14 × 36" blank for the sides (A). With the glue dry, sand it smooth, and cut the sides to the size shown in the Materials List.

2 Install a ⅝" dado blade in your tablesaw, and cut the dadoes and rabbets, as shown in **Drawing 1**.

Note that the sides are mirror images of each other, not identical.

3 Mark the ends and midpoint of the curved cutout at the bottom of each side (A). Flex a thin strip of wood to connect the three points of each curve, and mark the curve with a pencil. Bandsaw just to the waste side of the line, then sand to the line as shown in **Photo A**.

4 Mark the centers of the two square mortises on the outside face of each

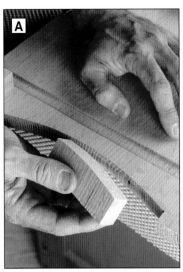

Make a custom sanding block by sticking adhesive-backed 120-grit sandpaper to a piece of the curve's waste material.

1 CARCASE

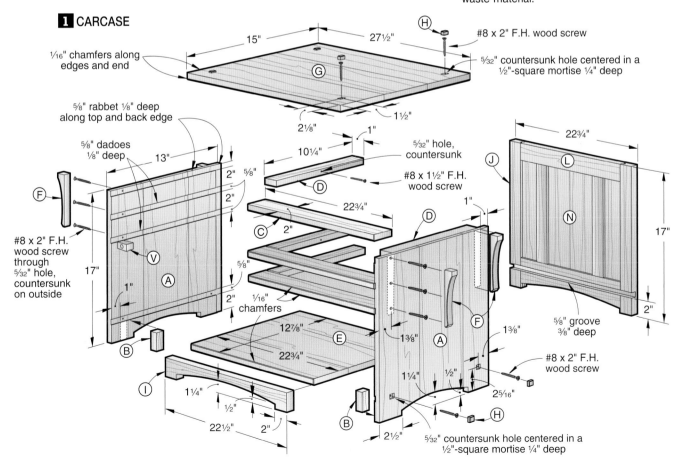

side (A). The mortises are centered on the width of the dadoes for the bottom (E). Remove most of the waste with a ½" Forstner bit, then square the corners with a chisel. Drill a $\frac{5}{32}$" countersunk hole centered in each of the mortises.

5 Drill $\frac{5}{32}$" countersunk holes centered in the rail/drawer runner rabbet and dadoes of each side, as shown in **Drawing 1**.

6 Cut the two glue blocks (B), and glue and clamp them to the front inside faces of the sides (A), as shown in **Drawing 1**.

Make the remaining carcase components

1 Plane ¾" stock to $\frac{5}{8}$" thick for the rails (C) and the drawer runners (D). Check the stock's fit in the dadoes in the sides (A). Cut the parts to size.

2 Chuck a chamfering bit in your table-mounted router, and rout $\frac{1}{16}$" chamfers around each rail's front edge. Keep this router-table setup for chamfering other parts.

3 Plane enough lumber to $\frac{5}{8}$" thick to edge-join a $\frac{5}{8} \times 14 \times 24$" blank for

the bottom (E). With the glue dry, cut the bottom to size. Rout $\frac{1}{16}$" chamfers around the front edge.

4 Cut four ¾ × 1¼ × 5⅛" blanks for the corbels (F). Make four photocopies of the full-size corbel pattern on *page 182*. Use spray adhesive to adhere them to the blanks. Bandsaw and sand the corbels to the pattern line. Rout $\frac{1}{16}$" chamfers along the edges, as shown on the pattern.

5 Edge-join a ¾ × 16 × 29" blank for the top (G). After the glue dries, cut it to size and sand it smooth. Rout $\frac{1}{16}$" chamfers along the edges and ends. Drill and chisel square mortises, and drill centered holes as shown in **Drawing 1**.

6 Cut a ½ × ½ × 10" blank for the plugs (H). Sand $\frac{1}{16}$" chamfers around each end. Use a fine-toothed handsaw to cut a ⅜"-long plug from each end of the blank. Repeat the chamfering and cutting until you have eight plugs.

7 Cut a ¾ × 2 × 23" blank for the apron (I), and set it aside. It will be trimmed to finished size after the carcase is assembled.

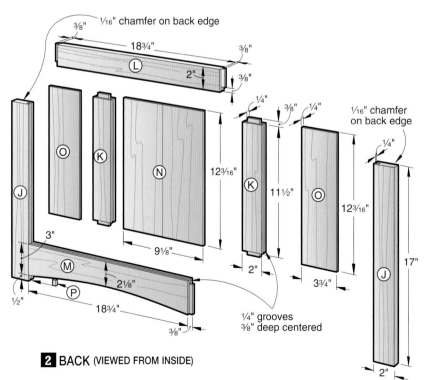

2 BACK (VIEWED FROM INSIDE)

Make the back

1 Cut the outer stiles (J), inner stiles (K), top rail (L), and bottom rail (M) to size.

2 Install a ¼" dado blade in your tablesaw, and cut centered grooves in one edge of parts J, L, and M, and both edges of part K.

3 Install a ⅜" dado blade in your tablesaw, and adjust it to cut ¼" deep. Screw an auxiliary extension to your tablesaw's miter gauge. Clamp a stopblock to the extension to control the cuts. Using a test piece the same thickness as the stiles and rails, form a ⅜"-long tenon. Test the fit in the stile and rail grooves, and make any necessary adjustments. When you are satisfied with the fit, cut tenons on the ends of the inner stiles (K), top rail (L), and bottom rail (M).

4 Referring to **Drawing 2**, mark the cutout on the lower edge of the bottom rail. As with the cutout in the sides (A), cut and sand it to shape.

5 Resaw ¾"-thick stock, then edge-join and plane a ¼ × 10 × 26" blank for the center panel (N) and outer panels (O). Cut the panels to size. To allow for wood movement, the panels are 1/16" shorter and ⅛" narrower than the maximum groove-to-groove dimensions.

SHOP TIP

How to Cut a Perfectly Centered Groove

It's easy to make a perfectly centered groove in the edge of a board. Set your rip fence by careful measurement, then make a test groove in scrapwood that matches the thickness of your stock. Turn off the saw, and put the opposite face of the scrapwood against the fence. If the blade aligns perfectly with the groove just cut, you're centered. If the blade doesn't line up, as shown at right, adjust your fence and repeat the test with a new piece of scrap.

Note: Turn off saw before checking fence position, as shown here.

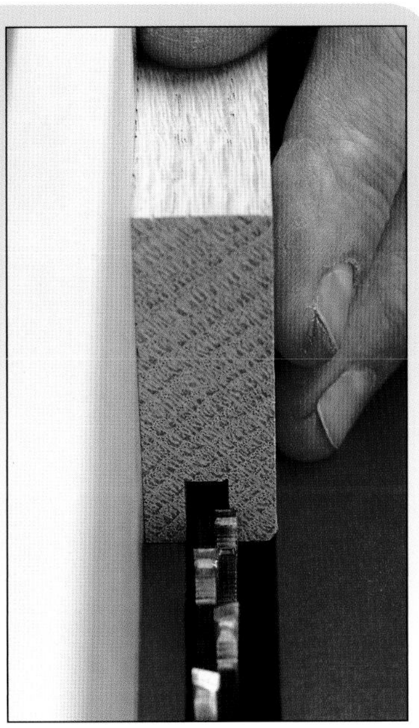

Materials List

FINISHED SIZE					
Carcase	**T**	**W**	**L**	**Matl.**	**Qty.**
A* sides	¾"	13"	17"	EQO	2
B glue blocks	¾"	¾"	2"	QO	2
C rails	⅝"	2"	22¾"	QO	3
D drawer runners	⅝"	1"	10¼"	QO	6
E* bottom	⅝"	12⅞"	22¾"	EQO	1
F corbels	¾"	1¼"	5⅞"	QO	4
G* top	¾"	15"	27½"	EQO	1
H* plugs	½"	½"	⅜"	QO	8
I* apron	¾"	2"	22½"	QO	1
Back					
J outer stiles	¾"	2"	17"	QO	2
K inner stiles	¾"	2"	12¼"	QO	2
L top rail	¾"	2"	19½"	QO	1
M bottom rail	¾"	3"	19½"	QO	1
N* center panel	¼"	9⅛"	12 3/16"	EQO	1
O* outer panels	¼"	3¾"	12 3/16"	QO	2
P* fillers	¼"	⅜"	½"	QO	2
Door					
Q outer stiles	¾"	2"	8⅜"	QO	2
R rails	¾"	2"	19⅛"	QO	2
S inner stiles	¾"	2"	5⅛"	QO	2
T* center panel	¼"	9"	5 1/16"	EQO	1
U* outer panels	¼"	3⅝"	5 1/16"	QO	2
V* stops	¾"	¾"	1"	QO	2
Drawers					
W fronts/backs	½"	1 15/16"	22 7/16"	QO	4
X sides	½"	1 15/16"	12⅛"	QO	4
Y bottoms	¼"	11⅞"	21 15/16"	OP	2
Tote					
Z sides	½"	2"	22"	QO	2
AA ends	½"	2"	10½"	QO	2
BB divider	½"	1⅝"	21½"	QO	1
CC* brackets	½"	1½"	5"	QO	2
DD handle	¾"-diam.		6¼"	WO	1
EE bottom	¼"	10½"	21½"	OP	1

*Parts initially cut oversize. See the instructions.

Materials Key: EQO–edge-joined quartersawn white oak, QO–quartersawn white oak, OP–oak plywood, WO–white oak dowel.

Supplies: #4 × ½" flathead wood screws (2), #8 × 1-½" flathead wood screws (6), #8 × 2" flathead wood screws (14), #6 × ½" flathead wood screws (2), 22 × 28" poster board (2), double-faced tape, fabric. Hardware: ⅞" tapered ring pulls, 2 × 11/16" plain-end no-mortise hinges, ⅜" rare-earth magnets and matching magnet cups, 1" copper rose-head boat nails (1 lb. box).

6 Glue and clamp the back together, positioning the edges of the inner stiles (K) 3⅛" from the outer stiles (J). Secure each panel with a drop of glue in the upper and lower rail grooves, centered on the width of each panel. Make certain that the assembly is square and flat. Rip a ¼ × ⅜ × 10" strip for the fillers (P), and cut them to length. Glue them into the grooves, as shown in **Drawing 2**.

7 Install a ⅝" dado blade in your tablesaw, and cut a ⅜"-deep groove in the inside face of the back, as shown in **Drawing 1**. Rout ¹⁄₁₆" chamfers on the outside back edges of the outer stiles (J) and bottom rail (M).

Assemble the carcase

1 Apply glue to the vertical rabbets at the rear inner edge of each side (A), and clamp the back in place, aligning the dadoes and groove that receive the bottom (E). Slide the bottom into position, check that its front edge is ⅛" proud of the front edges of the sides, and clamp it in place. Using the holes in the square counterbores as guides, drill pilot holes and drive in the screws.

2 To position the no-mortise hinges on the bottom (E), measure the distance between the sides (A), and cut a ¾ × 1½" piece of scrapwood to this length. (Ours is 22½".) Tape the large leaf of each hinge 2¹⁄₁₆" from each end of the scrapwood, and apply double-faced tape to the other leaf, as shown in **Photo B**. Position the scrapwood flush with the front edges of the sides. Press down, adhering the double-faced taped leaves to the bottom's front edge. Pivot the scrapwood forward, exposing the hinge leaves. Drill pilot holes, and remove the hinges.

3 Position the rails (C) in the dadoes and rabbets in the sides with their front edges ⅛" proud of the sides' front edges. Using the countersunk holes in the sides as guides, drill pilot holes and drive the screws as shown in **Photo C**.

4 Referring to **Drawing 1**, drill counter-sunk ⁵⁄₃₂" holes centered in the length of each drawer runner (D). Center the runners in the dadoes and rabbets in the sides (A), leaving a ⅛" gap at the front and back. Using the holes in the runners as guides, drill pilot holes in the sides. Applying glue only at their centers, screw the runners to the sides.

5 Center the top (G) on the carcase assembly, and using the holes in

To position the hinges on the bottom (E), tape their large leaves to a spacer. Apply double-faced tape to the small leaves. Press them in place, keeping the spacer flush with the sides' edges.

With the back panel glued and clamped between the sides and the bottom screwed in place, drill pilot holes, and drive in the screws that fasten the rails.

the counterbores as guides, drill pilot holes in the upper end of each side (A). Drive in the screws to fasten the top.

6 Place a drop of glue in the counterbores in the sides (A) and the top (G), and tap in the plugs (H).

7 Check the dimension between the sides (A), retrieve the apron (I) blank, and cut it to finished length. Referring to **Drawing 1**, mark the ends and mid-point of the curve on the apron. Following the same procedure you used for the sides and back, mark, saw, and sand the cutout to shape.

8 Turn the carcase assembly upside down on your workbench, and glue the apron (I) to the bottom (E) and the glue blocks (B). While the carcase is still upside down, glue the corbels (F) into place, as shown in **Drawing 1**. The front corbels hide the rail-screw heads. Apply glue only to the corbels' long edges. Use masking tape to hold them in place while the glue dries.

Make the paneled door

1 The door is ⅛" smaller in length and width than the carcase open-ing. Our opening measures 8½ × 22½". If yours differs,

make the necessary adjust-ments to the door parts. Cut the outer stiles (Q), rails (R), and inner stiles (S) to size. Referring to **Drawing 3** and following the same procedure you used for the back assembly, cut the grooves and tenons in the door parts.

2 Resaw ¾"-thick stock, then edge-join and plane a ¼ × 10 × 12" blank for the center panel (T) and outer panels (U). Cut the panels to size. Dry-assemble the door parts to check their fit. As with

the back, the panels are under-sized. Position the edges of the inner stiles (S) 3" from the outer stiles (Q). When you're satisfied with the fit, glue and clamp the door together in the same manner as the back. Make sure the door is flat and square. After the glue dries, drill a centered pull hole in the top rail, and set the door aside.

3 Cut a ¾ × ¾ × 10" blank for the stops (V). Referring to **Drawing 4**, drill counterbores and pilot holes ½" from each end, and

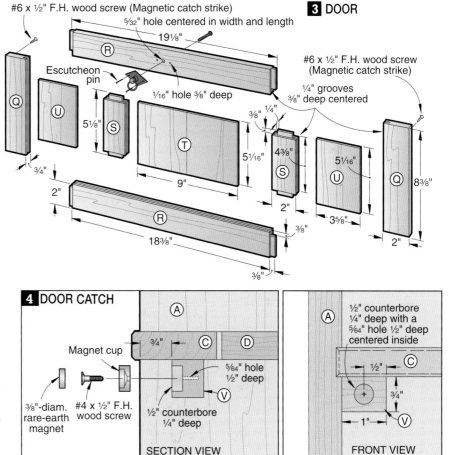

then cut the stops to size. Screw the magnet cups in place, but do not insert the magnets. Glue the stops to the underside of the lower rail (C) as shown.

Make a pair of drawers

1 Plane ¾" stock to ½" thick for the drawer fronts/backs (W) and the drawer sides (X). Cut the parts to size. Cut a ¼" groove ¼" deep in parts W and X for the drawer bottom (Y), as shown in **Drawing 5**.

2 Form the lock-rabbet joint shown in **Drawing 5a** by following the four-step sequence shown in **Drawing 6**. Use a ¾ × 6 × 6" follower block to prevent chip-out and to steady the narrow parts when making the cuts. Use a zero-clearance insert for your tablesaw when making the cuts in

Step 1. Drill holes for the drawer pulls, as shown in **Drawing 5**.

3 Cut the bottoms (Y) to size, and dry-assemble the drawers to check the fit of the parts. Glue and clamp together the drawers, making certain they are flat and square.

Craft a handy tool tote

1 Plane ¾" stock to ½" thick for the sides (Z), ends (AA), divider (BB), and brackets (CC). Cut the sides, ends, and divider to size. Cut the groove in the sides and ends for the bottom (EE), as shown in **Drawing 7**.

2 Cut the rabbets in the ends of the sides (Z), the dado at the midpoint of each end (AA), and the handle notches in the divider (BB), as shown in

Drawing 7. Rout ¹⁄₁₆" chamfers on these parts as shown.

3 Cut ½ × 1½ × 5½" blanks for the brackets (CC). Make two copies of the full-size bracket pattern on *page 182*, and adhere them to the blanks with spray adhesive. Drill the ¾" holes, and scrollsaw and sand the brackets to shape. Rout the ¹⁄₁₆" chamfers, as shown in the pattern.

4 Cut the handle (DD) from a length of ¾" oak dowel, and sand a ¹⁄₁₆" chamfer at each end.

5 Slip the brackets (CC) into the notches in the divider (BB). Drill pilot holes through the brackets and divider, and drive in the copper nails. Insert the handle (DD) through the holes in the brackets, drill pilot holes, and drive in the nails. Set the handle assembly aside.

6 Cut the bottom (EE) to size. Glue and clamp the sides and ends to the bottom, then drill nail pilot holes in the corners, as shown in **Drawing 7**. Drive in the nails.

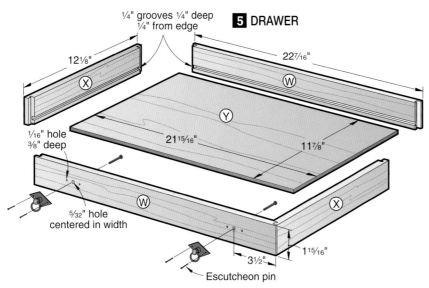

5 DRAWER

¼" grooves ¼" deep ¼" from edge

12⅛"

22⁷⁄₁₆"

X

W

Y

21¹⁵⁄₁₆"

11⅞"

¹⁄₁₆" hole ⅜" deep

W

X

⁵⁄₃₂" hole centered in width

1¹⁵⁄₁₆"

3½"

Escutcheon pin

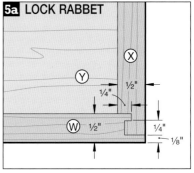

5a LOCK RABBET

X

Y

½"

¼"

W

½"

¼"

⅛"

6 HOW TO CUT A LOCK-RABBET JOINT

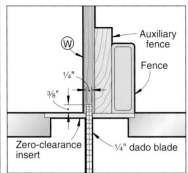

STEP 1: Cut centered grooves in both ends of the fronts and backs.

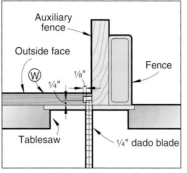

STEP 2: Remove part of the inside lip of the grooves just cut.

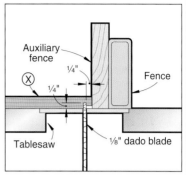

STEP 3: Cut ⅛"-deep rabbets in the ends of the drawer sides.

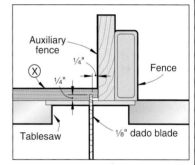

STEP 4: Cut a ⅛" saw kerf to form the interlocking notch.

Apply the finish and assemble

1 Apply the stain of your choice to achieve the Arts and Crafts look. (We used Salem maple.) After the stain dries, brush on two coats of a satin polyurethane, lightly sanding with 220-grit sandpaper after the first coat.

2 Fasten the pulls with their machine screws. Align the escutcheons, as shown on **Drawings 3** and **5**. Using the holes in the escutcheons as guides, drill pilot holes for the escutcheon pins. Drive in the pins.

7 TOTE

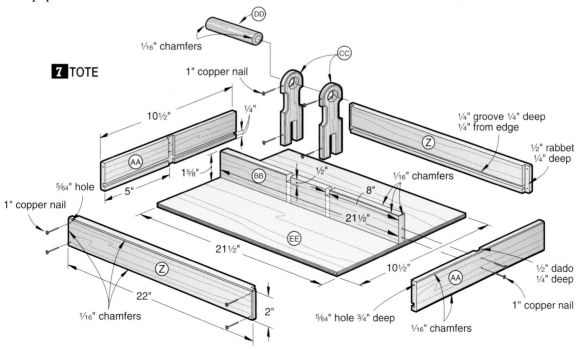

3 Screw the hinges to the bottom (E), and flip them open. Pull the chest to the edge of your workbench. With the door held straight down, position the hinge leaves on its bottom edge. Centering the door on its opening, drill pilot holes and drive in the screws.

4 Press magnets into the cups. To position the screws that act as catch strikes, stick #6 × ½" flathead wood screws to the centers of the magnets. Press the door against them, marking their positions. Drill countersunk pilot holes and drive in the screws.

5 To line the bottom of the drawers and the tote, cut pieces of poster board ⅛" smaller in length and width than the inside dimensions of the drawers and tote. Apply double-faced tape to the bottom of the poster board around its perimeter. Cut fabric 2" larger in length and width than the poster board. Green felt works well here. Center the poster board, top down, on the fabric, and trim the corners, as shown in **Drawing 8**. Fold the fabric onto the tape. Place the liners in the drawers and tote. Slide the divider assembly into the dadoes in the tote's ends. Drill pilot holes, and drive in the copper nails.

Now your tools have a new home and a cool new way to travel.

COLONIAL PIPE BOX

In the 1700s, pipe smokers kept their supplies in boxes similar to this one—clay pipes stood in the top compartment and tobacco lay in the drawer. Today, even in non-smoking households, it can be used to hold candles, matches, or anything else that suits your fancy.

Materials List

Part	T	W	L	Matl.	Qty.
	FINISHED SIZE				
A back	5⁄8"	6"	16"	P	1
B sides	5⁄8"	4 3⁄8"	12"	P	2
C bottoms	5⁄8"	3 3⁄4"	6"	P	2
D front panel	5⁄8"	6 5⁄16"	6 1⁄2"	P	1
E drawer front	5⁄8"	3 3⁄8"	6 1⁄2"	P	1
F drawer sides	7⁄16"	3 1⁄16"	3 11⁄16"	P	2
G drawer back	7⁄16"	3 1⁄16"	5 1⁄16"	P	1
H drawer bottom	7⁄16"	2 7⁄8"	5 1⁄16"	P	1

Material Key: P–pine.

Supplies: 5⁄8" diameter brass knob, 4d finishing nails (or square-cut nails), barn red flat paint.

1 From a 3⁄4 × 7 1⁄4 × 96" pine board, cut a piece 72" long, and plane it to 5⁄8" thick for parts A-E. Set the remaining wood aside. Cut a blank for the back (A) to the size listed in the Materials List. Referring to the Back on the Parts View drawing *opposite,* lay out the top profile, and mark the locations of the 1⁄2" hanging hole and the 5⁄32" nail pilot holes. Scrollsaw or bandsaw the top profile, then sand to the layout lines. Drill the holes, where marked. Sand a 1⁄16" round-over, as shown in the Exploded View drawing.

2 Cut two blanks for the sides (B) to the size listed, and fasten them together with double-faced tape. Referring to the Side on the Parts View Drawing, lay out the top arc, and mark the locations of the 5⁄32" nail pilot holes. Saw and sand the arc to the layout lines, and drill the pilot holes, where marked, through both pieces. Separate the two sides.

3 Cut the bottoms (C) to size, then finish-sand parts A, B, and C. Glue and clamp together the back (A), sides (B), and bottoms (C), as shown on the Exploded View drawing. Cut 3 1⁄8"-long spacers, and insert them between the bottoms to keep them aligned while gluing.

EXPLODED VIEW

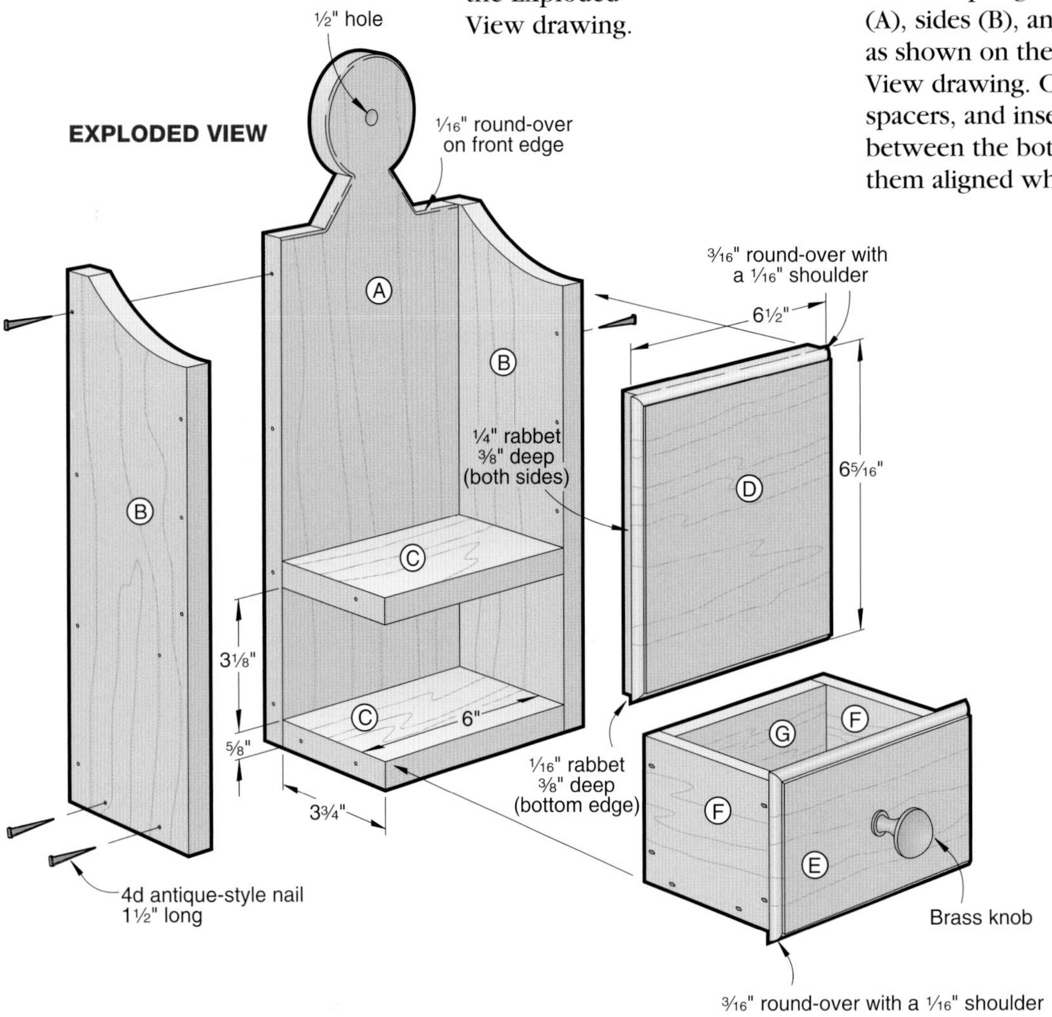

1⁄2" hole
1⁄16" round-over on front edge
A
B
B
C
C
3⁄16" round-over with a 1⁄16" shoulder
6 1⁄2"
6 5⁄16"
D
1⁄4" rabbet 3⁄8" deep (both sides)
3 1⁄8"
5⁄8"
6"
3 3⁄4"
1⁄16" rabbet 3⁄8" deep (bottom edge)
G
F
F
E
Brass knob
4d antique-style nail 1 1⁄2" long
3⁄16" round-over with a 1⁄16" shoulder

Hold the nails with needle-nose pliers to keep them vertical when you drive them.

4 When the glue is dry, remove the clamps and, using the ⁵⁄₃₂" holes previously drilled in the sides and back as guides, drills the pilot holes to a total depth of 1-½". Drive the 4d nails (antique-style, square-cut nails if you can obtain them), as shown in **Photo A.** Align the length of the roughly rectangular nail heads with the grain on the sides, and across the grain on the back. Drive the heads slightly below the surface of the wood.

Make two panels and a drawer

1 Cut the front panel (D) and drawer front (E) to the size listed. Install a ³⁄₁₆" round-over bit in your table-mounted router, and adjust it to make a bead with a ¹⁄₁₆" shoulder. Rout all four edges of both fronts.

2 Install a dado blade in your tablesaw, and cut rabbets in the bottom edge of the front panel (D), as

PARTS VIEW

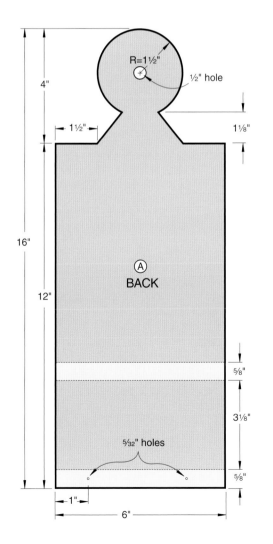

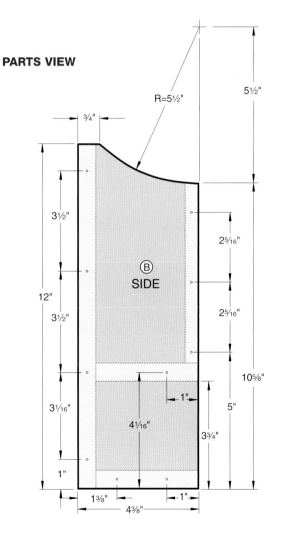

shown in the Side View drawing, and in the side edges, as shown in the Exploded View drawing. Next, cut rabbets in the top and bottom edges of the drawer front (E), as shown in the Side View drawing and in the side edges, as shown in the Drawer Exploded View drawing. Drill the knob pilot hole in the center of the drawer front. Finish-sand parts D and E.

3 Glue and clamp the front panel (D) in place. When the glue is dry, remove the clamps and, as before, drill the pilot holes, and drive the nails.

4 Plane the piece of pine previously set aside to 7/16" thick for the drawer sides (F), drawer back (G), and drawer bottom (H). Cut the parts to the sizes listed, and finish-sand them.

5 Glue and clamp the drawer together, as shown on the Drawer Exploded View drawing. When the glue is dry, drill the pilot holes and drive the nails. Align the length of the nail heads with the grain. Drive the nails deep so the heads do not protrude.

Apply a time-worn finish

1 Soften the sharp edges of the drawer front and the edges and corners of the box with sandpaper to give them a well-used look. Apply stain and let dry.

2 Apply a flat paint (we used milk paint) over the stain. When the paint has dried, rub through it on some of the corners and edges that would have seen wear with 0000 steel wool until the stain shows through. Rub the lacquer coating off the brass knob and give it a dull sheen. It will darken with age and handling. Install the knob, and rub away some of the drawer-front paint around it.

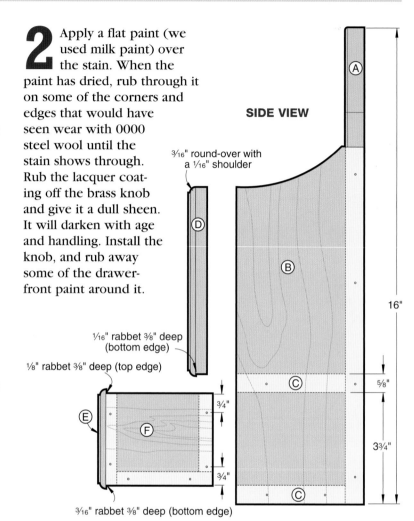

SIDE VIEW

3/16" round-over with a 1/16" shoulder

16"

5/8"

3 3/4"

3/4"

3/4"

1/16" rabbet 3/8" deep (bottom edge)

1/8" rabbet 3/8" deep (top edge)

3/16" rabbet 3/8" deep (bottom edge)

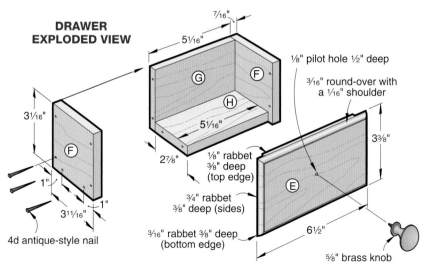

DRAWER EXPLODED VIEW

7/16"

5 1/16"

5 1/16"

3 1/16"

2 7/8"

1"

1"

3 11/16"

4d antique-style nail

1/8" pilot hole 1/2" deep

3/16" round-over with a 1/16" shoulder

3 3/8"

1/8" rabbet 3/8" deep (top edge)

3/4" rabbet 3/8" deep (sides)

3/16" rabbet 3/8" deep (bottom edge)

6 1/2"

5/8" brass knob

A "NUTTY" IDEA FOR A BOX

This nutcracker hides away in its own beautiful box between uses. Better yet, the box doubles as a nut bowl when the time comes to get cracking on some crunchy munchies.

Materials List

Part	Finished Size			Matl.	Qty.
	T	W	L		
A* box side	½"	4¾"	9¹⁄₁₆"	O	2
B* box end	½"	4¾"	6¹⁄₁₆"	O	2
C top, bottom	¼"	5⁷⁄₁₆"	8⁷⁄₁₆"	O	2
D** lever	¾"	1½"	7"	W	1
E** block	¾"	2"	1⅞"	W	1

*Initial dimensions shown.
**See full-size pattern for blank size.
Materials Key: O–oak; W–walnut.

Supplies: Brass sheet, ¹⁄₁₆ ×2×11"; brass flat-head wood screws, #4 ×¼" and #8 ×¾"; brass rod, ³⁄₁₆" diameter × 1" long; brass continuous hinge, ¾×12"; brass spring catch.

1 To match the wood's grain and color on the box sides, ends, top, and bottom, be sure to cut those parts from one board. You can get them all out of a piece that is ¾ × 6 × 52". Try to visualize how the parts will look together before you saw them to size.

2 Plane the board to ½" thick. Crosscut it to 32", saving the cut-off part.

3 Rip the 32"-long piece to 4¾" wide. Crosscut the box sides (A) and ends (B) sequentially from it, following the layout shown on the Cutting Diagram on *page 118.*

4 Mark identifying letters on the sides (A) and ends (B). Number the mating ends, as shown on the Cutting Diagram. Mark the bottom edges.

5 Plane the cut-off piece to ¼" thick, and cut the top and bottom (C) from it. Round the corners to a ¼" radius.

Cut the box joints with a simple tablesaw setup

1 Cut a piece of ¾"-thick scrapwood to 3 × 18" for an auxiliary miter-gauge fence. Also cut a piece of ⅛"-thick tempered hard-board to ½ × 1¼".

2 Install a blade that cuts a ⅛" kerf on your tablesaw. (We used an outside blade from a stackable dado set.) Adjust the blade elevation for a cutting depth of ½".

3 Clamp the auxiliary fence to your table-saw's miter gauge. Let the fence extend about 6" beyond the right side of the blade, with the miter gauge in the slot to the blade's left.

4 Cut a blade kerf in the auxiliary fence. Glue the ⅛ × ½ × 1¼" piece of hardboard into the kerf, with the end extending from the front face of the auxiliary fence, as shown in the Box Joint Cutting Jig drawing at *right*. This will be the index-ing pin for the jig.

5 After the glue dries, slide the fence to the right, locating the left side of the indexing pin ⅛" from the right side of the blade. Attach the fence to the miter gauge.

6 Raise the blade to a cutting depth of ¹⁷⁄₃₂", and saw a kerf through the auxiliary fence. The deeper cut makes the joint fingers longer than the thick-ness of the part. This allows you to sand them to final length after assembly, result-ing in a better-looking joint.

7 Saw test joints in scrapwood pieces that are the same width and thickness as the box sides and ends.

To cut a test joint with the jig, stack two pieces of stock face to face, and stand them on end in front of the miter-gauge jig. Align the right edges, and push the lower right cor-ner of the stack against the indexing pin on the jig. Cut through both pieces, but do not pull the jig and stock back past the blade. Instead, lift the workpieces away before returning the jig to make the next cut.

For the next cut, posi-tion the kerfs in the work-pieces over the jig's index-ing pin. Make the cut, again removing the workpieces before pulling the jig back. Continue until you've cut kerfs all along the end of the pieces.

CUTTING JOINTS IN SIDES AND ENDS

For the first cut, stack the sides and ends in pairs like this.

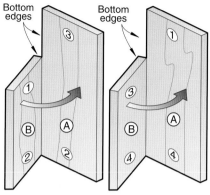

For the second cut, stack the sides and ends in pairs like this.

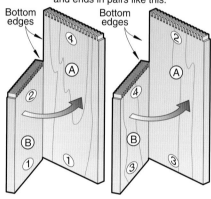

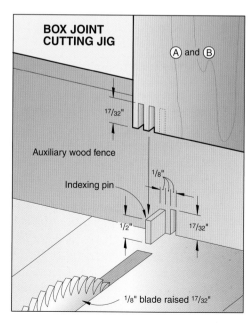

BOX JOINT CUTTING JIG

8 Check the fit of the joints by sliding the two parts together, placing the surfaces that were together toward the outside of the joint. (This helps hide any chip-out that might occur on the work-piece face that rides against the jig. Normally, the auxiliary fence minimizes chip-out.)

Tap the auxiliary fence to move the pin slightly toward the blade if the fingers are too wide, or away from the blade if they're too thin. Cut addi-tional test joints until you're satisfied with the results.

9 Cut the joints in parts A and B. When cutting them, stack the parts in mating pairs, as shown in the Cutting Joints in Sides and Ends illustration. Remember to keep the bot-tom edges of both pieces together and toward the right as you work.

10 After machining the joint fingers, rip parts A and B to about 4⅝". To determine the actual width of each side (A), count 19 fingers or spaces from the bottom up, and rip the waste off the top edge. Then count 19 fingers and spaces starting from the top on the ends (B), and rip them along the bottom. The sides (A) will then have a finger at the bottom and a slot at the top; the sides (B) will have a slot at the bot-tom and a finger at the top, as shown in the Box Joints illustration at *top right*.

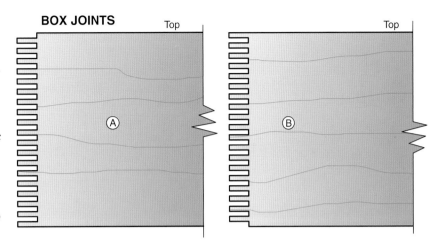

BOX JOINTS   Top   Top

Ⓐ   Ⓑ

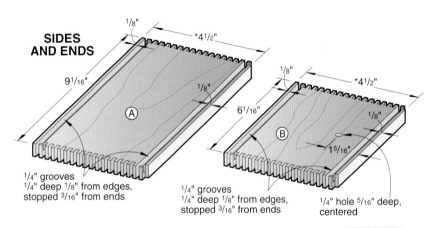

SIDES AND ENDS

1/8"   *4 1/2"
9 1/16"   1/8"   6 1/16"   Ⓐ

1/4" grooves 1/4" deep 1/8" from edges, stopped 3/16" from ends

1/8"   *4 1/2"   1/8"   Ⓑ   1 5/16"

1/4" grooves 1/4" deep 1/8" from edges, stopped 3/16" from ends

1/4" hole 5/16" deep, centered

* Dimensions may vary. See how-to instructions.

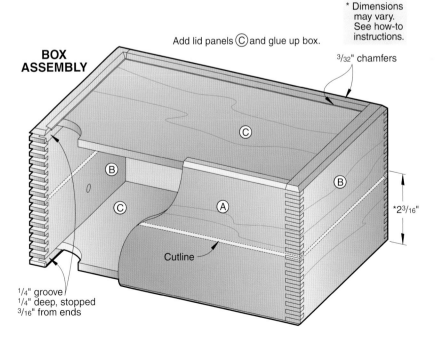

Add lid panels Ⓒ and glue up box.

BOX ASSEMBLY

3/32" chamfers

Ⓒ

Ⓑ   Ⓒ   Ⓐ   Ⓑ

*2 3/16"

Cutline

1/4" groove 1/4" deep, stopped 3/16" from ends

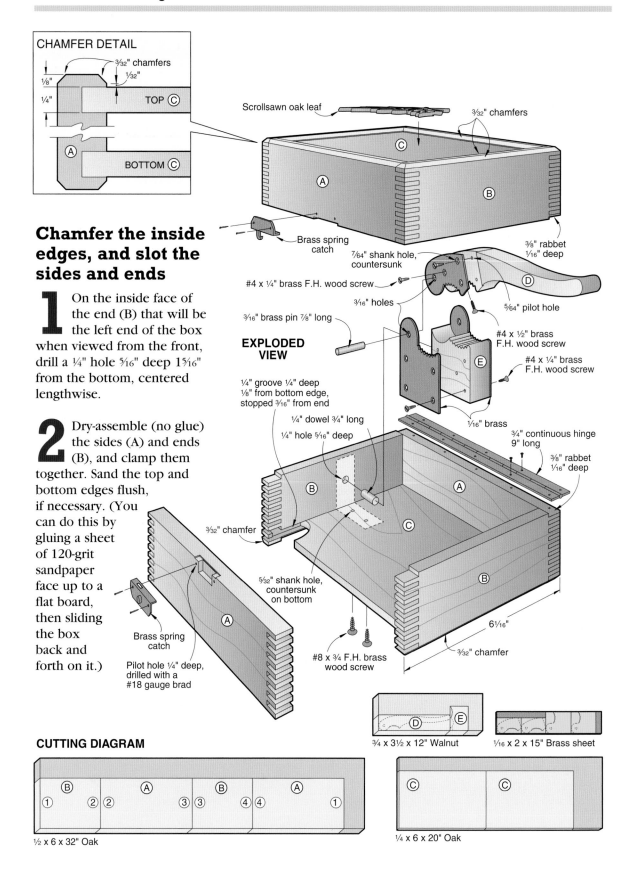

CHAMFER DETAIL

³⁄₃₂" chamfers
¹⁄₃₂"
¹⁄₈"
¹⁄₄"
TOP Ⓒ
Ⓐ
BOTTOM Ⓒ

Scrollsawn oak leaf

³⁄₃₂" chamfers

Ⓒ

Ⓐ

Ⓑ

³⁄₈" rabbet
¹⁄₁₆" deep

Chamfer the inside edges, and slot the sides and ends

1 On the inside face of the end (B) that will be the left end of the box when viewed from the front, drill a ¼" hole ⁵⁄₁₆" deep 1⁵⁄₁₆" from the bottom, centered lengthwise.

2 Dry-assemble (no glue) the sides (A) and ends (B), and clamp them together. Sand the top and bottom edges flush, if necessary. (You can do this by gluing a sheet of 120-grit sandpaper face up to a flat board, then sliding the box back and forth on it.)

Brass spring catch

⁷⁄₆₄" shank hole, countersunk

#4 x ¼" brass F.H. wood screw

³⁄₁₆" holes

³⁄₁₆" brass pin ⁷⁄₈" long

EXPLODED VIEW

¼" groove ¼" deep ⅛" from bottom edge, stopped ³⁄₁₆" from end

¼" dowel ¾" long

¼" hole ⁵⁄₁₆" deep

³⁄₃₂" chamfer

Brass spring catch

Pilot hole ¼" deep, drilled with a #18 gauge brad

Ⓐ

Ⓑ

Ⓒ

Ⓐ

Ⓑ

³⁄₃₂" chamfer

⁵⁄₃₂" shank hole, countersunk on bottom

#8 x ¾ F.H. brass wood screw

Ⓓ

⁵⁄₆₄" pilot hole

#4 x ½" brass F.H. wood screw

Ⓔ

#4 x ¼" brass F.H. wood screw

¹⁄₁₆" brass

¾" continuous hinge 9" long

³⁄₈" rabbet ¹⁄₁₆" deep

6¹⁄₁₆"

³⁄₃₂" chamfer

CUTTING DIAGRAM

Ⓓ   Ⓔ
¾ x 3½ x 12" Walnut

¹⁄₁₆ x 2 x 15" Brass sheet

Ⓑ   Ⓐ   Ⓑ   Ⓐ
① ② ② ③ ③ ④ ④ ①
½ x 6 x 32" Oak

Ⓒ   Ⓒ
¼ x 6 x 20" Oak

3 With a chamfer bit chucked in a table-mounted router, form a ⅛" chamfer around the inside and outside edges on the top and bottom. Unclamp and disassemble the box.

4 Now, form ¼" grooves ¼" deep ⅛" from each edge on the inside face of parts A and B, shown in the Sides and Ends illustration. Do this with a ¼" slot cutter bit and a table-mounted router. Stop the groove ³⁄₁₆" from each end of each part.

Scrollsaw a decorative ornament

1 Photocopy the Full-Size Oak Leaf pattern *below*. Using rubber cement or spray adhesive, adhere the copy to a piece of oak that measures ⅛ × 3 × 6".

2 If your scrollsaw has a large blade hole in the table, make a zero-clearance auxiliary table for it. To make one, cut a piece of ⅛" Baltic birch plywood large enough to cover the table. Then, saw into it from the back edge until its front edge lies flush with the front edge of the saw table. Affix it to the saw with double-faced tape.

3 Drill blade start holes as shown in the pattern. Scrollsaw the ornament with a #9 blade (.053 × .018", with 11½–14 teeth per inch).
 Begin cutting with the lines in the leaves. (The larger blade renders the sawn lines in the leaves more visible.) Then cut out the interior spaces between the leaves and, finally, saw around the outside of the pattern. Pay careful attention to the stopped lines.

4 Glue the ornament to the outer surface of the top (C). Apply white glue sparingly to minimize squeeze-out, center the cutout on the panel, and clamp, placing scrapwood over the ornament as a clamping pad.

5 After the glue sets, unclamp, and remove the pattern. Sand the cutout, rounding over the edges to create a sculptural effect. Sand carefully by hand, using 150-grit sandpaper. Finish-sand with a 180-grit flap sander.

Assemble the case

1 Finish-sand the inside surfaces of the sides (A), ends (B), and top and bottom (C). (It's easier to sand and finish the interior at this point than after you have assembled the box.)

2 Mask the fingers on parts A and B. Then apply two coats of clear finish, sanding between coats. (Lacquer spray works well here.)

3 After the finish dries, place a strip of masking tape at the base of the fingers on parts A and B. The tape will catch glue squeeze-out during assembly.

4 Assemble parts A, B, and C. (To allow enough time to fit all the joints together, we used slower-setting white glue.) Clamp the case, making sure the joints are pulled together snugly and the corners are square.

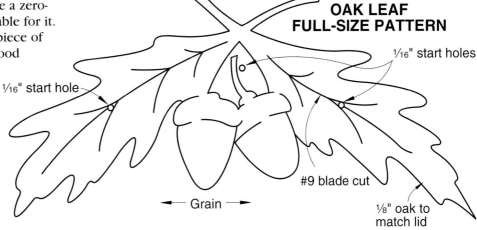

OAK LEAF FULL-SIZE PATTERN

¹⁄₁₆" start hole

¹⁄₁₆" start holes

← Grain →

#9 blade cut

⅛" oak to match lid

5 After the glue cures, sand the fingers flush on the outside.

Separate the lid and box, and add the hardware

1 Rip the case in half to separate the lid from the box. To do this on your tablesaw, position the fence to center the blade on the middle of the side and set the blade elevation slightly higher than ½".

Rip the ends. Place shims the same thickness as the width of the kerf in the ends, as shown in the illustration *below left.*(We held them in place with masking tape.) Then, rip the sides as shown.

2 Determine the height for the box (the bottom part) that will place a full finger at the top of each

side (A). (That measurement for our box was 2⅛".) Rip both the box and the lid to that dimension. Ideally, you'll then have a finger at the top of the box and a space at the bottom of the lid.

3 Rabbet the bottom and the lid for the hinge, as dimensioned in the Exploded View drawing. (We cut the rabbets on a table-mounted router, using a straight bit.) Drill pilot holes for the hinge, but do not install it yet.

4 Refer to the Catch Mortises drawing *below*, and lay out the mortises in the box and lid. Chisel the mortises. Test-fit the catch, but don't install it.

5 Finish-sand the exterior of the box and lid. Apply the finish.

The brass-bound walnut nutcracker comes next

1 On both sides of a ¾ × 3½ × 7¼" piece of wal-nut, form a ¹⁄₁₆"-deep rab-bet the full width of the stock and extending 2½" from one end. (We did this on a table-mounted router, employing a fence and a miter gauge.)

2 Cut four 2 × 2½" pieces of ¹⁄₁₆"-thick brass. (You can buy brass sheet from a hobby shop that caters to air-plane and railroad modelers.)

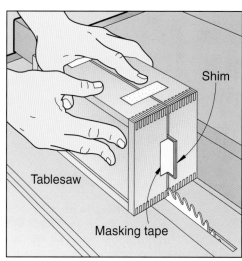

Cut the ends first when sawing the box bottom and lid apart. Shims inserted in the kerf will help keep the box from pinching on the blade.

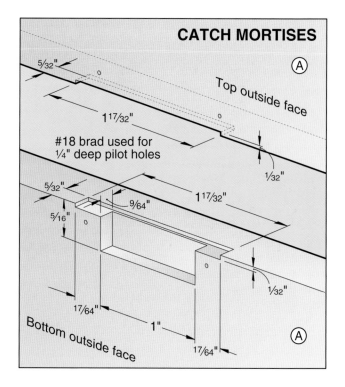

CATCH MORTISES

3 Photocopy the Full-Size Patterns for the lever (D) on *page 122*.

4 Using double-faced tape, fasten two brass pieces to the walnut stock, one on each side, as shown in the pattern. Adhere the pattern to the walnut-and-brass blank, placing it so the line on the lever (D) coincides with the edge of the brass.

5 Drill holes through the lever as shown. Bandsaw the lever using a ¼" fine-toothed blade.

6 Remove the brass pieces from the lever. Referring to the Lever Cover Parts View drawing, enlarge the screw holes and countersink them on the outside faces. Screw the brass to the lever.

7 Sand and file the handle to shape. A small triangular file works well to clean up the lever teeth. Rout a ⅛" chamfer around the edge

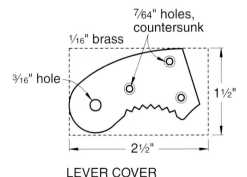

7/64" holes, countersunk
1/16" brass
3/16" hole
1½"
2½"

LEVER COVER
(2 needed)

PARTS VIEW

on both sides of the walnut lever handle (not the brass).

8 Affix the remaining two pieces of brass to the walnut stock as shown in the pattern. Adhere the Block Cover Full-Size pattern to the brass. Drill the 3⁄16" hole, as shown, and four 3⁄32" holes where the countersunk screw holes are called out. Bandsaw the part.

9 Remove the brass pieces. Enlarge and countersink the screw holes.

10 Adhere the Block Full-Size pattern to the cut-out block (E). Bandsaw the radius for the lever.

11 Sand the radius with a drum sander; then, attach the brass pieces to the block with screws. Sand and file the block to shape.

12 Locate and drill the dowel hole in the back of the block. To start, insert a dowel center in the ¼" hole in the box end (B), as shown *above right*. Place the back of the nutcracker block against the dowel point, and slide it back and forth to scribe a horizontal line across the block. Mark a center on the line at the middle of the block. There, drill a ¼" hole ½" deep.

Assemble the nutcracker and mount it in the box

1 Sand the lever's brass faces smooth and flush. Sand with progressively finer grits from 150 to 600 to bring up a shine. Finish-sand the walnut. Spray on two coats of clear lacquer, taking care to avoid runs on the brass.

2 After the finish dries, position the lever in the block opening. Slide a 15⁄16" length of 3⁄16" brass rod through the block and lever

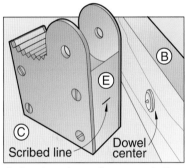

Scribed line   Dowel center

A dowel center scribes a centerline on the nutcracker block.

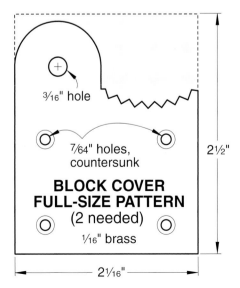

3/16" hole

7/64" holes, countersunk

BLOCK COVER FULL-SIZE PATTERN
(2 needed)
1/16" brass

2½"

2 1/16"

BLOCK FULL-SIZE PATTERN

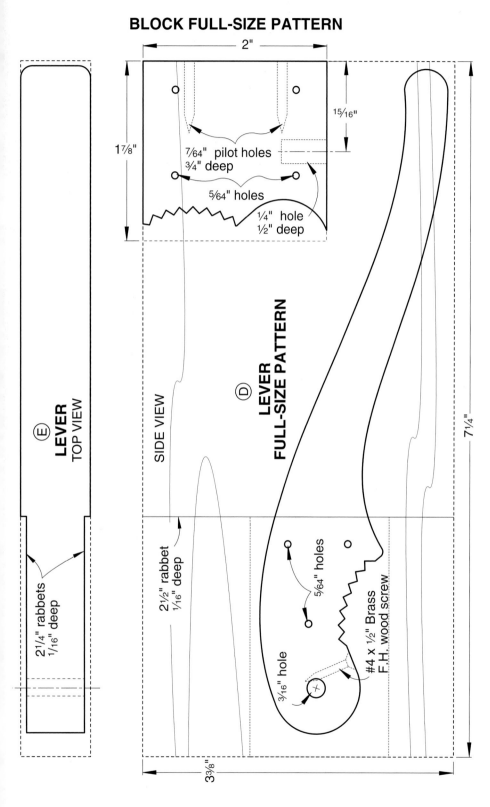

2"

1⅞"

15/16"

7/64" pilot holes
¾" deep

5/64" holes

¼" hole
½" deep

E
LEVER
TOP VIEW

2¼" rabbets
1/16" deep

SIDE VIEW

D
**LEVER
FULL-SIZE PATTERN**

2½" rabbet
1/16" deep

5/64" holes

#4 x ½" Brass
F.H. wood screw

3/16" hole

7¼"

3⅜"

holes. Check the lever movement. Open the lever all the way, and drill and countersink a ³⁄₃₂" hole, as shown in the pattern. Drive in a #4 × ½" flathead brass wood screw to lock the pin in place.

3 File the ends of the rod flush with the brass block sides. Polish the sides to match the lever. Spray a clear finish on the block.

4 Now, mount the nutcracker. First, lay out the centers and drill two ⁵⁄₃₂" holes through the box bottom (C) for the nutcracker mounting screws. Countersink the holes on the outside of the box.

5 Glue a ¾" length of ¼" dowel rod into the ¼" hole in the box. Glue and clamp the nutcracker block to it.

6 Guiding through the holes in the box bottom, drill pilot holes ¾" deep into the nutcracker block. Drive in two #8 × ¾" flathead wood screws.

7 Install the hinge and catch. Now get cracking!

MAGAZINE KEEPERS

Why keep magazine back issues in a messy pile when you can make some nifty cases like these? They're a classy end to clutter for standard 8 × 10½" publications.

Materials List

Part	Finished Size			Matl.	Qty.
	T	W	L		
A* side	¼"	11⅛"	9⅛"	M	2
B* back	¼"	11⅛"	4½"	M	1
C* front	¼"	4"	4½"	M	1
D bottom	½"	4"	8⅝"	M	1

*Make oversize initially, then cut to finished size in accordance with how-to instructions.

Materials Key: M–mahogany

Supplies: Drawer pull with card holder, semi-gloss clear lacquer.

1 This project calls for ¼"-thick stock 11½" wide. You can also use ¼" hardwood plywood, but if you want to employ a solid hardwood (we used mahogany), here's how. First, joint one edge of a ¾ × 6 × 30" board. Then resaw it into two ⅜"-thick pieces.

2 Edge-glue the two resulting pieces along the jointed edges, making sure that both sawn surfaces are facing up. (This is called bookmatching.)

3 Plane the book-matched stock to ¼" thick. Plane several pieces of scrapwood to the same thickness for setting up the box-joint jig later.

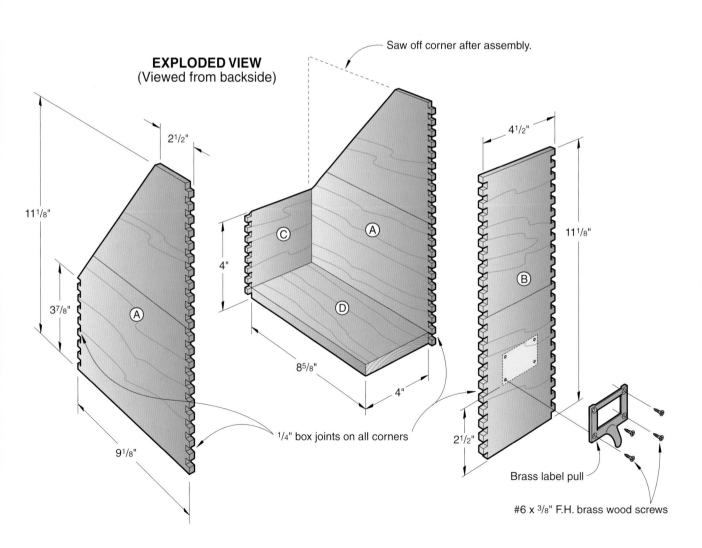

EXPLODED VIEW
(Viewed from backside)

Saw off corner after assembly.

2½"

11⅛"

3⅞"

9⅛"

A

4"

C   A

D

8⅝"

4"

¼" box joints on all corners

4½"

11⅛"

B

2½"

Brass label pull

#6 x ⅜" F.H. brass wood screws

4 Rip the piece to 11½". Refer to the Materials List and cut parts A, B, and C to finished length plus ¹⁄₁₆". (The extra length allows you to make the joint fingers ¹⁄₃₂" longer. You can then sand the joints flush after assembly.) Leave the parts' overwidth at 11½" for now. Mark a bottom edge on each piece.

Tackle the box joints next

1 Install a ¼" dado blade on your tablesaw. Adjust the saw's cutting depth to ⁹⁄₃₂". Lay out the box joints on the stock.

2 If you're utilizing a box-joint jig of some type, install it and set up for ¼" fingers ⁹⁄₃₂" long, following applicable instructions.

3 Saw fingers in two pieces of scrapwood, and test the joint for fit. Adjust and retest as necessary.

4 With the jig properly adjusted, saw fingers on both ends of parts A, B, and C, starting with a finger at the bottom of each side (A) and mating fingers on parts B and C.

5 Rip the sides (A) and back (B) to finished width, sawing the waste off the top edge. (For appearance, you could make the parts slightly wider if necessary to avoid cutting through a finger.) Cut the front (C) to the same width as A and B, but not to the finished width shown. Sand the inside faces.

Build the box, and cut a corner

1 From scrapwood, cut four clamping cauls, two that measure ¾ × 7¾ × 11¼" and two that are ¾ × 2¾ × 11¼".

2 Cut the bottom (D) to the dimensions shown in the Materials List. Dry-assemble parts A, B, C, and D to check fit.

3 Apply white glue to the inside edges of each joint finger, using a small brush. (White glue's longer open time allows you to glue and assemble all the joints before it starts to dry.) Apply glue along the edges and ends of the bottom.

4 Assemble the file box. Position the clamping cauls on the sides and ends, and clamp the assembly with band clamps. (We used three.) Ensure that the bottom is flush and the joints are tight. Clamp until the glue dries. Sand the joints flush.

5 Lay out the angled cutting line on one side of the file box. Bandsaw the angle, cutting with a fine-toothed blade. (To minimize chip-out, apply wide masking tape along the cutting line on the inside of the side that will be up when you saw and the outside of the one that will be on the bottom.) Plane or sand the sawn edge smooth and straight.

6 Finish-sand the box, using progressively finer sandpaper from 150- to 320-grit. Sand slight round-overs on the opening's edges.

7 Apply a clear finish. (We sprayed on several coats of semigloss lacquer, sanding between coats.)

8 Attach a brass file handle as shown. Make the pilot holes for the screws by punching with an awl.

A PERFECT BOX FOR YOUR PHOTOS

Say cheese! Don't dig out the dog-eared manila envelope to show your favorite photos to family and friends. Build this birds-eye maple-topped beauty instead.

1 Cut the bottom (A) and the back (B) to the sizes listed on the Materials List. Chuck a ½" straight bit in your table-mounted router and adjust it to cut ¼" deep. Using the fence to limit the cut, make multiple passes to rout the ½"-wide rabbet along the bottom's rear edge, and the ¾"-wide rabbets along the front and ends, as shown in **Drawing 1**. Then rout the ¾" rabbets on the ends of the back, as shown on **Drawing 1a**. Sand the rabbets smooth. Finish-sand the bottom and back to 320 grit.

2 Form the ends of the hinge notch in the back (B) by cutting ⅜"-deep kerfs in the top edge, ¾" from each end. To prevent chip-out, back your cuts with an auxiliary extension attached to your tablesaw miter gauge.

3 Now, complete the notch by routing between the kerfs. To do this, raise your ½" router bit to make a ⅜"-deep cut, and position your router table fence to expose ⅛" of the bit. From the bit's center, measure 8⅛" in each direction, and clamp stopblocks to the fence. Rout a ⅛ × ⅜" rabbet in the back, as in **Photo A**. Turn the part over and repeat. Reposition the fence to expose 5⁄16" of the bit. With the back's inside face against the fence, make a final pass, completing the hinge notch. (Making the ⅛"-deep cuts first reduces the chance of chipping.) Clean up the ends of the cut with a chisel. Glue and clamp the back to the bottom, maintaining a 90° angle.

4 Cut stock ½ × 2¼ × 25" for the ends (C) and front (D). (To resemble a book's pages, we selected a piece of straight-grained ash, cutting one edge parallel to the grain before ripping it to final width.) To get the grain to wrap continuously around the corners, miter-cut the parts to length in the sequence end-front-end. Finish-sand the front and ends, then glue and clamp

Materials List

Part	FINISHED SIZE T	W	L	Matl.	Qty.
A bottom	½"	7½"	9½"	B	1
B back	½"	2¼"	9½"	B	1
C* ends	½"	2¼"	7"	A	2
D* front	½"	2¼"	9"	A	1
E* lid sides	½"	1⅞"	9½"	B	2
F* lid ends	½"	1⅞"	7½"	B	2
G* corner tabs	3⁄32"	1½"	3"	M	4

*Parts initially cut oversize, see the instructions.

Materials Key: B–birdseye maple, A–ash, M–mahogany.

Supplies: #2×⅜" brass flathead wood screws (4), glue, finish, single-strength glass.

Hardware. 13⁄16" brass-plated turn buttons; ⅜×8" stop hinge w/screws; ½×⅛" self-adhesive bumpers.

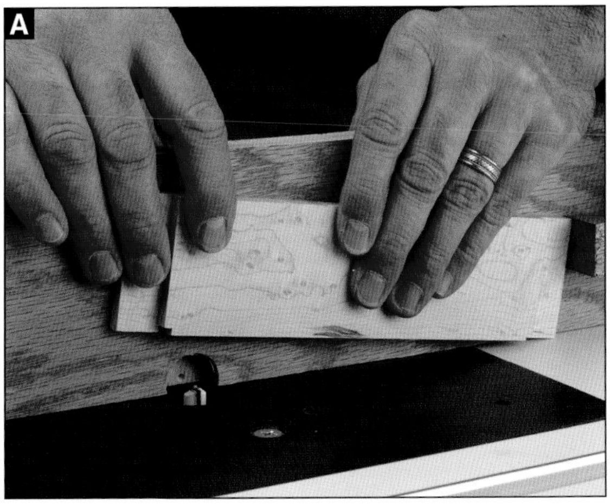
A

With its right end against one stopblock, lower the back (B) onto the running bit. Then move the back to the left until it contacts the other stopblock.

cutting diagram

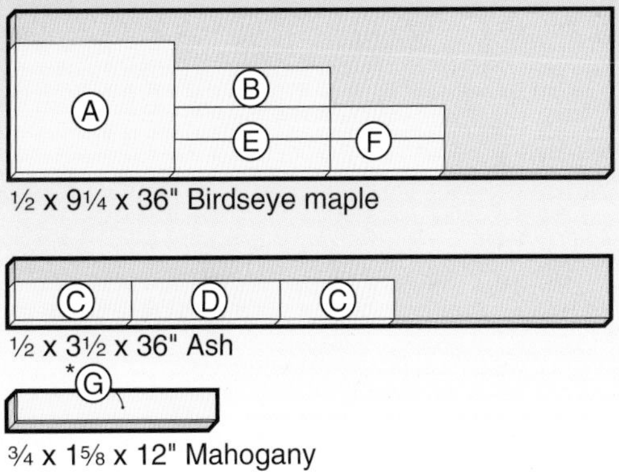
A
B
E
F
½ x 9¼ x 36" Birdseye maple
C
D
C
½ x 3½ x 36" Ash
*G
¾ x 1⅝ x 12" Mahogany

*Plane or resaw to thickness listed in the Bill of Materials.

1a RABBET/NOTCH DETAIL

¼"

¼" round-over
sanded after
assembly

⅜"

1⅞"

Ⓑ

2¼"

¹⁄₁₆" round-
over, sanded
after assembly

¾"

1b END SECTION VIEW DETAIL

Ⓔ

Ⓒ

Ⓑ

Ⓐ

Rout the corner tab recesses, making
multiple passes until the frame's corners
ride against the fence.

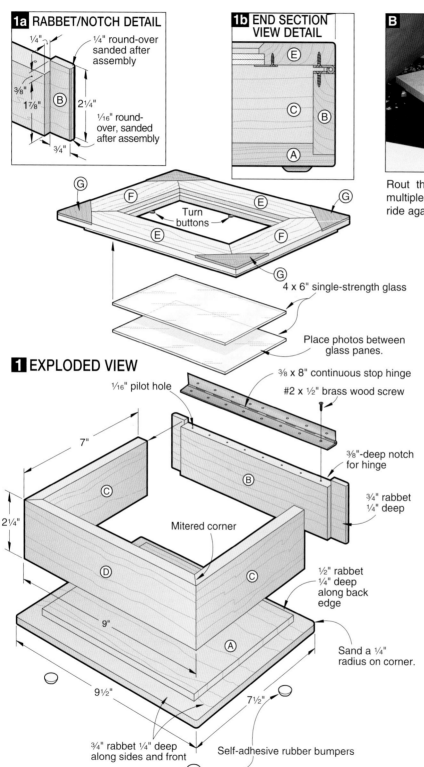

Ⓖ

Ⓕ

Ⓔ

Ⓖ

Turn
buttons

Ⓔ

Ⓕ

Ⓖ

4 x 6" single-strength glass

Place photos between
glass panes.

1 EXPLODED VIEW

¹⁄₁₆" pilot hole

⅜ x 8" continuous stop hinge

#2 x ½" brass wood screw

⅜"-deep notch
for hinge

7"

Ⓑ

¾" rabbet
¼" deep

2¼"

Ⓒ

Mitered corner

Ⓒ

Ⓓ

½" rabbet
¼" deep
along back
edge

9"

Ⓐ

Sand a ¼"
radius on corner.

9½"

7½"

¾" rabbet ¼" deep
along sides and front

Self-adhesive rubber bumpers

them into the rabbets in
the bottom and back.

Add a picture-frame lid

1 First, cut two pieces
½ × 1⅞ × 20" for
the lid sides (E) and
lid ends (F). Rout ⅛ × ¼"
rabbets and ⅛" chamfers,
as shown in **Drawing 2**.
Finish-sand the pieces,
then miter-cut one lid side
and one lid end from each
piece. Glue and clamp the
lid frame together.

2 Chuck a ½" straight
bit in your table-
mounted router, and
adjust it to cut ¹⁄₁₆" deep.
Position the fence parallel
to the miter-gauge slot,
and 1½" from the bit's outside edge. With the glue
dry, and the miter gauge at
45° rout shallow recesses
across the lid's corners, as
shown in **Photo B**.

3 Flip the frame over and, in the same manner as the bottom, rout a $^{13}/_{16}$"-wide rabbet along the ends and front edge, as shown in Drawing 2a. There is no rabbet along the rear edge. Finish-sand the rabbet.

4 Resaw a $^{3}/_{32}$"-thick strip from a $^{3}/_{4} \times 1^{5}/_{8} \times 12$" piece of mahogany. Cut four oversize triangles for the corner tabs (G). Ease one top long edge of each triangle with a sanding block. Glue and clamp them into the corner recesses in the lid. When the glue dries, sand the tabs flush with the lid's edges.

5 Sand $^{1}/_{4}$" radii on the lid's corners, as shown on Drawing 2b. Retrieve the box, and sand matching radii on the bottom's corners, including the back's ends.

Finish up the details

1 Position the hinge so that the knuckle is flush with the back and the lid's rear edge, as shown in Drawing 1b, and drill the screw pilot holes. Drill screw pilot holes for the turn buttons. Cut two pieces of single-strength glass to fit the lid's rabbeted opening.

2 Soften the edges of the lid, bottom, and the inside end of the back with a sanding block forming $^{1}/_{16}$" round-overs. Apply two coats of a wiping varnish or penetrating oil, rubbing between coats with 0000 steel wool.

3 Screw the turn buttons and the hinge in place, and adhere the bumpers to the bottom. For safe handling when changing pictures, sand the edges of the glass panes with 320-grit sandpaper.

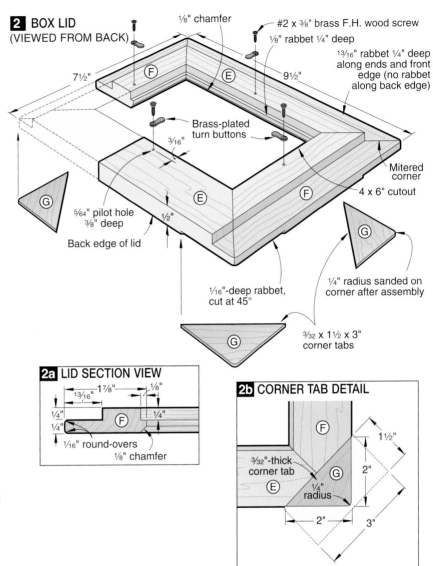

2 BOX LID (VIEWED FROM BACK)

$^{1}/_{8}$" chamfer

#2 x $^{3}/_{8}$" brass F.H. wood screw

$^{1}/_{8}$" rabbet $^{1}/_{4}$" deep

$^{13}/_{16}$" rabbet $^{1}/_{4}$" deep along ends and front edge (no rabbet along back edge)

7½"

9½"

Brass-plated turn buttons

$^{3}/_{16}$"

Mitered corner

4 x 6" cutout

$^{5}/_{64}$" pilot hole $^{3}/_{8}$" deep

½"

Back edge of lid

$^{1}/_{16}$"-deep rabbet, cut at 45°

¼" radius sanded on corner after assembly

$^{3}/_{32}$ x 1½ x 3" corner tabs

2a LID SECTION VIEW

1$^{7}/_{8}$"

$^{13}/_{16}$"

$^{1}/_{8}$"

¼"

¼"

¼"

$^{1}/_{16}$" round-overs

$^{1}/_{8}$" chamfer

2b CORNER TAB DETAIL

1½"

2"

3"

2"

$^{3}/_{32}$"-thick corner tab

¼" radius

FIRST-CLASS LETTER BOX

Don't misplace the mail...put it in it's place. It looks great in cherry, but build it to harmonize with your own surroundings. The floral motif adds a nice homey touch.

1 Photocopy the full-size patterns for the end panels (A) and dividers (B, C) shown *opposite* and for the front panel (D) and back panel (E) *on page 183*. (Make two copies of the pattern that shows parts D and E, and note the necessary size alterations.)

2 Cut two ⅜ × 3 × 4½" blanks for the end panels (A). Temporarily laminate them with double-faced tape, with the good faces to the outside. Adhere the pattern to the top of the stack, using rubber cement or spray adhesive.

3 Bandsaw or scrollsaw the outline. Sand or plane the straight edges and bottom true, then separate the parts.

4 Rout a ⅜" half round-over along both faces on the top (curved) and

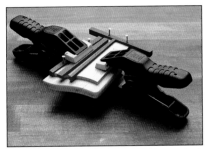

Scrapwood spacers (the dark pieces) help position the front and back dividers when gluing the end assemblies.

a fence to the table, aligning its face with the cutting edge at the top of the bit (right below the pilot bearing).

5 Cut two ⅛ × 1¼ × 3½" blanks for the front dividers (B), and temporarily laminate them with double-faced tape. Next, saw two ⅛ × 1 × 4" blanks for the back dividers (C) , and tape them together.

6 Adhere the divider patterns (B, C) to the top of the appropriate stack of blanks. Cut out the dividers. Sand a slight round-over along the top outside edge of each divider.

front (sloped) edge of each part. To do that, install a ⅜" round-over bit in your table-mounted router. Adjust the cutting depth to center the top of the bit's cutting edge (not the pilot) on the edge of the stock, as shown in the Half Round-Over detail on *page 132 (bottom)*. Clamp

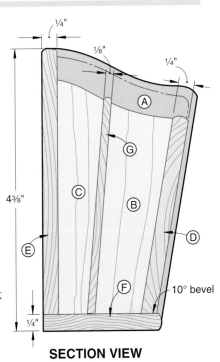

SECTION VIEW

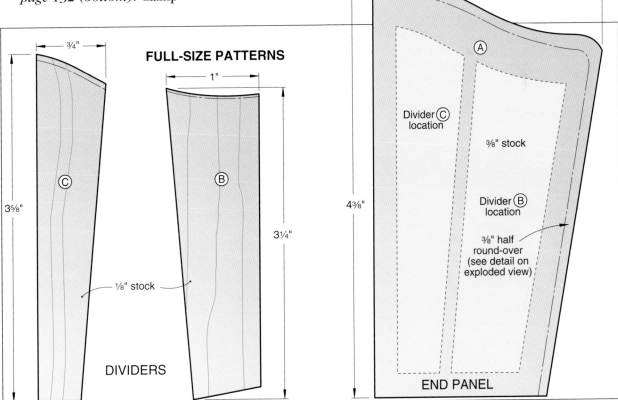

FULL-SIZE PATTERNS

DIVIDERS

END PANEL

Materials List

Part	Finished Size			Matl.	Qty.
	T	W	L		
A* end panel	⅜"	2½"	4⅜"	C	2
B* front divider	⅛"	1"	3¼"	C	2
C* back divider	⅛"	¾"	3⅝"	C	2
D* front panel	¼"	3¹³⁄₁₆"	10"	C	1
E* back panel	¼"	4⅛"	10"	C	1
F bottom	¼"	1¹⁵⁄₁₆"	10"	C	1
G center panel	⅛"	3¼"	10"	C	1

*Make parts oversize initially, then cut to finished dimensions in accordance with instructions.
Material Key: C–cherry

Supplies: woodworker's glue, clear finish.

7 Glue the dividers to the end panels, positioning them to form a groove in the middle and rabbets along the top, bottom, front, and back, as shown in the Exploded View drawing. Be sure to assemble the two ends (A, B, C) as a mirror-image pair.

To glue the dividers in place accurately, tack ¼"-wide spacers to the inside face of each end panel (A), as shown in the photo on *page 131*. Align the outside edge of one spacer flush with the bottom of part A, the outside edge of the other flush with the back edge of A. Cut a ⅛" spacer for

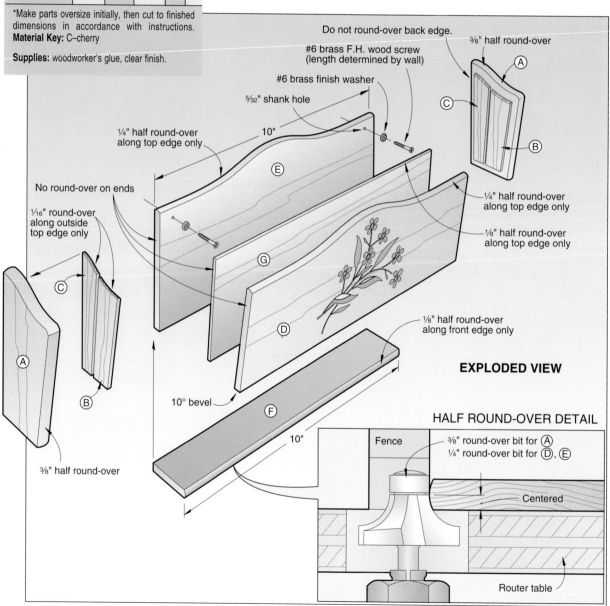

Do not round-over back edge.

#6 brass F.H. wood screw
(length determined by wall)

#6 brass finish washer

⅝₃₂" shank hole

⅜" half round-over

Ⓐ

Ⓒ

Ⓑ

¼" half round-over along top edge only

10"

Ⓔ

No round-over on ends

¼" half round-over along top edge only

¹⁄₁₆" round-over along outside top edge only

Ⓒ

Ⓖ

⅛" half round-over along top edge only

Ⓐ

Ⓓ

⅛" half round-over along front edge only

Ⓑ

10° bevel

Ⓕ

10"

EXPLODED VIEW

⅜" half round-over

HALF ROUND-OVER DETAIL

Fence

⅜" round-over bit for Ⓐ
¼" round-over bit for Ⓓ, Ⓔ

Centered

Router table

the groove, then glue and clamp the parts as shown. (We used another piece of scrap-wood as a clamping caul for the back divider because the face of the part was lower than the spacer behind it.) Remove the spacer from the groove as soon as the glue begins to tack.

Scrollsaw a decorative design

1 Cut a ¼ × 4 × 10" blank for the front panel (D). Adhere the full-size pattern to the blank, aligning it along the straight ends and bottom edge.

2 Scrollsaw the design in the face of the panel. To do that, first drill a 3⁄32" blade-start hole for each of the interior cuts. Notice that you don't need to drill entry holes in most of the narrow stems; you can saw into the stems from the leaves.

Thread the scrollsaw blade through the start hole in the left leaf (where the callout arrow on the pattern points), and cut out the leaf and stem. (We sawed the design using a #4 blade, .035 × .015", with 15 teeth per inch.) Continue around the pattern to make all the cutouts.

3 Scrollsaw or bandsaw the front panel's curved top. If you cut it with a bandsaw, stay slightly outside the pattern line, and sand to the line for a smoother edge.

4 Form a half round-over along the top of the front panel.

Make a few more parts and assemble

1 Cut a ¼ × 4½ × 10" blank for the back panel (E). Transfer the pattern line for the top contour to the blank, and cut it out. Form a half round-over along the top edge of the panel. If you plan to hang the letter holder on a wall, drill 5⁄32" screw holes as shown.

2 Cut the bottom (F) and center panel (G) to the dimensions shown on the Materials List. Sand a half round-over along the front edge of the bottom and along the top edge of the center panel. Sand all parts with grits from 120 to 220.

3 Dry-assemble the parts to check for fit. For easiest assembly, join the ends (A, B, C) and bottom (F). Then add the back (E), front (D), and center panel (G). Disassemble the parts, then glue and clamp the letter holder together. Clean off any glue squeeze-out.

4 Finish-sand the assembled letter holder. Apply three coats of semigloss lacquer, sanding between coats with 320-grit sandpaper.

To hang the letter holder, drive #6 brass flathead wood screws with finish washers into the wall or other appropriate anchors.

BATTER UP! FOR A BASEBALL CARD BOX

You'll get seamless results inlaying this box's lid, making splined corners without a jig, and creating mating rabbets. And you'll end up with a project that belongs in the majors. A must for serious collectors, this box holds about 300 standard 2½ × 3½" sports cards!

CUTTING DIAGRAM

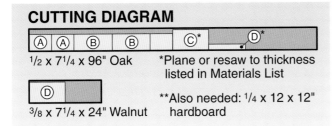

$\frac{1}{2}$ x $7\frac{1}{4}$ x 96" Oak

$\frac{3}{8}$ x $7\frac{1}{4}$ x 24" Walnut

*Plane or resaw to thickness listed in Materials List

**Also needed: $\frac{1}{4}$ x 12 x 12" hardboard

Materials List

Part	Finished Size			Matl.	Qty.
	T	W	L		
A ends	$\frac{1}{2}$"	$5\frac{1}{8}$"	$7\frac{1}{2}$"	O	2
B sides	$\frac{1}{2}$"	$5\frac{1}{8}$"	$12\frac{3}{4}$"	O	2
C divider	$\frac{1}{4}$"	2"	$12\frac{1}{4}$"	O	1
D top assembly	$\frac{3}{8}$"	$6\frac{3}{4}$"	12"	O/W	2*
E bottom	$\frac{1}{4}$"	$6\frac{3}{4}$"	12"	H	1

*Start with one piece each of oak and walnut to make the inlaid-top assembly. Please read all instructions before cutting.

Materials Key: O—oak; W—walnut; H—hardboard.

1 Plane or resaw a piece of $5\frac{1}{2} \times 48$" oak to $\frac{1}{2}$" thick. Rip to $5\frac{1}{8}$" wide, and sand the face that will be inside of the box. Mark the unsanded face with a piece of masking tape. Chuck a $\frac{1}{4}$" straight bit into your table-mounted router, and set the bit $\frac{3}{16}$" above the table. Next, adjust the fence $\frac{1}{8}$" from the inner edge of the bit, and rout grooves into the sanded face for the top and bottom as shown in the Section View drawing on *page 136 (bottom).*

2 Adjust the height of the router bit to $\frac{1}{4}$" above the surface of the table, and set the fence to $1\frac{1}{4}$" from the inner edge of the bit. Then, rout a groove into the same face of the stock as the grooves you cut in Step 1.

NOTE: By studying the Section View, you can see that this groove will eventually become a rabbet in the top assembly. This rabbet will mate with another rabbet formed when you separate the lid as one of the last steps.

3 Tilt your tablesaw blade to 45°, and miter-cut the ends (A) and sides (B) of the box to the lengths shown in the Materials List.

4 Rout a stopped dado centered in each box end as shown in the Routing the Stopped Dado drawings *below left.* Use a chisel to square the end of each dado.

Make the divider, top, and bottom

1 Dry-assemble (no glue) the box ends and sides with a band clamp to check the fit of the miters. Double-check the dimensions of the divider (C), then rip and crosscut it to size.

2 Double-check the size of the top (D) and bottom (E). Refer to the Section View to see that these parts do not bottom

ROUTING THE STOPPED DADO

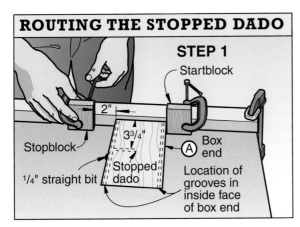

STEP 1

Startblock

Stopblock

2"

$3\frac{3}{4}$"

Stopped dado

$\frac{1}{4}$" straight bit

(A) Box end

Location of grooves in inside face of box end

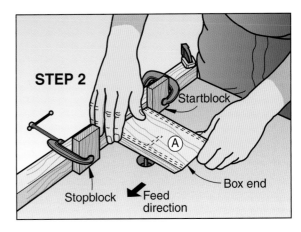

STEP 2

Startblock

(A)

Stopblock

Feed direction

Box end

out in the grooves. These pieces are ripped and cross-cut ⅛" shorter and more narrow than the maximum groove-to-groove dimension.

3 To make the inlaid top, start by ripping and crosscutting one piece each of walnut and oak to size from ⅜"-thick stock.

4 Make a photocopy of the full-sized scene for the top from the patterns shown on *pages 184–185*. Adhere the patterns to the walnut stock with spray adhesive, then use a utility knife to trim the paper flush with the edges of the stock. Next, use masking tape to join the walnut and oak blanks face-to-face, with edges and ends flush. Set this assembly aside for now.

5 Use masking tape to join scrap cutoffs into a test blank. Put a No. 5 blade into your scrollsaw, and tilt your scrollsaw table (2° is a good starting point) to make the first test cut as shown in the Test Cut drawing on *page 138 (top)*. If your scrollsaw table tilts left (as you face it), cut clockwise; if the table tilts right, cut counterclockwise. If the test inlay piece does not seat fully into the base stock, decrease the tilt angle. If the inlay piece goes too deep, increase the tilt. *NOTE: Change the tilt angle of the table in very small increments between test cuts.* Do not use sideways pressure on the blade because that can

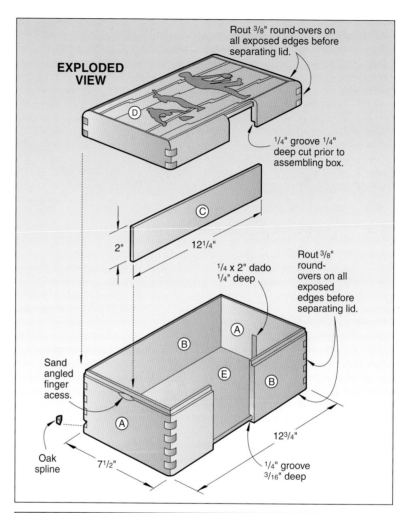

EXPLODED VIEW

Rout ³/₈" round-overs on all exposed edges before separating lid.

¼" groove ¼" deep cut prior to assembling box.

Ⓓ

Ⓒ

2"

12¼"

¼ x 2" dado ¼" deep

Rout ³/₈" round-overs on all exposed edges before separating lid.

Ⓐ

Ⓑ

Ⓐ

Ⓔ

Ⓑ

Sand angled finger acess.

Oak spline

7½"

12¾"

¼" groove ³/₁₆" deep

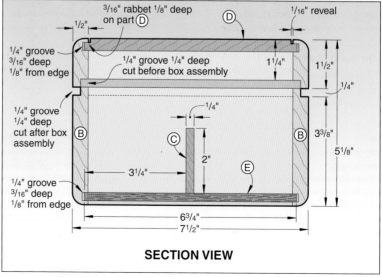

³/₁₆" rabbet ⅛" deep on part Ⓓ

1/2"

Ⓓ

1/16" reveal

¼" groove ³/₁₆" deep ⅛" from edge

¼" groove ¼" deep cut before box assembly

1¼"

1½"

¼"

¼" groove ¼" deep cut after box assembly

Ⓑ

¼"

Ⓒ

2"

Ⓑ

3³/₈"

5⅛"

¼" groove ³/₁₆" deep ⅛" from edge

3¼"

6¾"

7½"

Ⓔ

SECTION VIEW

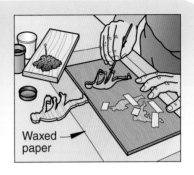

Waxed paper

distort the effective angle of the cut. Do not hurry this test procedure—your completed inlay will not fit any better than your test cut.

6 When you are satisfied with the test cut, drill angled blade start holes through the top assembly as shown in the pattern. Use a hand-held drill, "eyeballing" the angle, or use a bevel gauge. Be sure that the tilt of the blade start holes corresponds with the tilt direction of your saw table.

7 Cut the inlay pieces, and then remove the pattern. Next, separate the walnut and oak stock. Use a toothpick to apply a thin coat of glue on the cut oak edges, then press the walnut inlays into place. Let the glue dry, then sand both faces of the inlay assembly. See the Shop Tip *above* for an idea about using the scraps to make another box lid.

8 Chuck a ⅜" straight bit into your table-mounted router, and set it ⅛"

above the table. Adjust your fence to make a cut 3⁄16" wide. Make a test cut in scrap stock to verify the setting, checking the fit of the piece into the groove in the box. Rout the rabbet along the ends and edges of the inlaid top.
NOTE: Make sure that you rout the rabbets with the inlaid top facedown on the router table. Otherwise, all of the players will become southpaws!

9 Rip and crosscut the bottom from ¼"-thick plywood. Dry-clamp the box assembly with the divider, top, and bottom in place. When you are satisfied with the fit, glue and clamp the assembly with two band clamps. Adjust the position of the top so that there is a consistent reveal as shown in the Section View. Check that the assembly is square and flat, then allow the glue to dry.

Rout the spline slots

1 Tilt your tablesaw blade to 45°, and bevel-rip scrapwood for the eight blocks shown in the Routing the Spline Slots drawing *below*. Return the blade to vertical, and cut the blocks 5" long. Attach them to the box assembly with double-faced tape.

ROUTING THE SPLINE SLOTS

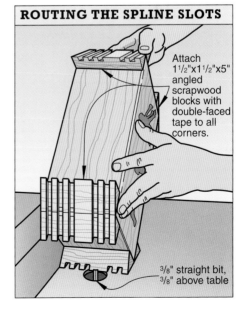

Attach 1½"x1½"x5" angled scrapwood blocks with double-faced tape to all corners.

⅜" straight bit, ⅜" above table

2 Chuck a ⅜" straight bit into your table-mounted router, and set it ⅜" above the table. Clamp a 4"-high fence to your router table ⅜" from the inner edge of the bit. Holding the bottom of the box against the fence as shown in the Routing the Spline Slots drawing, rout a slot through the scrapwood blocks and across each corner. Next, turn the box so that the top is against the fence, and repeat the process. See the Spline Locations drawing *below* for reference. Adjust the fence to 1⅛" from the bit, and rout slots with the top against the fence, then with the bottom against the fence. Rout the two remaining sets of slots (for a total of six at each corner) by holding the bottom against the fence when it is positioned at 1⅞" and 2⅝" from the bit. Remove the scrapwood blocks.

3 Plane a 1¼ × 24" length of oak to ⅜" thick, working it to a snug fit in the spline slots. Rip a ½"-wide strip, then crosscut 24 splines ¾" long. Glue the splines into the slots, making certain that each spline is fully seated into the bottom of the slot. Let the glue dry.

4 Trim the splines flush with the ends and sides with a fine-toothed saw (we used an offset backsaw). Then sand the assembly.

5 Chuck a ⅜" round-over bit into your table-mounted router. Next, round-over all edges of the box assembly. Then sand the box to final smoothness.

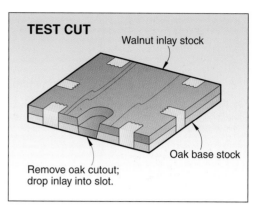

TEST CUT

Walnut inlay stock

Oak base stock

Remove oak cutout; drop inlay into slot.

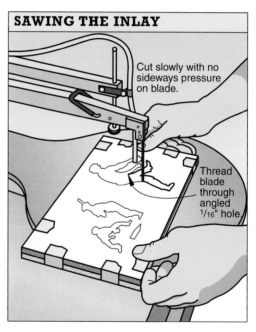

SAWING THE INLAY

Cut slowly with no sideways pressure on blade.

Thread blade through angled 1/16" hole.

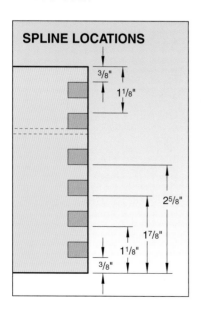

SPLINE LOCATIONS

3/8"

1 1/8"

2 5/8"

1 7/8"

1 1/8"

3/8"

SHOPTIP

Use a scrap cutoff from the side to double-check the set-up for the lid separation as shown in the drawing here. You'll be able to check the position of the fence and height of the bit quickly and accurately.

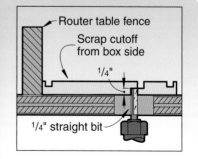

Router table fence

Scrap cutoff from box side

1/4"

1/4" straight bit

SHOP TIP

Use a utility knife to free a lid that does not separate after routing the grooves. You'll probably discover that your router set-up was off by a tiny amount, and that only a few wood fibers are holding the lid in place. Cut cleanly all around the box, resisting the temptation to twist the lid free. Twisting will rip the wood fibers, forcing you to sand the area smooth.

Separate the lid, then finish

1 Chuck a ¼" straight bit into your table-mounted router, and set it ¼" above the table. Clamp a fence 3⅜" from the inside edge of the bit. See the Shop Tip on *page 138* for a good way to double-check this set-up.

2 Rout the grooves in the sequence shown in the Separating the Lid drawing *below*. After you rout each groove, use masking tape to hold a ¼ × ¼" spacer in the groove. The spacers prevent the grooves from pinching shut. See the Shop Tip *(left)* for advice on dealing with a lid that doesn't separate completely.

3 Build the jig shown in the Sanding Jig Exploded View *below*. Chuck a 2½" sanding drum into your drill press, and sand an angled finger-hold centered in each box end as shown in the Exploded View.

4 Finish sand as necessary, and apply your choice of a clear finish. Put on three coats, and sand between with 320-grit sandpaper, removing dust with a tack cloth. (After the first coat of finish, we filled the blade start holes in the lid with colored wood putty.)

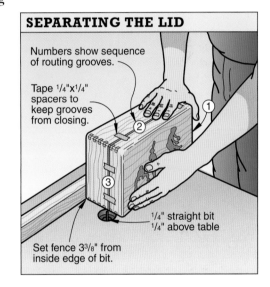

SEPARATING THE LID

Numbers show sequence of routing grooves.

Tape ¼"x¼" spacers to keep grooves from closing.

¼" straight bit ¼" above table

Set fence 3⅜" from inside edge of bit.

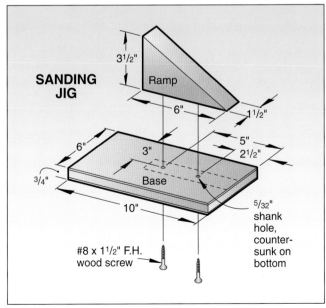

SANDING JIG

3½"

Ramp

6"

1½"

6"

5"

3"

2½"

¾"

Base

10"

5/32" shank hole, countersunk on bottom

#8 x 1½" F.H. wood screw

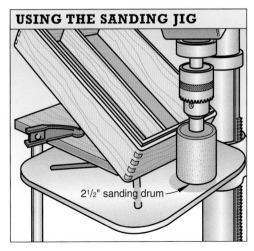

USING THE SANDING JIG

2½" sanding drum

CLASSIC CANDLE BOX

If you've steered clear of dovetail joinery because if its precision and perceived difficulty, here's a great project. With just a simple jig and handsaws, you'll be able to achieve the look of old-world craftsmanship.

1 From a 60" length of ½ × 5½" cherry stock, rip and crosscut a piece to 3½ × 36". Lay out and crosscut two side panels (A) and two end panels (B) in A-B-A-B order, so that the grain will run continuously around the box. Then, make reference marks on the mating surfaces. *Note: These dimensions accommodate 10"-long*

candles. If you intend to use candles of different length, simply add 1¼" to the candle length to determine the new lengths of the side panels, lid, and bottom panel.

2 Next, make the simple clamping jig shown in the drawing on *page 143*. To do this, rip and crosscut two 1¹⁄₁₆ × 8" pieces of

1¹⁄₁₆"-thick hardwood stock. Then, cut two 8" lengths of ⅛ × 1" aluminum angle. Adhere one of these to each hardwood piece with double-faced tape; then, with the same tape, join the assemblies face-to-face. Next, lay out centered ⁹⁄₃₂" holes 1" from each end on the back face of one hardwood piece. Drill through both aluminum angles and hardwood pieces. Then, attach the jig sides using a ¼ × 4" carriage bolt, split washer, and wing nut in each hole.

Mark and saw out the pins and tails

1 Make four photocopies of the full-size pin pattern shown *below*, and adhere a copy to each end of both end panels. Then, mark a stop line across each end panel ½" in from each end, and clamp one of them into your jig so that the stop line is flush angle faces. Clamp the other end of the stock into your bench vise. Now, use a dovetail saw to make the ver-

tical cuts as shown in the drawing *below (top)*, keeping your blade on the waste side of each line. Use a guide block to keep the saw vertical.

2 Next, use a fret saw fitted with a #5 scroll-saw blade to saw out the waste as shown in the drawing *below left,* making

progressively more horizontal angle cuts until your blade is flush with the jig surface. Repeat this procedure for each end of both end panels.

3 To saw the tails in the side panels, first match each side-panel end with its mating end-panel end. Then, use a sharp pencil to

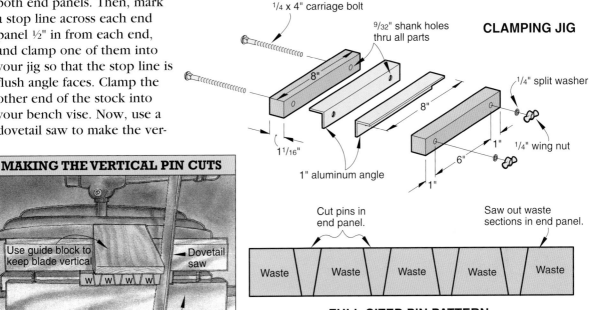

MAKING THE VERTICAL PIN CUTS

Use guide block to keep blade vertical
Dovetail saw
w = waste
Clamping jig secured in vise

MAKING THE HORIZONTAL PIN CUTS

#5 scrollsaw blade in fret saw

CLAMPING JIG

FULL-SIZED PIN PATTERN

Part		Initial Size			Matl.	Qty.
		T	W	L		
A	side panels	½"	3½"	11¼"	C	2
B	end panels	½"	3½"	5¼"	C	2
C	lid	3/16"	4¾"	11"	C	1
D	bottom	3/16"	4 11/16"	10 11/16"	C	1

Materials Key: C—cherry.

Supplies (for jig): 2—⅛×1×8" aluminum angles; 2—¼×4" carriage bolts, split washers, and wing nuts; double-faced carpet tape.

trace each set of pins onto the inside face of the side panel. To do this, lay the side panel flat on your bench, and stand the end panel on it. Square and align the two pieces before you trace. After tracing, use a combination square

to transfer the ends of the traced pins onto the side-panel ends.

4 Clamp the side panel into your jig so that the bottoms of the traced pins are flush with the angle faces. This time, mark the pin sections as waste, and repeat the sawing procedures used in the previous step. When you've sawed tails in both ends of each side panel, dry-assemble the four panels, tapping the parts lightly until they slide together. Watch for tight spots in the joints, and don't force the pieces

together. Adjust the fit as necessary, using a triangular file.

Rout the grooves and assemble

1 First, rip ⁵⁄₁₆" off the top edge of one end panel to allow the lid to slide. Then, fit your table-mounted router with a ³⁄₁₆" straight bit and fence. Rout grooves along the end panels as shown and dimensioned on the Exploded View drawing. *Note: Check the pins to make sure you're routing the inside faces. Rout only a bottom-panel groove in the end panel you just ripped.*

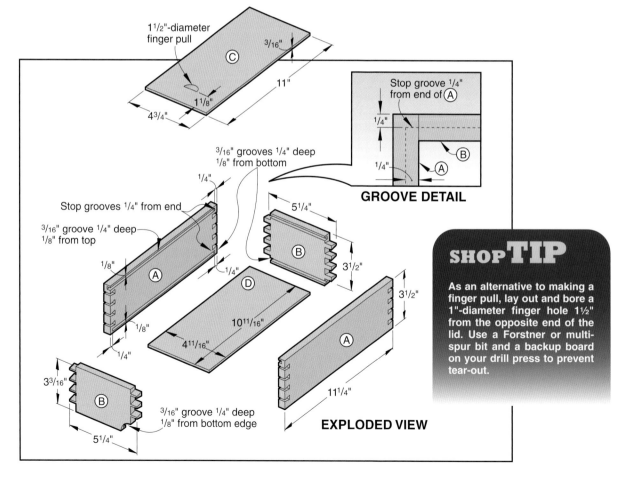

GROOVE DETAIL

Stop groove 1/4" from end of Ⓐ

EXPLODED VIEW

1 1/2"-diameter finger pull — Ⓒ

3/16"

11"

1 1/8"

4 3/4"

3/16" grooves 1/4" deep 1/8" from bottom

5 1/4"

Ⓑ

3 1/2"

Stop grooves 1/4" from end

3/16" groove 1/4" deep 1/8" from top

1/4"

1/8"

Ⓐ

1/4"

Ⓓ

10 11/16"

4 11/16"

1/8"

1/4"

3 3/16"

Ⓑ

5 1/4"

3/16" groove 1/4" deep 1/8" from bottom edge

3 1/2"

Ⓐ

11 1/4"

2 Rout the lid groove in one side panel using the groove-routing setup shown in the drawing *below*. To do this, clamp a stopblock to your router-table fence to the left of the bit as shown. ***Note:*** *Make sure you position the lid grooves so that their open ends will mate with the open-topped end panel you ripped in the previous step.* Feed one of the side panels from right to left over the bit, using the block to stop the cut ¼" from the right end. Next, remove the stopblock, and position a start-block to the *right* of the bit as shown. Butt the right end of your other side panel up against the startblock, lower the left end down onto the spinning bit, and rout the groove clear through the right end.

3 To rout the bottom-panel groove in the two side panels, reclamp the left-hand stopblock, keeping your right-hand startblock in position. As in the previous step, butt the right end of each panel up against the startblock and lower the left end down onto the bit, but this time use the stop-block to stop the cut ¼" from the right end of both side panels.

4 Plane or resaw a 24" length of stock to ³⁄₁₆" thick. Then, rip and cross-cut the lid (C) and bottom (D) to the dimensions listed on the Materials List.

5 Sand the bottom-panel ends so they'll fit in the stopped grooves. Then, finish-sand the inside faces of the side, end, and bottom panels. Glue and clamp these parts, allowing the bottom panel to float in the grooves without glue.

Put a lid on, and apply the finish

1 To make the fingerpull on the lid, first chuck a 1½" diameter drum sander into your drill press and elevate the table to 1" below the bottom of the drum. Clamp on a fence and a stopblock as shown *above*.

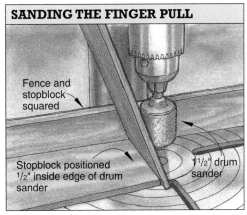

SANDING THE FINGER PULL

Fence and stopblock squared

Stopblock positioned ½" inside edge of drum sander

1½" drum sander

Then, brace the lid against your fence and stopblock, and ease the lid into the drum sander until the bottom of the pull is ⅛" deep. (We used calipers to check the depth during this operation so as not to sand all the way through the lid.)

2 Sand the lid top face until the lid slides smoothly in its groove. Then, finish-sand all surfaces requiring it, and apply the finish of your choice. Two coats of a clear penetrating oil worked well on this cherry box.

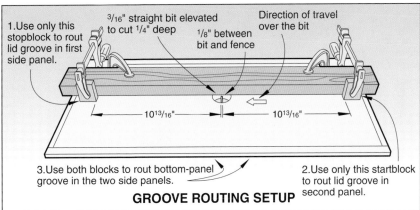

1.Use only this stopblock to rout lid groove in first side panel.

³⁄₁₆" straight bit elevated to cut ¼" deep

⅛" between bit and fence

Direction of travel over the bit

10¹³⁄₁₆"   10¹³⁄₁₆"

3.Use both blocks to rout bottom-panel groove in the two side panels.

2.Use only this startblock to rout lid groove in second panel.

GROOVE ROUTING SETUP

FLIP-UP PEN BOX

Open the lid and this box pops a pair of writing instruments into view. Although it's designed to accommodate two pens (or a pen and pencil) about ½" in diameter and a little less than 6" long, you can adjust the dimensions for fatter or longer pens.

1 Trim a 2 × 1⅝ × 10" blank of hardwood (moradillo is shown here) to 6¼" long. Draw index marks on one end of the blank, as shown in the Cutting the Box Top and Bottom drawing *opposite (top)*.

2 Saw a ¼"-thick slice off the top of the blank and a ⅛"-thick piece off the bottom. Make the cuts with a bandsaw or on a tablesaw equipped with a thin-kerf blade in order to preserve grain continuity on the box as much as possible. Plane or sand the saw marks off the mating surfaces, and set the top and bottom aside until later.

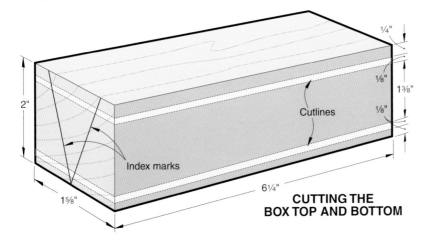

CUTTING THE BOX TOP AND BOTTOM

3 Saw two deep dadoes across the body, as shown in the drawing on *page 171*. To do this, install a ⅜" dado blade on your tablesaw, and set the cutting depth to 1⅜". Attach an extended fence to the miter gauge. Clamp stopblocks to the fence 5⅛" from each side of the dado blade, and saw the dadoes as shown in **Photo A**.

Install an extended miter-gauge fence to saw the deep dadoes in the body.

4 Saw dadoes in the edge of the lid for the hinges, shown in the Lid, Body, and Bottom and Exploded View drawings. To saw them, change to a ⁵⁄₁₆" dado blade, and set the cutting depth at ¼".

Install a new auxiliary fence on the miter gauge or move the used one over so you'll have solid wood behind the lid when you cut the dadoes. This will help minimize tearout.

To locate the dadoes accurately, place the body against the fence, and center the dado in the body over the narrower dado blade. Clamp a stopblock to the fence at the opposite end of the body, as shown in **Photo B**. Repeat for the other dado. Verify which edge to cut by checking the index marks, and then saw the dadoes in the lid.

The body dadoes help when setting stopblocks for sawing hinge dadoes in the lid.

Rout the body and make the lid

1 Rout a ³⁄₁₆" round-over along the top back edge of the body (the dadoed side). Do the job on a table-mounted router. To bridge the dadoes, set a fence flush with the router bit's pilot.

2 Using a ½" round-nose bit in the table-mounted router, rout the pen grooves in the body as shown. To rout them, position a fence on the router table ¼" from the bit. Clamp stopblocks to the fence 5⅝" from each side of the bit. Clamp a straight-edged board to the table parallel to the fence, and 1⅝" from it. This will help keep the body against the fence throughout the routing.

Rout the grooves in small depth increments—start at about ⅛" deep and increase the depth by about that much each pass. Make a pass at each depth with each face against the fence to form the two grooves.

3 Now, make the lid hinges. Start with two ¼ × ⁵⁄₁₆ × 1⁹⁄₁₆" pieces of stock that match the rest of the parts. You can cut the hinge blanks from the cut-off end of the blank.

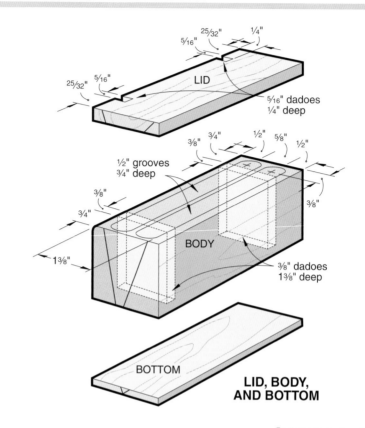

LID, BODY, AND BOTTOM

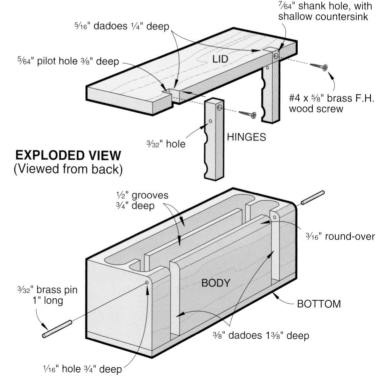

EXPLODED VIEW (Viewed from back)

4 Tape the pieces together edge to edge, referring to the Hinge Full-Size Pattern on *page 173,* and sand the pen recesses as shown. (We did this with sandpaper wrapped around a ½"-diameter dowel rod.)

5 Glue the hinges into the lid dadoes. (Epoxy works well here.) Position the hinges perpendicular to the lid in both directions. (See the Exploded View and Side Section View drawings.)

6 After the epoxy cures, sand off the squeeze-out on the top and back of the lid. You can pare away squeeze-out on the inside of the lid and sides of the hinges with a sharp chisel.

7 Drill a ⁵⁄₆₄" hole ⁵⁄₈" deep at the middle of each hinge, centered on the edge of the lid. Enlarge the holes through the hinge arms to ⁷⁄₆₄", and countersink them—shallow enough that the screw slot will be above the surface.

8 Drive a screw into each hole, and file the heads flush with the arms, as shown in **Photo C**. Tape the tip of the file to keep it from gouging the wood.

Tape on the end of the file protects the lid when filing the screws flush.

Insert a cardboard spacer between the body and lid when drilling hinge holes.

Write the last chapter

1 Mark the location of the hinge pin on each end of the body. Refer to the Side Section View and Exploded View drawings for placement.

2 Place the lid on the body, and slide a shim about ¹⁄₃₂" thick between them. (We used cardboard from the back of a notepad.) Clamp the parts together, keeping the edges and ends flush.

3 Drill the hinge hole on each end. Clamp the body/lid assembly to a fence on the drill-press table for accurate drilling, as shown in **Photo D**. Unclamp the assembly.

4 Glue the bottom to the body. Double-check your alignment marks before gluing for the best grain match.

5 Finish-sand the top and inside of the body, the underside of the lid, and the hinge arms. Clamp the lid to the body again, with the shim in place, and drive in the hinge pins. File the pin ends flush with the body. Unclamp and remove the shim.

6 Sand the sides and ends flush, and finish-sand all exterior surfaces. (We sanded with progressively finer grits, ending with 320.) Break the sharp edges slightly by block-sanding.

7 Apply two or more coats of a clear oil finish, and go find your favorite pen or pencil.

HINGE ARM FULL-SIZE PATTERN
(2 needed)

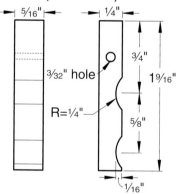

⁵⁄₁₆"   ¼"
³⁄₃₂" hole
¾"
1⁹⁄₁₆"
R=¼"
⁵⁄₈"
¹⁄₁₆"

END SECTION VIEW

Lid

Hinge pin

Hinge arm

TOP VIEW

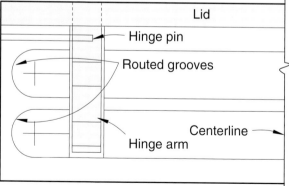

Lid

Hinge pin

Routed grooves

Centerline

Hinge arm

6

Boxes with Flair to Spare

*H*ow exactly do we define "flair" as it pertains to the boxes in this chapter? Well, simply put, it's that special something—that unusual or unexpected feature that makes a project unforgettable. So as you review the last four boxes in this book, decide for yourself what makes each one truly unique.

A BEVELED BEAUTY

This is a jewelry box in a league of its own. But you might be surprised to learn that building it requires mostly a very straightforward technique that you can achieve with an ordinary tablesaw.

1 From ¾" hardwood stock (bird's-eye maple was the choice here), cut a piece of wood to 2½" wide by 50" long for the box front, back, and ends (A, B). Next, cut a piece of ¾" stock to 1" wide by 50" for the base pieces (C, D). We used cherry for these.

2 With the surfaces and ends flush, clamp and glue the ¾ × 2½ × 50" cherry to one edge of the ¾ × 2½ × 50" maple. Remove the glue once it has formed a tough skin. Later, remove the clamps and

excess glue, and sand both surfaces until smooth.

3 To house the bottom panel (E) later, cut a ⅛" groove ¼" deep, and ⅛" from the bottom edge (in the cherry) on the inside surface in the 50"-long edge-joined strip.

4 Using a stop to help keep the lengths consistent, miter-cut the four box pieces (A/C, B/D) to length. (It's a good idea to test-cut scrap stock first to verify an

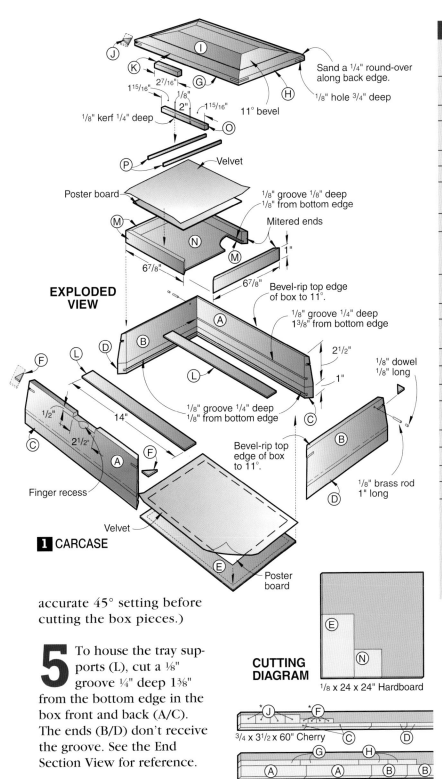

Sand a ¹/₄" round-over along back edge.

¹/₈" hole ³/₄" deep

11° bevel

2⁷/₁₆"

1¹⁵/₁₆"

¹/₈"

2"

1¹⁵/₁₆"

¹/₈" kerf ¹/₄" deep

Velvet

Poster board

¹/₈" groove ¹/₈" deep ¹/₈" from bottom edge

Mitered ends

1"

6⁷/₈"

6⁷/₈"

Bevel-rip top edge of box to 11°.

EXPLODED VIEW

¹/₈" groove ¹/₄" deep 1³/₈" from bottom edge

2¹/₂"

1"

¹/₈" dowel ¹/₈" long

¹/₈" groove ¹/₄" deep ¹/₈" from bottom edge

Bevel-rip top edge of box to 11°.

¹/₈" brass rod 1" long

14"

¹/₂"

2¹/₂"

Finger recess

Velvet

1 CARCASE

Poster board

Materials List

Part	Finished Size			Matl.	Qty.
	T	**W**	**L**		
A* front & back	³/₄"	2¹/₂"	15¹/₂"	BM	2
B* ends	³/₄"	2¹/₂"	8¹/₂"	BM	2
C* base front & back	³/₄"	1"	15¹/₂"	C	2
D* base ends	³/₄"	1"	8¹/₂"	C	2
E bottom	¹/₈"	7⁷/₁₆"	14⁷/₁₆"	H	1
F spline blanks	¹/₈"	1"	2"	C	4
LID					
G* front & back frame members	³/₄"	1¹/₄"	13¹⁵/₁₆"	BM	2
H* end frame members	³/₄"	1¹/₄"	6⁷/₈"	BM	2
I panel	³/₄"	5¹/₁₆"	12¹/₈"	BM	1
J spline blanks	¹/₈"	1¹/₄"	3"	C	4
K handle	⁷/₁₆"	1⁷/₃₂"	2⁷/₁₆"	C	1
TRAY					
L supports	¹/₈"	³/₄"	14"	BM	2
M* front back & ends	³/₈"	1"	6⁷/₈"	BM	4
N bottom	¹/₈"	6⁵/₁₆"	6⁵/₁₆"	H	1
DIVIDER					
O center	³/₈"	¹/₂"	6¹/₈"	BM	1
P strips	¹/₈"	¹/₄"	6¹/₈"	BM	2

*Initially cut parts oversized. Then, trim each to finished size according to the how-to instructions.

Supplies: ¹/₈" dowel stock, ¹/₈" brass rod, poster board, velvet, clear finish.

Materials Key: BM–bird's-eye maple, C–cherry, H–hardboard

accurate 45° setting before cutting the box pieces.)

5 To house the tray supports (L), cut a ¹/₈" groove ¹/₄" deep 1³/₈" from the bottom edge in the box front and back (A/C). The ends (B/D) don't receive the groove. See the End Section View for reference.

CUTTING DIAGRAM

¹/₈ x 24 x 24" Hardboard

³/₄ x 3¹/₂ x 60" Cherry

³/₄ x 5¹/₂ x 96" Bird's-eye maple

6 Fit your tablesaw with a dado blade and your miter gauge with a wooden extension. Now, cut a ½" notch, 2½" long, centered in the top edge of the box front (A).

7 To form the finger recess at the notch, mount a ¾" drum sander in your drill press and sand a recess centered and angled in the notch as shown in the Exploded View drawing.

8 Cut the box bottom (E) to size from ⅛" hardboard.

9 Finish-sand the inside surface of the box pieces with 220-grit sandpaper.

10 Using band clamps, glue and clamp the box together, checking for tight miter joints and square.

11 Tilt your tablesaw blade 11° from center, position the tablesaw fence, and with the bottom of the box riding against the fence, bevel-rip the top edges (not the sides) of the box. See the Exploded View for reference.

Add the corner splines

1 Follow the Spline-Cutting Jig drawing to build a jig.

Use a spline-cutting jig to support and angle the box for cutting the ⅛" kerfs in the corners.

2 Cut a ⅛" kerf 1⅛" deep, and 2⅞" from the bottom edge at each corner of the box as shown in **Photo A**. (We used a large spring clamp to hold the box tightly against the jig.)

3 From ⅛" cherry (or, you can resaw thicker stock), cut four corner splines (F) to 1 × 2". Glue one into each ⅛" corner kerf. Lightly tap the splines into the kerfs so there will be no glue line evident later. Later, trim and sand the splines flush with the outside of the box.

Construct the lid

1 Cut a piece of ¾" maple to 1¼" × 46" for the lid frame (G, H).

2 Cut a ¼" groove ⅜" deep, centered along one edge of the

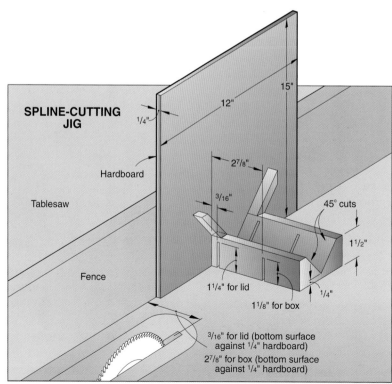

SPLINE-CUTTING JIG

Hardboard

Tablesaw

Fence

15"

12"

1/4"

2⅞"

3/16"

45° cuts

1½"

1¼" for lid

1⅛" for box

1/4"

3/16" for lid (bottom surface against 1/4" hardboard)

2⅞" for box (bottom surface against 1/4" hardboard)

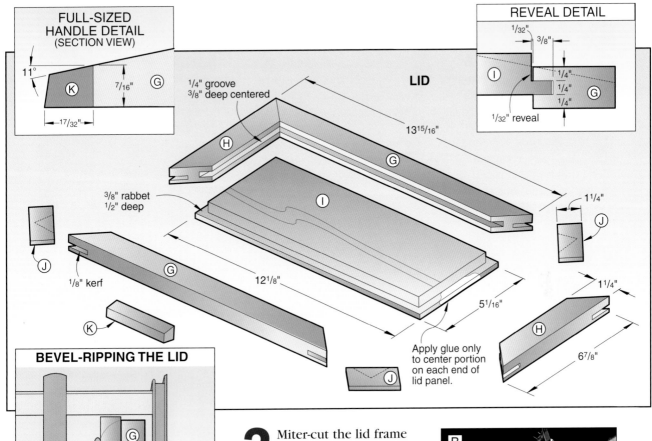

FULL-SIZED HANDLE DETAIL
(SECTION VIEW)

11°

K

7/16"

G

17/32"

REVEAL DETAIL

1/32"

3/8"

I

1/4"

G

1/4"

1/4"

1/32" reveal

LID

1/4" groove
3/8" deep centered

H

G

13¹⁵/₁₆"

1¹/₄"

J

3/8" rabbet
1/2" deep

I

J

1/8" kerf

G

12¹/₈"

5¹/₁₆"

1¹/₄"

H

6⁷/₈"

K

Apply glue only
to center portion
on each end of
lid panel.

J

BEVEL-RIPPING THE LID

Fence rider

G

I

Blade
tilted 11°

Fence

3¹/₄"

7/16"

Tablesaw

G

46"-long maple strip. This groove will house the lid panel (I) later. See the Lid drawing for reference.

3 Miter-cut the lid frame members (G, H) for a frame that will fit tightly into the box opening.

4 Cut the lid panel (I) to size. Cut ⅜" rabbets ½" deep along the top surface of each edge of the panel so the panel fits into the grooves cut in the lid frame pieces (G, H). As noted on the Reveal detail, the panel should not fit tightly inside the frame. This will allow for expansion and contraction.

5 Glue and clamp the lid together, checking for square and that an equal reveal exists between

Use the spline-cutting jig to support the lid when cutting a kerf in each corner of the lid.

the panel and lid frame. To allow for wood movement, the lid panel should be glued in place only on the center portion of each end (as shown in the Lid drawing).

6 Using the spline-cutting jig, cut a ⅛" kerf 1¼" deep in each corner of the lid 3⁄16" from the bottom surface of the lid, as shown in **Photo B**.

7 From ⅛" cherry, cut four spline blanks (J) measuring 1¼ × 3" each. Glue and clamp a spline in each corner of the lid. Later, trim the splines flush with the outside edges of the lid.

8 Tilt your tablesaw blade 11° from vertical, and raise it 3¼" above the

surface of the saw table as shown in the "Bevel-Ripping the Lid" drawing. Clamp a fence rider to the lid as shown. Bevel-rip the top surfaces of the lid as shown in **Photo C**.

9 Sand a ¼" round-over along the top back edge of the lid as shown in the End Section View and Exploded View drawings.

10 Cut the handle (K) to size, and sand an 11° angle on its top surface. See the Handle

With the blade tilted at 11°, bevel-rip the top surfaces of the lid. A fence rider helps to support the piece.

detail for reference. Glue and clamp the handle, centered, to the front edge of the lid.

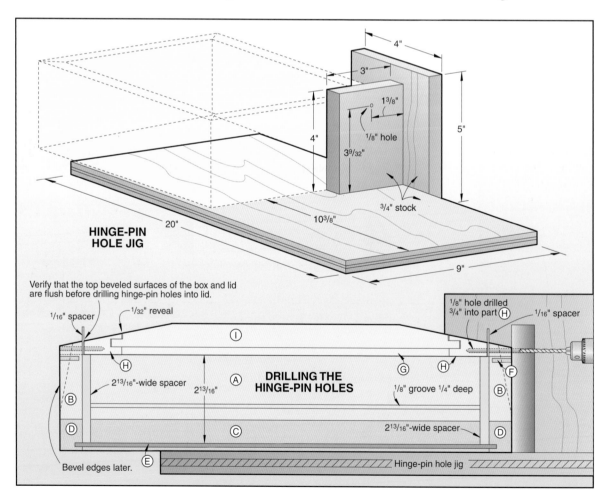

Sand the top and bottom surfaces of the handle flush with those of the lid.

Drill the hinge-pin holes

1 Cut the pieces for the jig as dimensioned on the Hinge-Pin Hole Jig drawing. Carefully mark the centerpoint, and use a brad-point bit in your drill press to drill a ⅛" hole through the center piece. Assemble the jig.

2 As shown in the Drilling the Hinge-Pin Holes drawing, use spacers on the inside of the box to support the lid so that the 11° bevels on the top surface of the lid are flush with the top beveled edges of the box. Use ¹⁄₁₆" spacers to center the lid in the box opening. Using a brad-point bit to eliminate bit wander, drill ⅛" holes through the box ends (B) and ¾" into the rear lid corners.

3 Temporarily slide a 2"-long brass pin into each guide hole. Open and close the lid to check the fit of the pins. Remove the pins and crosscut the pins to 1" long each.

Bevel-rip the outside surfaces

1 Tilt your carbide-tipped tablesaw blade 9° from center, and carefully position the fence so you'll

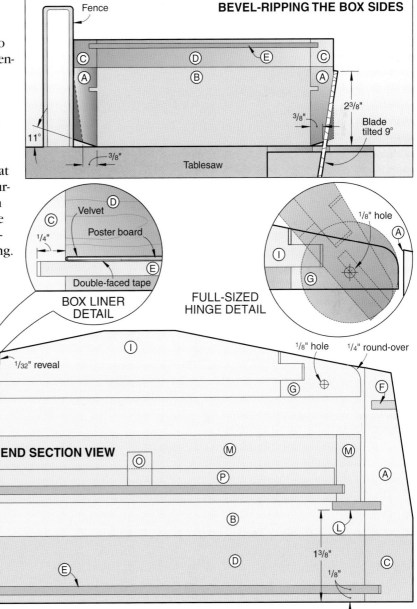

BEVEL-RIPPING THE BOX SIDES

Fence

Ⓒ Ⓓ Ⓔ Ⓒ
Ⓐ Ⓑ Ⓐ

11°

2³⁄₈"

3⁄₈"

Blade tilted 9°

3⁄₈"

Tablesaw

BOX LINER DETAIL

Velvet
Poster board
Ⓒ Ⓓ
1/4"
Ⓔ
Double-faced tape

FULL-SIZED HINGE DETAIL

1/8" hole
Ⓐ
Ⓘ
Ⓖ

END SECTION VIEW

1/32" reveal
1/8" hole   1/4" round-over
Ⓘ
Ⓖ   Ⓖ   Ⓕ
11°
9°
Ⓜ   Ⓜ   Ⓜ
Ⓞ
Ⓟ
Ⓐ
Ⓐ
3¹⁄₂"
Ⓝ   Ⓑ
Ⓛ   Ⓛ
Ⓒ   Ⓒ
Ⓓ
1³⁄₈"
Ⓔ
1/8"

leave a ⅜"-thick wall thickness after making the cut as shown in the Bevel-Ripping the Box Sides drawing. With the box upside down, bevel-rip the front and back of the box as shown in the drawing.

2 As shown in **Photo D**, attach a long wooden extension to your miter gauge. Verify that the extension is square to the blade. Secure a stop (we used a handscrew clamp) to the extension to ensure equal cuts on both ends. Also, clamp the box to the extension to hold it steady when making the cut.

3 Sand the outside surfaces of the box to remove any saw marks.

The supports, tray, and divider

1 Cut the tray supports (L) to size, but do not glue them in place yet.

2 Cut a piece of ⅜" stock to 1" wide by 32" long. Cut a ⅛" groove ⅛" deep, ⅛" from the bottom edge on the inside surface of the long strip. This groove will house the tray bottom (N) later.

3 Miter-cut the tray front, back, and ends (M) to length from the 32" strip. Cut the tray bottom (N) to size and dry-fit the assembly. The tray should measure ⅛" less front to back than the box opening. You'll need this

Attach a wooden extension to your miter gauge, and square it with the table-saw blade. Then, bevel-rip the ends of the box.

for clearance when removing the tray.

4 Cut the divider pieces (O, P) to size. Cut a pair of ⅛" kerfs in the center divider piece (O) for the two single strips (P) to fit into snugly. Glue the three strips together to form the divider.

The finishing touches

1 Finish-sand the box, tray, lid, and divider.

2 To add fabric to the bottom of the box and tray, cut pieces of posterboard ¹⁄₁₆" less in length and width than the openings. Adhere double-faced tape along the edges to what will be the bottom side of the posterboard. See the Box liner detail for reference.

3 Cut black velvet to the size of the posterboard plus 1" in each direc-

tion. Using spray adhesive, secure the fabric, centered onto the top side of the posterboard.

4 Remove the backing from the tape and wrap the velvet around the posterboard and secure it against the tape. Leave enough of the tape exposed so that it will stick to the bottom of the box and the tray later. See the Box liner detail for reference.

5 Fit a 1" long brass pin into each guide hole. Drive the pins in all the way and plug the hole with a piece of ⅛" dowel. Sand the end of the protruding dowel flush.

6 Apply the finish. The box shown was double-coated with a clear penetrating oil. After the finish has thoroughly dried, fit the fabric bottoms in place. Then, glue the tray supports (L) in place.

CROWN MOLDING BOXES

With their elegant curves and classic proportions, these delightful boxes look like the work of a master sculptor. But actually, they're made with basic crown molding that's available at any home center. The trick is in the jigs, and even they're not very complicated. Give one of the designs a try and you'll be hooked.

A tale of three boxes

A   B   C

Believe it or not, these boxes were made from crown molding of the same size and profile, with only slight building modifications. **Box A** is made of red oak with an oak handle. **Boxes B** and **C**, made of cherry, have cardinal wood and Corian handles, respectively.

We made boxes A and B in the same way, but we positioned the crown moldings upside down in the jigs when cutting the parts for box B (relative to how we positioned them when making box A). With box C, we laid the moldings at a flatter angle in the miter-gauge jig. Doing this made Box C more upright.

Get your jig ready

Before you begin, look over the plans for the two jigs you'll need—the Miter-Gauge Jig and the Sliding Table Jig—shown on *page 159.* You can use these to make crown molding boxes of any height or width. Just give it a try and you'll quickly forget about the process of calculating degree angles for compound miters. Plus, they can handle molding up to 4⅝" wide.

As you can see in "A tale of three boxes," *above,* changing the position of the workpieces in the jigs can dramatically change the appearance of your box. Continue on to learn how to make the box in the large photo on *page 157.* Once you've got the technique down, feel free to go and experiment with your own configurations.

Ready to try one?

1 Our finished box will measure about 8" wide by 10" long. From a piece of 4¼"-wide crown molding, cut two pieces 8½" long and two pieces 10½" long. Cut them in the same sequence that they'll follow around the box—side, end, side, end—and number each one near the bottom edge. (This way, the grain will seem to "run" continuously around the box.)

Set your tablesaw blade to 45°, or just a hair over, to make sure that the outside points of the miters will be tight. Slip the miter-gauge jig into the right-hand slot of the tablesaw, and load one of the four pieces into it. Lean the molding against the rear fence at the steepest angle that will still allow the blade to cut

through it, and then measure the distance between the lower edge and the front fence. Cut a spacer to that width, and put it between the workpiece and the fence, as shown in the "Determining the Spacer Size" drawing.

The edge that sits higher in the jig will become the top edge of the finished box; the lower edge will be at the bottom. Double-check that before making each cut. Now, with the workpiece wedged firmly between spacer and fence, cut a miter. Do the same at one end of each of the four pieces.

2 To miter the opposite ends, flip one of the shorter pieces so it's leaning against the front fence, and place the spacer between the workpiece and the rear fence. Line it up with the blade and clamp a stop-block at the other end. You don't have to measure a thing. Cut that miter, take the piece out, and cut the second short piece exactly the same way without moving the stopblock.

Remove the stopblock and follow the same procedure for the longer pieces. Tape the four pieces together to check the fit.

Add the feet and a bottom

3 Along the bottom edge of each workpiece, measure in 1" from each end and make a mark. Draw a line parallel to the bottom edge and 1" up from that edge. With a compass set to a 1" radius, scribe a curve up to the line.

Use a scrollsaw or bandsaw to cut close to that line. Install a 2" drum in your spindle sander or on your drill press, and sand to the line as shown in the photo on *page 160.*

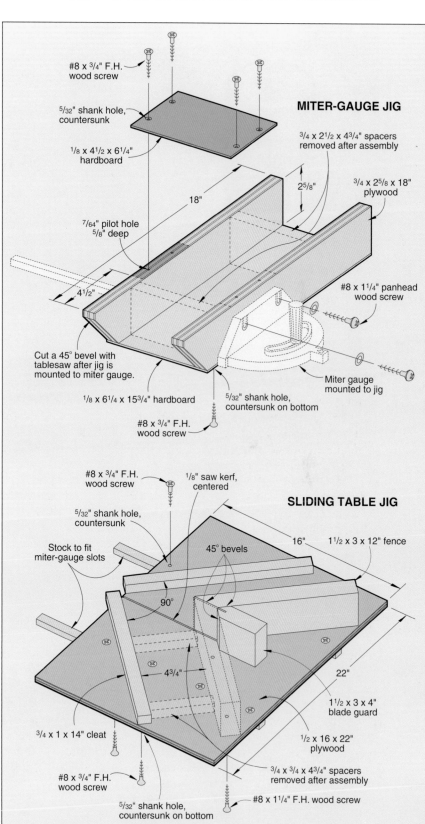

MITER-GAUGE JIG

#8 x 3/4" F.H. wood screw

5/32" shank hole, countersunk

1/8 x 4 1/2 x 6 1/4" hardboard

3/4 x 2 1/2 x 4 3/4" spacers removed after assembly

3/4 x 2 5/8 x 18" plywood

2 5/8"

18"

7/64" pilot hole 5/8" deep

4 1/2"

Cut a 45° bevel with tablesaw after jig is mounted to miter gauge.

1/8 x 6 1/4 x 15 3/4" hardboard

5/32" shank hole, countersunk on bottom

#8 x 3/4" F.H. wood screw

#8 x 1 1/4" panhead wood screw

Miter gauge mounted to jig

SLIDING TABLE JIG

#8 x 3/4" F.H. wood screw

1/8" saw kerf, centered

5/32" shank hole, countersunk

Stock to fit miter-gauge slots

45° bevels

90°

16"

1 1/2 x 3 x 12" fence

4 3/4"

22"

1 1/2 x 3 x 4" blade guard

1/2 x 16 x 22" plywood

3/4 x 1 x 14" cleat

#8 x 3/4" F.H. wood screw

5/32" shank hole, countersunk on bottom

3/4 x 3/4 x 4 3/4" spacers removed after assembly

#8 x 1 1/4" F.H. wood screw

When forming the legs, use a fence with a drum or spindle sander to sand a straight edge and smooth radius.

isn't important. Just set the sliding bevel gauge and use it to set your tablesaw blade.

With the feet of each piece against the rip fence and the molding profile facing up, saw a ⅛"-wide kerf about ⅛" above the leg cutout and ³⁄₁₆" deep at its shallow side. Do this on all four pieces. Measure the lengths of those kerfs to find the dimensions of the bottom, and cut a piece of ⅛" plywood or solid wood to fit.

After test-fitting, glue together the sides, ends, and bottom of the box. Hold them together with masking tape and a band clamp until the glue dries. Make sure the top edges are lined up at the corners. It's easier to sand away imperfections if they're on the bottom.

As shown in the drawing *below*, use a sliding bevel gauge and a straightedge to determine the angle for the kerf that holds the box bottom. Again, the number of degrees

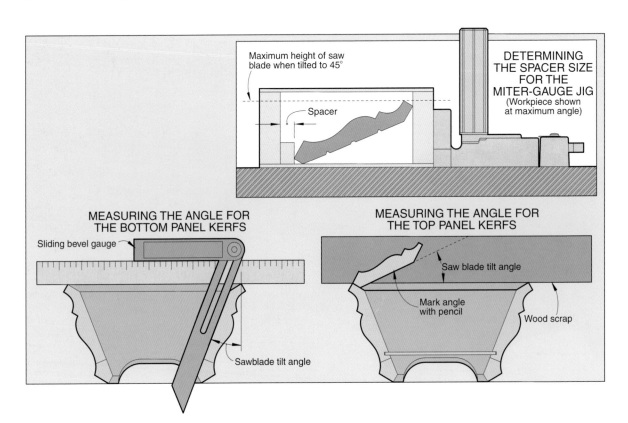

Maximum height of saw blade when tilted to 45°

Spacer

DETERMINING THE SPACER SIZE FOR THE MITER-GAUGE JIG
(Workpiece shown at maximum angle)

MEASURING THE ANGLE FOR THE BOTTOM PANEL KERFS

Sliding bevel gauge

Sawblade tilt angle

MEASURING THE ANGLE FOR THE TOP PANEL KERFS

Saw blade tilt angle

Mark angle with pencil

Wood scrap

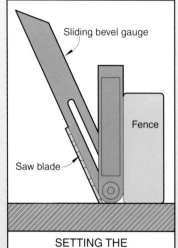

SETTING THE
SAW BLADE ANGLE
FOR THE TOP PANEL KERFS

Hold the back side of the molding against your tablesaw's fence to cut the kerf that holds the panel in the center of the lid.

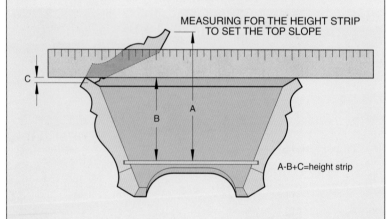

MEASURING FOR THE HEIGHT STRIP
TO SET THE TOP SLOPE

A−B+C=height strip

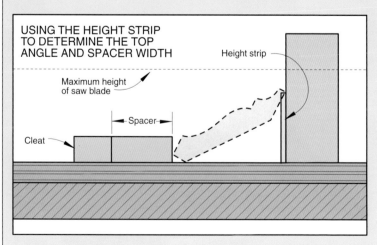

USING THE HEIGHT STRIP
TO DETERMINE THE TOP
ANGLE AND SPACER WIDTH

Top it off

4 As you choose molding stock for the lid, keep in mind that the lid pieces cannot meet in the center of the box. That's

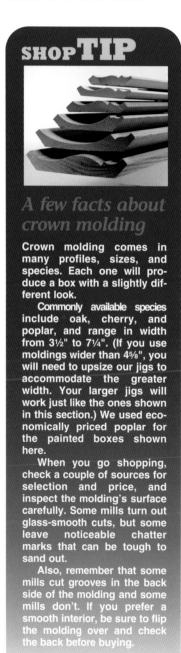

SHOP**TIP**

A few facts about crown molding

Crown molding comes in many profiles, sizes, and species. Each one will produce a box with a slightly different look.

Commonly available species include oak, cherry, and poplar, and range in width from 3½" to 7¼". (If you use moldings wider than 4⅝", you will need to upsize our jigs to accommodate the greater width. Your larger jigs will work just like the ones shown in this section.) We used economically priced poplar for the painted boxes shown here.

When you go shopping, check a couple of sources for selection and price, and inspect the molding's surface carefully. Some mills turn out glass-smooth cuts, but some leave noticeable chatter marks that can be tough to sand out.

Also, remember that some mills cut grooves in the back side of the molding and some mills don't. If you prefer a smooth interior, be sure to flip the molding over and check the back before buying.

because there must be a panel at least 1" wide in the center of the lid for mounting a handle. For the box in this example, 3½"-wide crown molding will do the trick. If the box were a bit wider, the 4¼"-wide stock used for the base might work for the lid as well.

From the 3½" crown molding, cut two pieces 8½" long and two pieces 10½" long. As before, cut in a side-end-side-end sequence and number the pieces.

Also cut a scrap of that molding 1" long and tape it to the box so that its bottom edge fits snugly against the bevel of the box. Lay a straight piece of scrapwood across the box and mark the angle of your scrap molding on it. (See the Measuring the Angle for the Top Panel Kerfs drawing.) Set the sliding bevel gauge to that angle, and use it to set the tablesaw blade, with the handle of the gauge against the rip fence as shown in the Setting the Saw Blade Angle for the Top Panel Kerfs drawing.

Saw kerfs in each lid piece to receive the top panel. To do so, hold the flat side of the molding against the fence, and cut a slot ⅛" wide and ³⁄₁₆" deep, at least ⅛" from the edge that will be the highest part of the lid. See the photo on *page 161 (top)*.

5 Place the sliding table jig in the slots of your tablesaw, and set the blade at exactly 90°. To find the correct angle for the miter cut, again use a piece of scrap

Attach four cleats at right angles to each other to hold the lid pieces in position on a plywood clamping platform.

Apply glue to the mitered edges and squeeze them together with the help of some scrap stock and clamps.

molding 1" long taped to the box. With a straightedge across the box, measure as shown in the illustration on *page 161 (middle)*. Cut a piece of scrap to a length that equals *A-B+C*. Hold this height strip flat against the left fence of the jig, and draw a line along the top edge.

Tilt one of the molding pieces against the fence so that it just covers the line, and measure the gap between the workpiece and the cleat. Cut a spacer to fit that gap. See the drawing on *page 161 (bottom)*. Cut a miter at one end of each of the four pieces, pressing the piece firmly between the fence and spacer each time.

Hold one of the longer lid pieces against the side of the box and mark its finished length, which should be about 10" in this example.

Moving to the right-hand side of the sliding table jig, put the spacer against the cleat and set the workpiece so the blade meets the mark. Clamp a stopblock to the fence and against the point of the mitered end. Cut the miter.

Repeat the procedure for the other long piece, and follow the same steps for the two shorter pieces. Again, the bottom edge of the lid goes at the bottom when cutting. Cut a piece of ⅛" plywood or solid wood to fit the lid kerfs.

6 To make a clamping jig for the lid, screw two pieces of scrap to a piece of plywood at right angles, hold the lid together, and set it into that corner. Screw two more scrap pieces into the plywood so they are tight against the lid, as shown in the photo on *page 162 (top)*.

Take the lid out, glue the miters, and replace the lid assembly into the clamping jig. A board or two on top, held down by clamps, will force the miters snugly together as shown on *page 162 (bottom)*.

7 For a handle, we suggest a "fin" made of ¼–½" stock, cut to the length of the lid panel and about ½–1" wide. This would be a fine time to use a piece of exotic scrapwood or Corian. Attach the handle with brass screws from the bottom side of the panel.

8 Apply the finish of your choice. Paint works well for woods lacking showy grain patterns, but if you want to show off the grain, apply several coats of oil and top it off with paste wax.

A ROOMY JEWELRY BOX

The excellent spline-jointed drawers (all 12 of them) give this dresser-top jewelry chest a Shaker-style look. You can achieve these splines using a simple jig. Because you'll need a few different thicknesses of solid stock, be prepared to do some planing or resawing.

Cut the sides and top pieces

1 Cut the side panels (A) to 7⅝ × 13". Now, rip a strip ⅜" wide off the front edge of each side panel.

Crosscut the narrow strip to 12¹³⁄₁₆" long. See the Side Panel drawing for reference.

2 Lay out the locations and cut ⅜" dadoes ³⁄₁₆" deep on the inside face

of each side panel as shown in the Side Panel drawing. Then, cut a ³⁄₁₆" rabbet ³⁄₁₆" deep along the top outside edge of each piece. Next, cut a ³⁄₁₆" rabbet ⅛" deep along the back inside edge of each side panel.

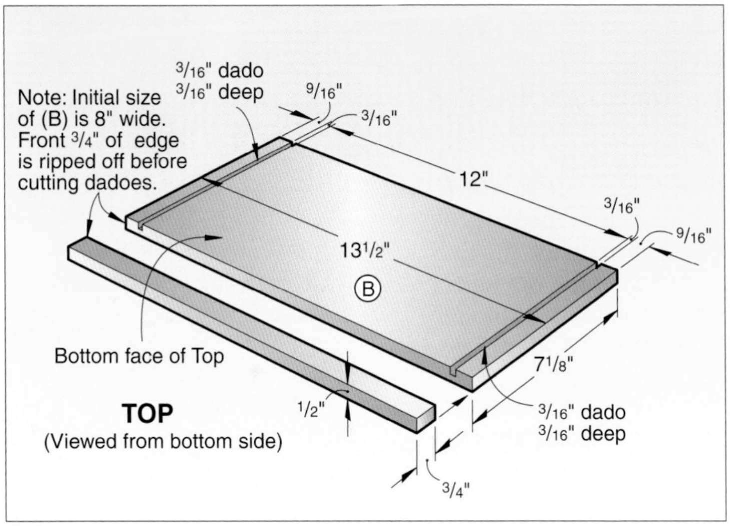
Note: Initial size of (B) is 8" wide. Front 3/4" of edge is ripped off before cutting dadoes.
3/16" dado
3/16" deep
9/16"
3/16"
12"
3/16"
9/16"
13 1/2"
B
Bottom face of Top
7 1/8"
1/2"
3/16" dado
3/16" deep
3/4"
TOP
(Viewed from bottom side)

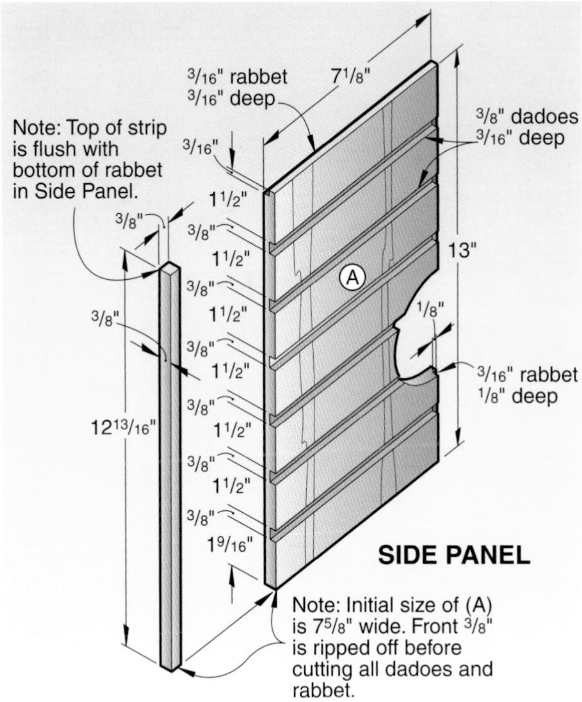
3/16" rabbet
3/16" deep
7 1/8"
Note: Top of strip is flush with bottom of rabbet in Side Panel.
3/8" dadoes
3/16" deep
3/16"
1 1/2"
3/8"
3/8"
1 1/2"
3/8"
1 1/2"
3/8"
1 1/2"
3/8"
1 1/2"
3/8"
1 1/2"
3/8"
1 9/16"
12 13/16"
13"
A
1/8"
3/16" rabbet
1/8" deep
SIDE PANEL
Note: Initial size of (A) is 7 5/8" wide. Front 3/8" is ripped off before cutting all dadoes and rabbet.

Materials List

Part	Finished Size T	Finished Size W	Finished Size L	Matl.	Qty.
BASIC ASSEMBLY					
A* sides	3/8"	7 1/2"	13"	EC	2
B* top	1/2"	7 7/8"	13 1/2"	EC	1
C shelves	3/8"	7 3/8"	12 3/8"	EC	6
D bottom rail	3/8"	1 9/16"	12"	C	1
E back	1/8"	12 3/8"	12 13/16"	BP	1
TRIM					
F* front	1/2"	1 3/4"	13 3/4"	C	1
G* sides	1/2"	1 3/4"	8"	C	2
DRAWERS					
H* fronts	3/8"	1 7/16"	4"	C	6
I* fronts	3/8"	1 7/16"	6"	C	4
J* fronts	3/8"	1 7/16"	12"	C	2
K sides	3/8"	1 7/16"	7 5/16"	C	24
L backs	3/8"	1 3/32"	3 5/8"	C	6
M backs	3/8"	1 3/32"	5 5/8"	C	4
N backs	3/8"	1 3/32"	11 5/8"	C	2
O bottoms	1/8"	3 5/8"	6 1/8"	BP	6
P bottoms	1/8"	5 5/8"	6 1/8"	BP	4
Q bottoms	1/8"	11 5/8"	6 1/8"	BP	2
DRAWER GUIDES					
R top	1/4"	3 7/32"	7"	H	6
S middle	1/4"	5 7/32"	7"	H	4
T bottom	1/4"	11 7/32"	7"	H	2

*Initially cut parts marked with an * oversized. Trim to finished size according to the instructions.

Materials Key: EC–edge-joined cherry, C–cherry, BP–birch plywood, H–hardboard.

Supplies: #17×3/4" brads, #18×1/2" brads, clear finish, solid brass knobs (14).

3 To hide the dadoes on the front edges of each side panel, glue the 3/8 × 3/8 × 12 13/16" strip (trimmed from the front edge in Step 1) against the front edge of each panel, keeping the surfaces flush and the top end of the strip flush with the shoulder of the rabbet. Later, remove the clamps and sand the panels.

4 Cut the top (B) to 8 × 13 1/2". Rip 3/4" from the front edge as shown in the Top drawing, and set the narrow piece aside for now.

5 Mark the locations and cut a pair of ³⁄₁₆" dadoes ³⁄₁₆" deep on the bottom side of the top piece. Glue the ½ × ¾ × 13½" strip against the front edge of the top piece. Later, remove the clamps and sand smooth.

6 Rout a ¼" cove along the bottom front and side edges of the top piece. Wrap sandpaper around a ½" dowel and sand the coves smooth.

Add the shelves and back

1 Cut the six shelves (C) to size.

2 Mark and cut a ³⁄₁₆ × ³⁄₈" notch on the front corners of each shelf. See the Shelf Notch detail (*below left*) for reference.

3 Dry-clamp the parts (A, B, C) to check the fit. Measure the opening and then cut the bottom rail (D) to size. Glue and clamp the parts, checking for square.

4 Measure the opening, and cut the back (E) to size from ⅛" birch ply-

wood. Set the back aside for now—we'll attach it later.

Cut and attach the trim

1 Cut a ½" piece of cherry to 1¾" wide by 32" long. Now, rout a ³⁄₈" cove along one edge.

2 From the 32"-long piece, miter-cut the front trim piece (F) and the side trim pieces (G) to length.

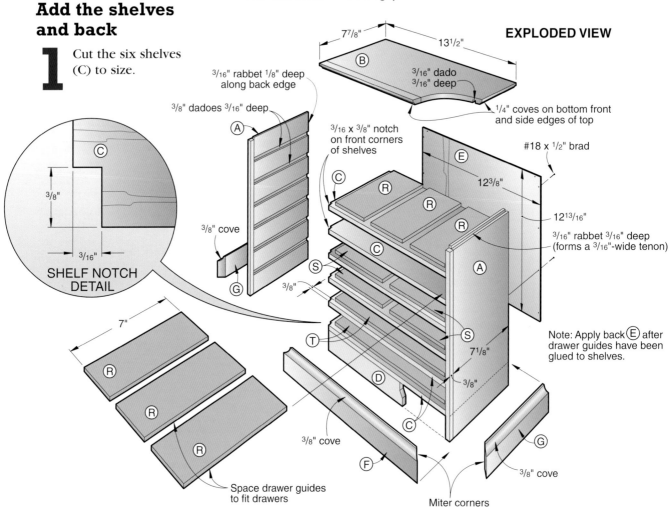

SHELF NOTCH DETAIL

³⁄₈"

³⁄₁₆"

C

EXPLODED VIEW

7⁷⁄₈"   13½"

B

³⁄₁₆" dado ³⁄₁₆" deep

³⁄₁₆" rabbet ⅛" deep along back edge

³⁄₈" dadoes ³⁄₁₆" deep

A

¼" coves on bottom front and side edges of top

³⁄₁₆ x ³⁄₈" notch on front corners of shelves

#18 x ½" brad

E

12³⁄₈"

12¹³⁄₁₆"

³⁄₈" cove

C

R

R

R

C

³⁄₁₆" rabbet ³⁄₁₆" deep (forms a ³⁄₁₆"-wide tenon)

S

G

³⁄₈"

A

7"

R

R

R

T

S

7⅛"

Note: Apply back E after drawer guides have been glued to shelves.

C

³⁄₈"

D

³⁄₈" cove

F

C

G

³⁄₈" cove

Space drawer guides to fit drawers

Miter corners

3 Glue and clamp the trim pieces to the case. Wrap sandpaper around a ¾" dowel and sand the coves smooth.

Add a dozen drawers

Note: We constructed our drawers using the sizes of pieces listed in the Materials List, creating a gap-free fit of the drawers in the case. Then, after positioning the drawer guides (R, S, T), we used a sanding block to sand the sides of each drawer for consistent ¹/₃₂" gaps as shown in the Front View drawing.

1 From ⅜"-thick stock, rip 1⁷/₁₆"-wide strips for the drawer fronts (H, I, J). Following the Cutting Diagram, cut adjoining drawer fronts end-to-end from the same piece of stock. Doing this will allow side-by-side drawers to have continuous grain across their fronts.

2 Using the Drawer drawing for reference, cut a ⅛" groove ³/₁₆" deep along the back edge of the long strips to be used for the drawer fronts.

3 Miter-cut the drawer fronts (H, I, J) to length.

4 Cut long lineal stock for the drawer sides (K). Cut a ⅛" groove ³/₁₆" deep, ⁷/₃₂" from the bottom edge of the long drawer-side

CUTTING DIAGRAM

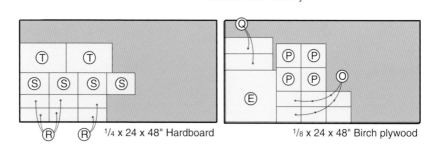

⅜ x 9¼ x 96" Cherry

(2) ⅛ x ⅜ x 24" for splines

⅜ x 9¼ x 96" Cherry

½ x 5½ x 60" Cherry

¼ x 24 x 48" Hardboard

⅛ x 24 x 48" Birch plywood

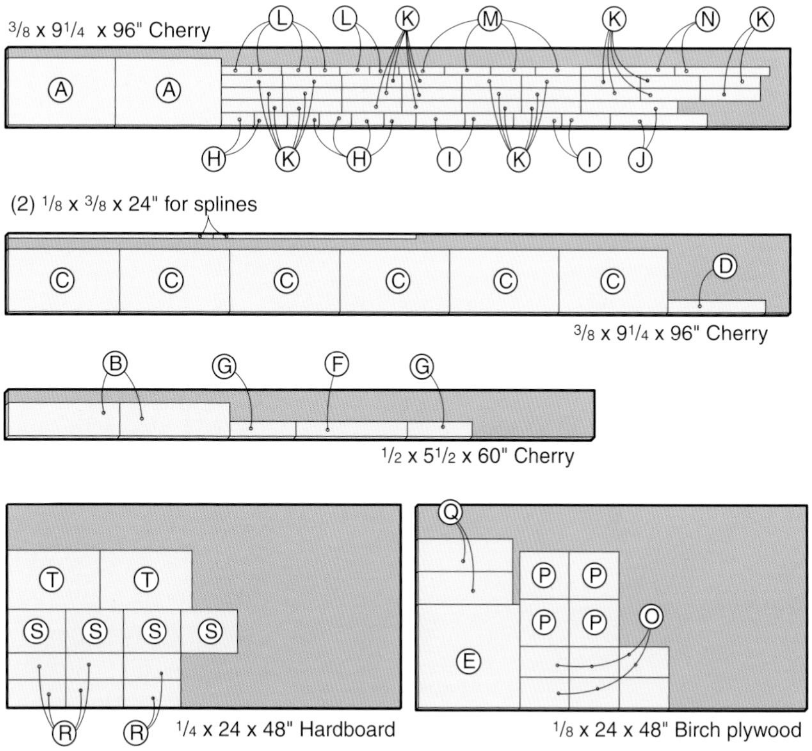

Measure diagonally and adjust until the measurements are perfectly equal, to ensure square drawers.

stock. Position the groove ⁷/₃₂" from the bottom edge to create a ¹/₃₂" gap between the bottom edge of the drawer fronts and the top edge of the shelves.

Cut and miter-cut the drawer sides to length. For housing the drawer backs later, cut a ⅜" dado in each drawer side as shown in the drawing.

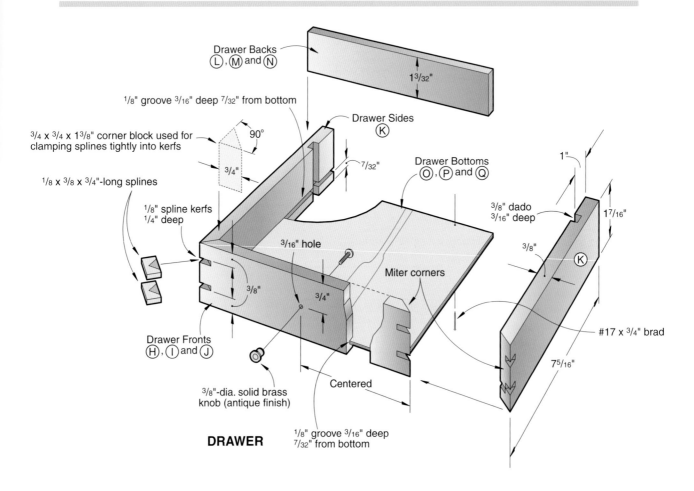

Drawer Backs
(L), (M) and (N)

$1^{3/32}$"

$1/8$" groove $3/16$" deep $7/32$" from bottom

$3/4$ x $3/4$ x $1^{3/8}$" corner block used for clamping splines tightly into kerfs

90°

Drawer Sides
(K)

$3/4$"

$7/32$"

Drawer Bottoms
(O), (P) and (Q)

1"

$1/8$ x $3/8$ x $3/4$"-long splines

$3/8$" dado
$3/16$" deep

$1^{7/16}$"

$1/8$" spline kerfs
$1/4$" deep

$3/8$"

$3/16$" hole

Miter corners

(K)

$3/8$"

$3/4$"

Drawer Fronts
(H), (I) and (J)

#17 x $3/4$" brad

$7^{5/16}$"

Centered

$3/8$"-dia. solid brass
knob (antique finish)

DRAWER

$1/8$" groove $3/16$" deep
$7/32$" from bottom

5 Cut the drawer backs (L, M, N) and bottoms (O, P, Q) to size.

6 Dry-clamp each drawer to check the fit. Then, glue and clamp each drawer, checking for square by measuring from corner to corner and adjusting until the opposing diagonal measurements are equal as shown in **Photo A**.

7 To reinforce the mitered corner joints and add the decorative joinery look, start by building the corner-kerfing jig

shown in the Corner Kerfing Jig drawing on *page 169.*

8 As shown in **Photo B**, cut a pair of $1/8$" spline kerfs $1/4$" deep in each front corner of each drawer. For flat bottom kerfs, you'll need to use a blade with a flat-top or triple-chip grind.

9 Cut two pieces of $3/8$"-wide $1/8$"-thick solid cherry stock to 24" long each. Now, crosscut 48 $1/8 \times 3/8 \times 3/4$" cherry splines from the strips. Cut several corner blocks to the size shown in the Drawer

drawing. Glue the splines in the kerfs using a corner block on the inside of the drawer, as shown in **Photo C**. (For an even distribution of pressure, we placed a small piece of scrap stock between the clamp head and the splines). Check that the splines bottom out in the kerfs. If they don't, you'll have an unsightly glue joint later.

10 Trim the splines to within about $1/16$" of the drawer front and sides, and then sand them flush.

Using the corner kerfing jig for support, cut a pair of kerfs in the front corners of each drawer.

Use corner blocks to prevent denting the inside of the drawers when pulling the splines snug into the kerfs.

Add the guides for evenly-spaced drawers

1 Cut the drawer guides (R, S, T) to size. The width of the guides needs to be equal to the distance between the drawer sides (K) minus $\frac{1}{32}$".

2 Slide the top three drawers into place and position the drawers so that you have an equal gap between the drawers and the sides (A) and the same gap between the drawers. Since the drawers were made to fit tight, you will have to sand the outside faces of the drawer sides to create the $\frac{1}{32}$" gaps. (For gaps of consistent sizes, we placed cereal-box cardboard between the drawers and between the drawers and jewelry box side panels. We used sandpaper wrapped around a block of wood to sand the outside surfaces of the drawers evenly.)

3 Working from the back of the case, slide the drawer guides into place. The guides should be $\frac{3}{8}$" (the same thickness as the drawer fronts) from the front of the case. Check for equal gaps and that the drawer fronts are flush with each other and the front of the case. Clamp (no glue) the guides in place from the back of the case. Push the drawers out the front without moving the guides. Use a sharp pencil to mark the location of the

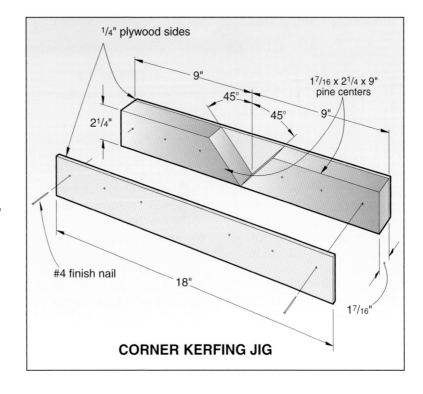

1/4" plywood sides

9"

45°

45°

$1^{7}/_{16}$ x $2^{1}/_{4}$ x 9" pine centers

9"

$2^{1}/_{4}$"

#4 finish nail

18"

$1^{7}/_{16}$"

CORNER KERFING JIG

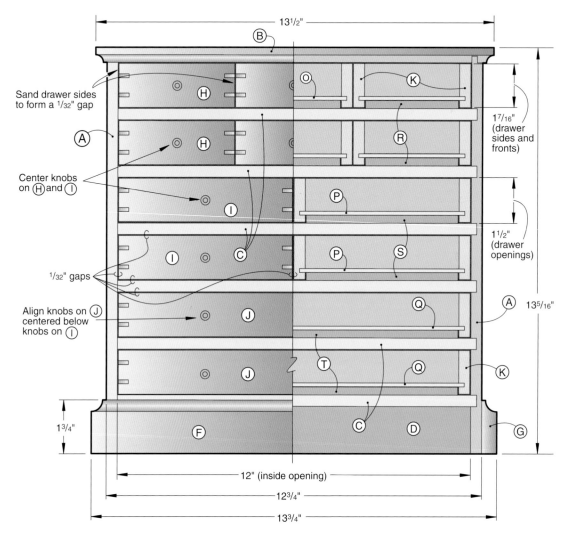

Sand drawer sides
to form a 1/32" gap

Center knobs
on (H) and (I)

1/32" gaps

Align knobs on (J)
centered below
knobs on (I)

13 1/2"

1 7/16"
(drawer
sides and
fronts)

1 1/2"
(drawer
openings)

13 5/16"

1 3/4"

12" (inside opening)

12 3/4"

13 3/4"

FRONT VIEW

guides on the shelves. Using a few drops of glue (no need to overdo it), glue the guides in place. Immediately reposition the drawers and spacers to verify that the guides are positioned correctly. Evenly spaced drawers depend on properly positioned guides, so take your time. Repeat the process to install the remaining guides.

4 After gluing all the guides in place, install the drawers, and mark the knob-hole centerpoints as shown in the Front View drawing. Note that the holes in drawer fronts I and J align. The machine screws supplied with the knobs are a bit too long for the 3/8"-thick drawer fronts, so trim each screw accordingly.

5 Remove the drawers from the assembled jewelry case. Finish-sand as necessary, clean off dust, and then apply a penetrating oil finish. While still wet, steel-wool the finish and wipe dry with a clean cloth. Let this dry, and repeat the process with a second coat to seal the wood. For added luster, apply two or so coats of 100% tung oil.

ASPEN-LEAF TREASURE CHEST

With this scaled-down strongbox, you can keep all your clutter at bay, yet still close at hand. It's shown here in stained pine with a unique, stenciled aspen-leaf motif on the lid (yes, there's a pattern included). It would look equally fine, though, made from a handsome hardwood.

1 Cut parts A, B, and C to the sizes shown in the Materials list. (We edge-joined two ⅜ × 3¼ × 10" pieces to make stock for part A.) Temporarily laminate both parts B together with double-faced tape.

Trace the lid curvature from the full-sized pattern on *page 169* onto the stacked end pieces. Bandsaw or scroll-saw slightly on the waste side of the line. Sand to the line and separate the pieces.

2 On the inside face of each part B, rout a ⅜" rabbet ¼" deep along both ends and the curved side. With a tablesaw, groove parts B and C to receive the bottom. See the Box Assembly drawing.

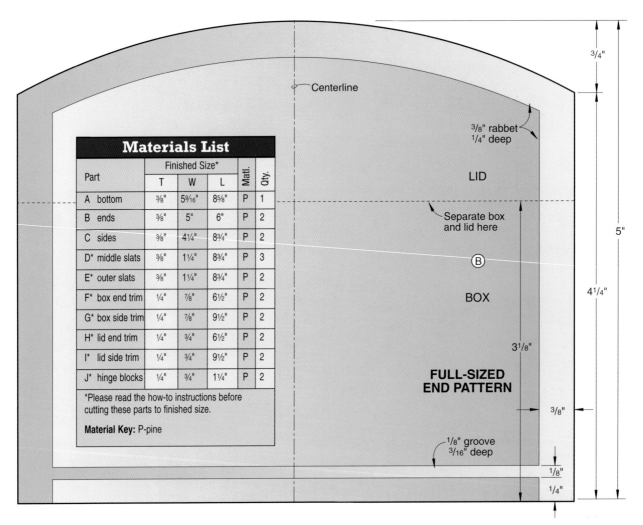

Centerline

³⁄₈" rabbet
¹⁄₄" deep

³⁄₄"

LID

Separate box
and lid here

Ⓑ

5"

BOX

4¹⁄₄"

3¹⁄₈"

**FULL-SIZED
END PATTERN**

³⁄₈"

¹⁄₈" groove
³⁄₁₆" deep

¹⁄₈"

¹⁄₄"

Materials List

Part	Finished Size*			Matl.	Qty.
	T	W	L		
A bottom	³⁄₈"	5⁹⁄₁₆"	8⁵⁄₈"	P	1
B ends	³⁄₈"	5"	6"	P	2
C sides	³⁄₈"	4¹⁄₄"	8³⁄₄"	P	2
D* middle slats	³⁄₈"	1¹⁄₄"	8³⁄₄"	P	3
E* outer slats	³⁄₈"	1¹⁄₄"	8³⁄₄"	P	2
F* box end trim	¹⁄₄"	⁷⁄₈"	6¹⁄₂"	P	2
G* box side trim	¹⁄₄"	⁷⁄₈"	9¹⁄₂"	P	2
H* lid end trim	¹⁄₄"	³⁄₄"	6¹⁄₂"	P	2
I* lid side trim	¹⁄₄"	³⁄₄"	9¹⁄₂"	P	2
J* hinge blocks	¹⁄₄"	³⁄₄"	1¹⁄₄"	P	2

*Please read the how-to instructions before
cutting these parts to finished size.

Material Key: P-pine

Mount a dado blade on the tablesaw, and cut a ¹⁄₄ × ¹⁄₄" rabbet around the bottom panel. Dry assemble parts A, B, and C. Glue the corner joints (but not the bottom), square the box, and clamp.

3 Tilt your tablesaw blade 5° from vertical, and bevel-rip one edge of a ³⁄₈ × 1³⁄₄ × 36" piece of pine. Re-adjust the fence for a 1¹⁄₄" cutting width, and bevel-rip the other edge to make stock for parts D. Bevel-rip one

edge of another piece of stock at 5°, then tilt the blade to 30° to bevel the other edge to make stock for parts E. Measure the top opening before trimming the parts.

4 Mask inside the box to catch any glue squeeze-out. Fit parts D and E, applying glue sparingly. Place waxed paper over the arched top, and clamp with rubber bands. When dry, contour-sand the top. (We held the box lengthwise against a belt

sander and rolled it from side to side.)

5 Before separating the lid, draw a pencil line from top to bottom on one end to serve as an index mark. Set the tablesaw cutting depth to ¹⁄₂". Referring to the drawing on *page 170 (top left)*, saw the box apart on both sides and both ends.

6 Now, make the trim for the box and lid. Form a ¹⁄₈" chamfer on one

SEPARATING THE BOX AND LID

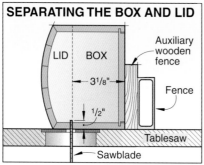

LID   BOX

Auxiliary wooden fence

Fence

3 1/8"

1/2"

Tablesaw

Sawblade

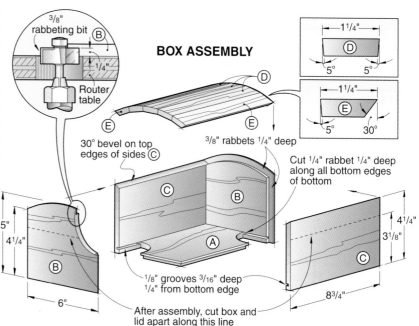

3/8" rabbeting bit   (B)

Router table

BOX ASSEMBLY

(D)

(D)

(E)   (E)

30° bevel on top edges of sides (C)

3/8" rabbets 1/4" deep

1 1/4"

(D)

5°   5°

1 1/4"

(E)

5°   30°

5"

4 1/4"

(B)

6"

(C)

(B)

(A)

Cut 1/4" rabbet 1/4" deep along all bottom edges of bottom

4 1/4"

3 1/8"

(C)

8 3/4"

1/8" grooves 3/16" deep 1/4" from bottom edge

After assembly, cut box and lid apart along this line

edge of a 1/4 × 3/4 × 36" strip and a 1/4 × 7/8 × 36" strip. (We used a chamfer bit and table-mounted router).

Measure and miter-cut parts F and G from the 7/8"-wide material. Refer to the Box Trim Leg Detail drawing, lay out the legs, and scrollsaw or bandsaw them. Measure and miter-cut the lid trim pieces H and I. Glue on the trim as shown in the Exploded View drawing.

When the glue dries, fit the lid to the box. Mark the box at the bottom of the lid trim. Remove the lid, and lightly sand the area above the mark to allow the top to open and close easily.

Cut the hinge blocks (J) to size, and glue on as shown. Sand the box. Attach 1 × 1" brass hinges as shown here. Then, sand the inside of the front lid trim as necessary for smooth opening.

7 The box shown here was finished with a sten-ciled Aspen leaf design using acrylic gel stains. See the pattern on the next page.

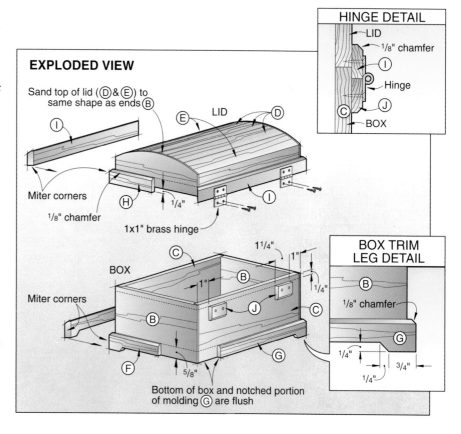

EXPLODED VIEW

Sand top of lid (D)&(E) to same shape as ends (B)

(I)

LID

(E)

(D)

(I)

Miter corners

1/8" chamfer

(H)

1/4"

1x1" brass hinge

(I)

BOX

(C)

(B)

Miter corners

(B)

(J)

(G)

(F)

5/8"

(G)

1 1/4"   1"

(C)   1/4"

1"

Bottom of box and notched portion of molding (G) are flush

HINGE DETAIL

LID

1/8" chamfer

(I)

Hinge

(C)   (J)

BOX

BOX TRIM LEG DETAIL

(B)

1/8" chamfer

(G)

1/4"   3/4"

1/4"

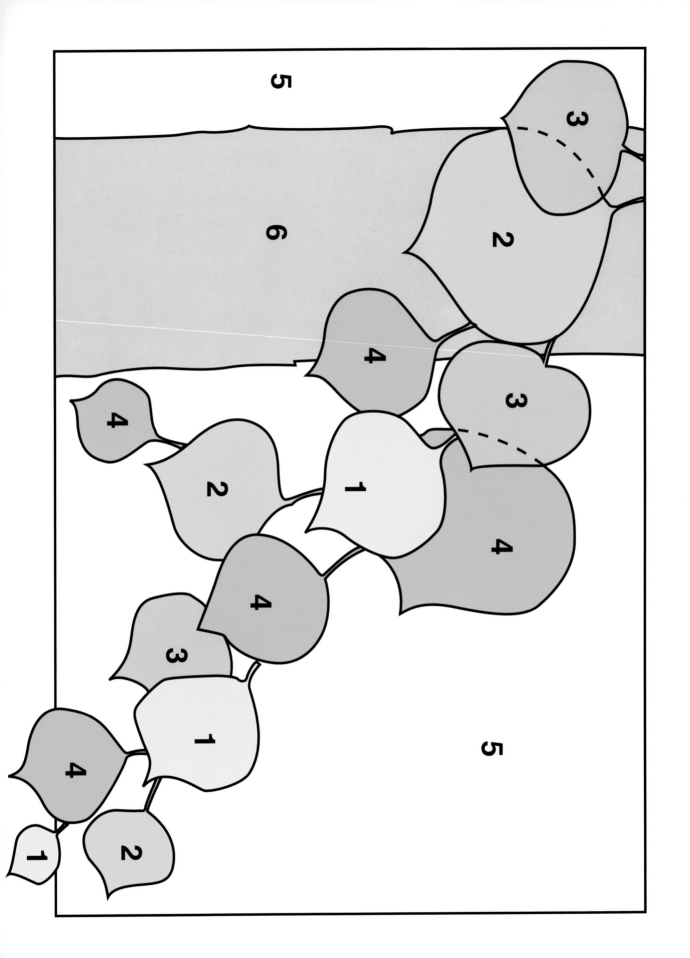

Patterns Appendix

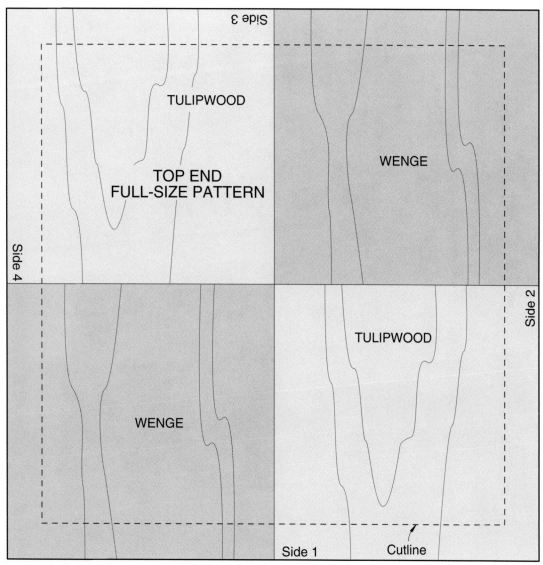

Note: Bottom end pattern is two strips of holly veneer butted together.

MARQUETRY MIRAGE
FULL-SIZED PATTERNS *(continued)*
Page 14

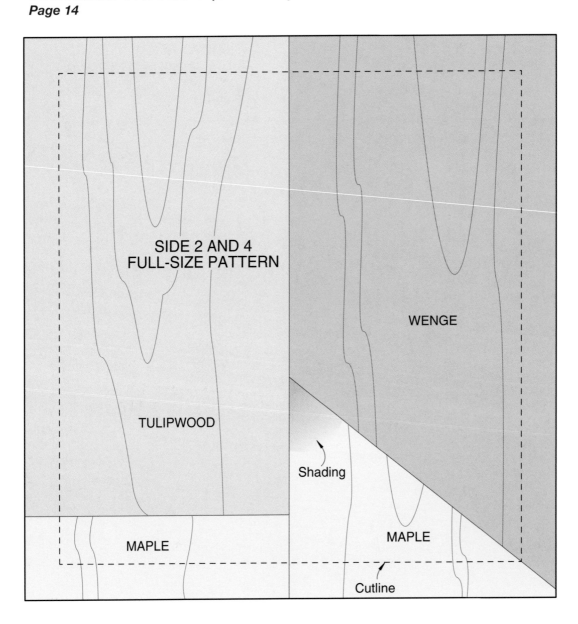

SIDE 2 AND 4
FULL-SIZE PATTERN

WENGE

TULIPWOOD

Shading

MAPLE

MAPLE

Cutline

MARQUETRY MIRAGE
FULL-SIZED PATTERNS *(continued)*
Page 14

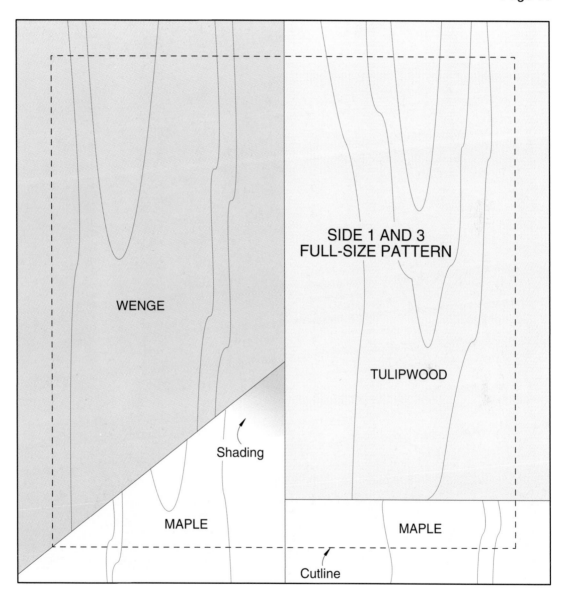

WENGE

SIDE 1 AND 3
FULL-SIZE PATTERN

TULIPWOOD

Shading

MAPLE

MAPLE

Cutline

A BOX WITH A BEAK
FULL-SIZED PATTERNS
Page 44

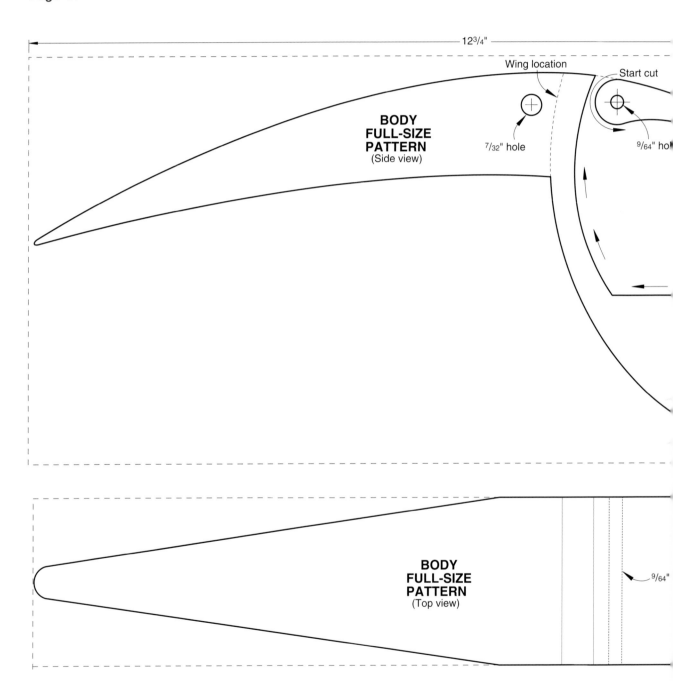

12³/₄"

Wing location

Start cut

**BODY
FULL-SIZE
PATTERN**
(Side view)

7/32" hole

9/64" hol

**BODY
FULL-SIZE
PATTERN**
(Top view)

9/64"

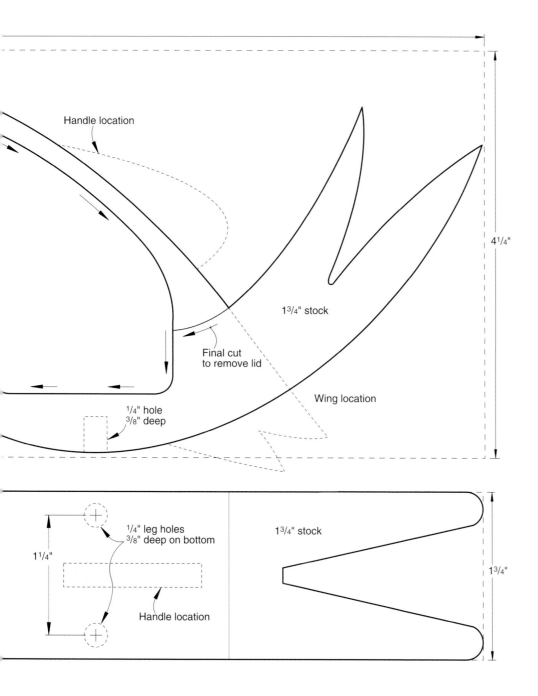

Handle location

1³/₄" stock

Final cut
to remove lid

Wing location

¹/₄" hole
³/₈" deep

4¹/₄"

¹/₄" leg holes
³/₈" deep on bottom

1³/₄" stock

1¹/₄"

Handle location

1³/₄"

A BOX WITH A BEAK
FULL-SIZED PATTERNS *(continued)*
Page 44

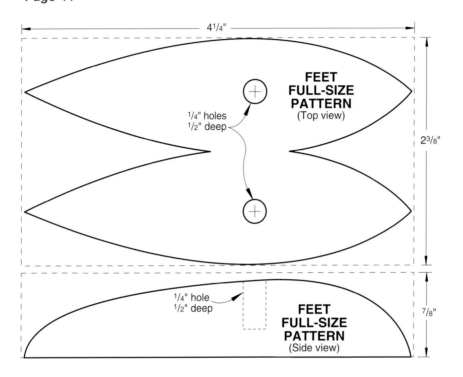

4¹/₄"

¹/₄" holes
¹/₂" deep

**FEET
FULL-SIZE
PATTERN**
(Top view)

2³/₈"

¹/₄" hole
¹/₂" deep

**FEET
FULL-SIZE
PATTERN**
(Side view)

7/₈"

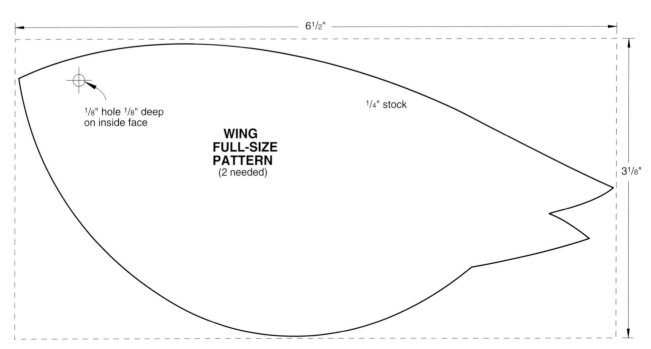

6¹/₂"

¹/₈" hole ¹/₈" deep
on inside face

¹/₄" stock

**WING
FULL-SIZE
PATTERN**
(2 needed)

3¹/₈"

POTPOURRI BOX
FULL-SIZED PATTERN
Page 68

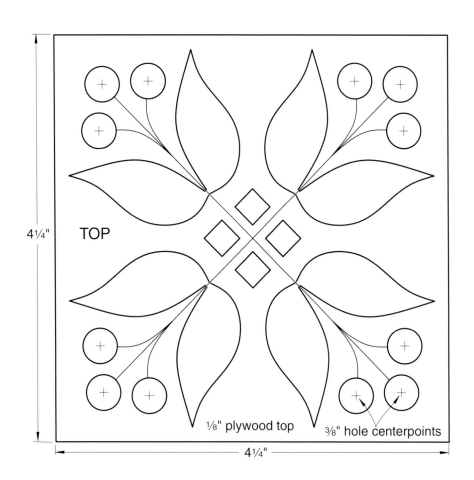

4¼"

TOP

4¼"

⅛" plywood top   ⅜" hole centerpoints

A TOOL CHEST THAT'S TOP DRAWER
FULL-SIZED PATTERNS
Page 102

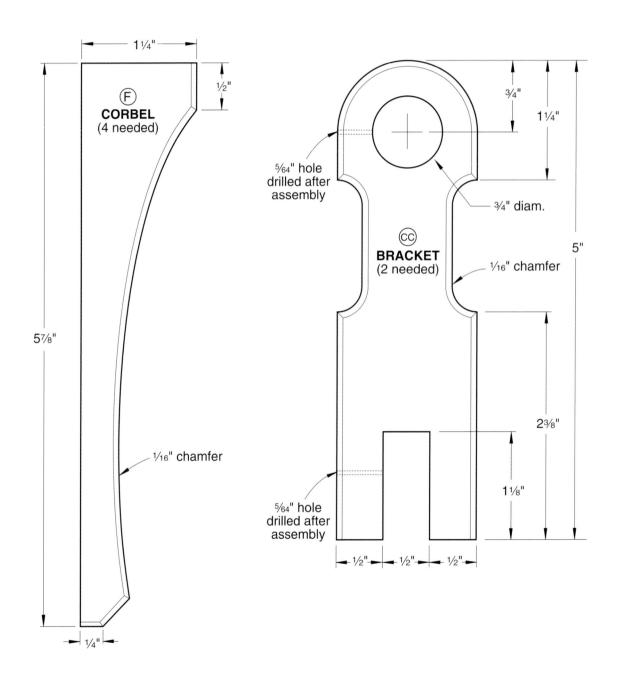

1¼"

½"

Ⓕ
CORBEL
(4 needed)

5⅞"

¹⁄₁₆" chamfer

¼"

¾"

1¼"

5/64" hole
drilled after
assembly

¾" diam.

ⒸⒸ
BRACKET
(2 needed)

¹⁄₁₆" chamfer

5"

2⅜"

1⅛"

5/64" hole
drilled after
assembly

½"   ½"   ½"

**FIRST-CLASS
LETTER BOX
PATTERN AT 75%
OF FULL SIZE**
Page 130

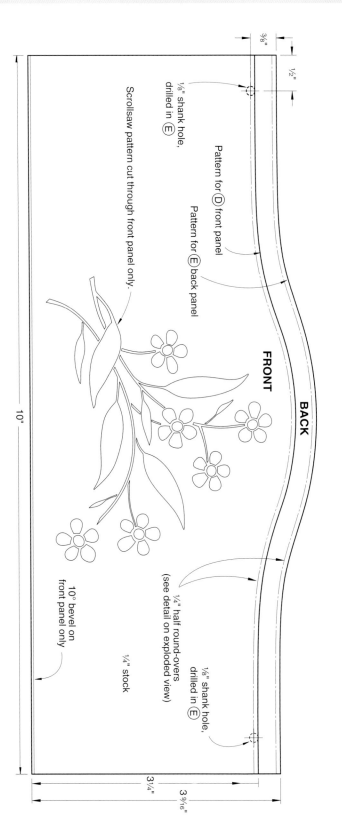

3/8"

1/2"

1/8" shank hole,
drilled in Ⓔ

Pattern for Ⓓ front panel

Pattern for Ⓔ back panel

Scrollsaw pattern cut through front panel only.

FRONT

BACK

10"

1/4" half round-overs
(see detail on exploded view)

1/8" shank hole,
drilled in Ⓔ

10° bevel on
front panel only

1/4" stock

3 1/4"

3 9/16"

BATTER UP! FOR A BASEBALL CARD BOX
FULL-SIZED SCENE PATTERNS
Page 134

$^3/_{16}$" rabbet $^1/_8$" deep after completing inlay

$^1/_{16}$" blade
start hole

$^1/_{16}$" blade
start hole

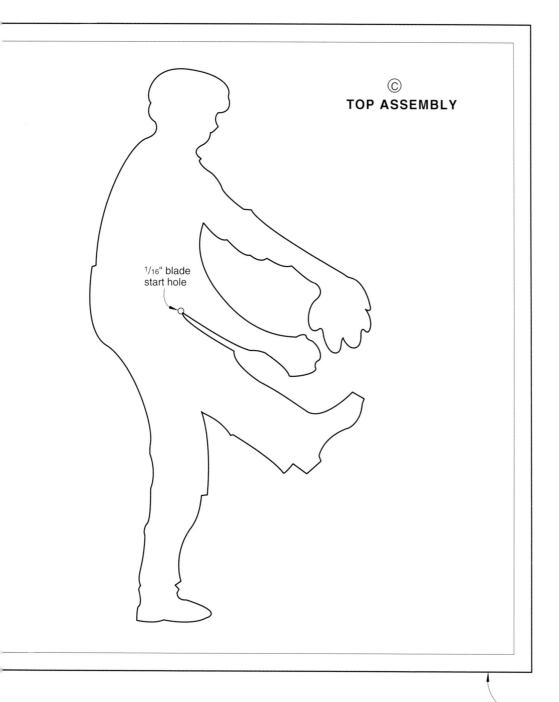

© TOP ASSEMBLY

$1/16$" blade start hole

$1/4$" -thick stock

BATTER UP! FOR A BASEBALL CARD BOX
FULL-SIZED SCENE PATTERNS *(continued)*
Page 134

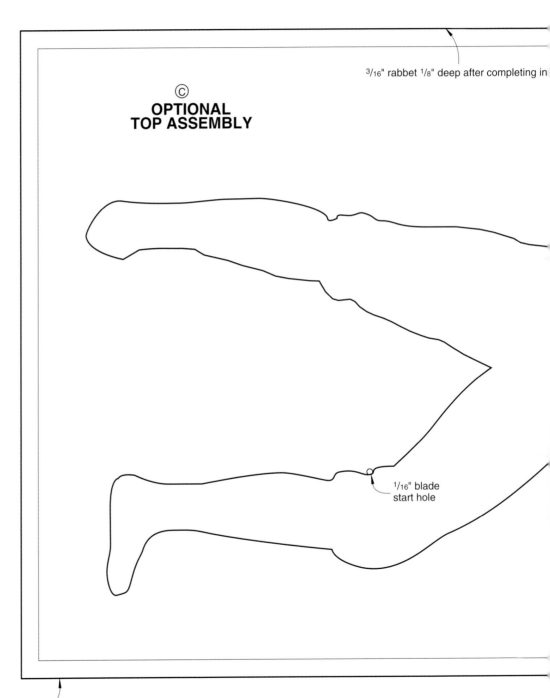

3/16" rabbet 1/8" deep after completing in

© **OPTIONAL TOP ASSEMBLY**

1/16" blade start hole

. 1/4" -thick stock

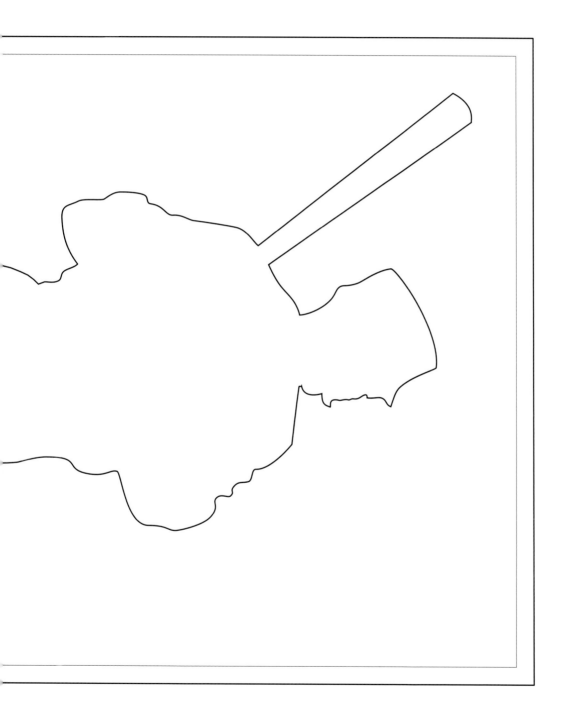

Index

A

Ammonia, creating patina with, 80–81
Arts-and-Crafts tool chest, 102–110, 182
Aspen-leaf treasure chest, 171–174

B

Bandsaw boxes
  basic types of, 33–34
  cutting, safety tips, 74
  with lift-out tray, 34
  with locking lid pin, 34, 40
  multiple, from one wood block, 35–39
  open, basic, 33
  overview, 31–32
  practicing making, 32
  securing stock for cutting, 59
  with sliding lid, 33
  techniques for, 35–39, 59, 60, 64, 65
  wood thickness and sawing speed, 60
Bandsaw box projects
  bird-shaped box, 44–46, 178–180
  bunny box, 63–66
  catch-all box, 51–54
  moon and stars box, 58–62
  rabbit-shaped box, 63–66
  sweetheart jewelry box, 47–50
  trinket treasure chest, 55–57
  whale-shaped box, 42–43
Baseball card box, 134–139, 184–187

Beveled jewelry box, 150–156
Bird-shaped box, 44–46, 178–180
Bunny box, 63–66

C

Candle box, 140–143
Catch-all box, 51–54
Colonial pipe box, 111–114
Contact cement, 9
Contemporary keepsake box, 71–76
Corners
  continuous grain at, 72
  splines for, 152
Coving edges, 28–29
Crown molding boxes, 157–163
Cutting
  crown molding, 158–159, 160–161
  inlay bandings, 5–7
  saw safety tips, 74
  veneer, 5–7, 10–11, 17

D

Diamond shapes, 20, 21–23
Dovetails
  candle box with, 140–143
  jewelry box with, 90–96
  keys and slots, 92–94
  marking and cutting pins/tails, 141–142
Drawers, boxes with
  pipe box, 111–114
  spline-jointed jewelry box, 164–170

tool chest, 102–110, 182
trinket treasure chest, 55–57
Dyed veneer, 13

F

Felt linings, 50
Figured veneer, 10, 12–13
Flat-cut veneer, 12
Flattening veneer, 10
Flexible veneer, 13
Flip-up pen box, 144–148

G

Glues/gluing veneers, 8–9, 19
Grooves in boards, centering, 105

H

Heart-shaped box. See Sweetheart jewelry box
Hinged boxes
  aspen-leaf treasure chest, 171–174
  beveled jewelry box, 150–156
  bird-shaped box, 44–46, 178–180
  catch-all box, 51–54
  flip-up pen box, 144–148
  keepsake box, 26–29
  nut box, 115–122
  patina-topped jewelry box, 77–85
  photo box, 126–129
  rabbit-shaped box, 63–66
  sweetheart jewelry box, 47–50

Hinged boxes (*continued*)
    trinket treasure chest, 55–57
Hinge-pin dowels, snug fit for,
    64

I

Inlay
    baseball card box, 134–139,
      184–187
    keepsake box, 26–29
    quilt-top wood box, 20–25
    types of, 13
Inlay bandings
    cutting, 5–7
    described, 13
Inlay faces, 13

J

Jewelry boxes
    beveled, 150–156
    dovetailed, 90–96
    moon and stars, 58–62
    patina-topped, 77–85
    with spline-jointed drawers,
      164–170
    stackable chest, 86–89
    sweetheart, 47–50
Jigs
    for crown molding, 158, 159
    for cutting splines, 100
    for miter cuts, 21, 158, 159

K

Keepsake box
    solid wood, contemporary,
      71–76
    veneer, 26–29

L

Leaf-shaped patina, 79–81

Letter box, 130–133, 183
Lidded boxes. *See also* Hinged
    boxes
    bandsaw box techniques,
      35–39
    baseball card box, 134–139,
      184–187
    basic bandsaw box with lock-
      ing lid pin, 34, 40
    basic bandsaw box with slid-
      ing lid, 33
    candle box, 140–143
    contemporary keepsake box,
      71–76
    crown molding boxes,
      157–163
    dovetailed jewelry box,
      90–96
    moon and stars box, 58–62
    potpourri box, 68–70, 181
    stackable jewelry chest,
      86–89
    standout box with splines,
      97–100
    whale-shaped box, 42–43
Linings, felt, 50

M

Magazine keepers, 123–125
Marquetry mirage, 14–19,
    175–177
Miters
    cuts for inlay, 7
    jigs, 21, 158, 159
Moon and stars box, 58–62

N

Nut box, 115–122

P

Paperback veneer, 13

Patina
    creating, with basic chem-
      istry, 79–81
    experiment suggestions, 81
    jewelry box, 77–85
Peel-and-stick veneer, 13
Pen box, 144–148
Photo box, 126–129
Pipe box, 111–114
Potpourri Box, 68–70, 181
Pressure-sensitive veneer, 13

Q

Quartersawn veneer, 13
Quilt-top wood box, 20–25

R

Rabbit-shaped box, 63–66
Rotary-cut veneer, 13

S

Scroll saw, 29, 133
Splines
    corner, 152
    jewelry box with, 164–170
    jig for, 100
    standout box with, 97–100
Stackable jewelry chest, 86–89
Standard (raw) veneer, 12
Standout box with splines,
    97–100
Stars and moon box, 58–62
Sweetheart jewelry box, 47–50

T

Tablesaw
    centering grooves in boards,
      105
    safety tips, 74
Tapers, forming, 74

Taping veneers together, 8
Tool chest, 102–110, 182
Trinket treasure chest, 55–57

U
Urea-formaldehyde resin, 9

V
Veneer
  buying, 12–13
  cracks, correcting, 10
  cutting, 5–7, 17
  dyed, 13
  figured, 10, 12–13
  finishing, 11
  flat-cut, 12
  flattening, 10
  flexible, 13
  gluing, to substrate, 8–9, 19
  illusion with, 16–18
  joining seams, 7–8
  jointing edges, 7
  laying out, 5
  paperback, 13
  peel-and-stick, 13
  pressure-sensitive, 13
  quartersawn, 13
  removing tape, 10
  repairing, 10
  rotary-cut, 13
  sanding, 10–11
  seams, 7
  shading, 16
  standard (raw), 12
  taping edges together, 8
  trimming and cleaning up, 10–11
  types of, 12–13
Veneered boxes
  keepsake box, 26–29
  marquetry mirage, 14–19, 175–177
  quilt-top wood box (veneer option), 20–25
Veneering
  basics of, 4–11
  glues, 9
  tools, 5

W
Whale-shaped box, 42–43
White glue, 9

Y
Yellow woodworker's glue, 9

METRIC EQUIVALENTS CHART (Inches to Millimeters and Centimeters)

MM=MILLIMETERS   CM=CENTIMETERS

INCHES	MM	CM	INCHES	CM	INCHES	CM
1/8	3	0.3	9	22.9	30	76.2
1/4	6	0.6	10	25.4	31	78.7
3/8	10	1.0	11	27.9	32	81.3
1/2	13	1.3	12	30.5	33	83.8
5/8	16	1.6	13	33.0	34	86.4
3/4	19	1.9	14	35.6	35	88.9
7/8	22	2.2	15	38.1	36	91.4
1	25	2.5	16	40.6	37	94.0
1 1/4	32	3.2	17	43.2	38	96.5
1 1/2	38	3.8	18	45.7	39	99.1
1 3/4	44	4.4	19	48.3	48	101.6
2	51	5.1	20	50.8	41	104.1
2 1/2	64	6.4	21	53.3	42	106.7
3	76	7.6	22	55.9	43	109.2
3 1/2	89	8.9	23	58.4	44	111.8
4	102	10.2	24	61.0	45	114.3
4 1/2	114	11.4	25	63.5	46	116.8
5	127	12.7	26	66.0	47	119.4
6	152	15.2	27	68.6	48	121.9

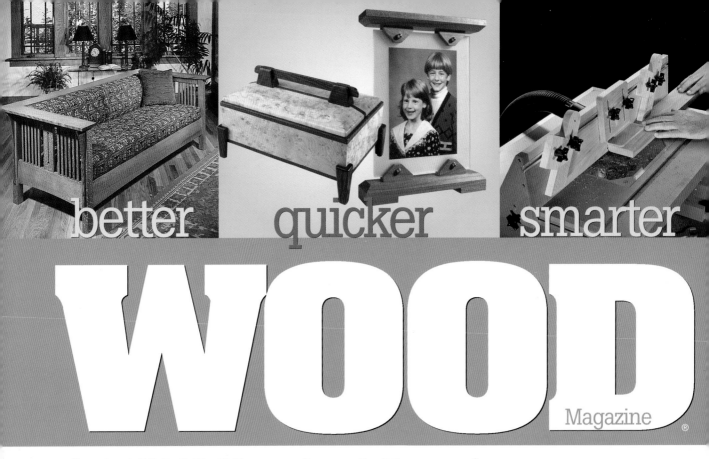

better quicker smarter

WOOD
Magazine ®

Only WOOD Magazine delivers the woodworking know-how you need, including ...

- Over 50 new shop-tested projects a year
- Time-saving tips and techniques
- Ingenious jigs and fixtures
- Full-size pull-out patterns
- America's best tool reviews
- Space-saving shop ideas

Apply glue beads 1" apart.
Custom cut corner cladding pieces to width to fit inside of icebox.

WOOD MAGAZINE
SHOP TESTED
APPROVED ™

This seal is your assurance that we build every project, verify every fact, and test every reviewed tool in our workshop to guarantee your success and complete satisfaction.

chamfer along top edge of doors

To get your best deal on WOOD, call 1-800-374-9663

or visit us online at
www.woodonline.com